D1436350

Moving

Pictures,

Migrating

Identities

Eva Rueschmann

University Press of Mississippi / *Jackson*

Moving

Pictures,

Migrating

Identities

www.upress.state.ms.us

The University Press of Mississippi is a member of the Association
of American University Presses.

Copyright © 2003 by University Press of Mississippi
All rights reserved
Manufactured in the United States of America

11 10 09 08 07 06 05 04 03   4 3 2 1

∞

Library of Congress Cataloging-in-Publication Data
Rueschmann, Eva, 1962–
    Moving pictures, migrating identities / Eva Rueschmann.
        p. cm.
Includes bibliographical references and index.
    ISBN 1-57806-542-9 (alk. paper)
1. Emigration and immigration in motion pictures. I. Title.
PN1995.9.E44   R84   2003
791.43'655–dc21   2002012428

British Library Cataloging-in-Publication Data available

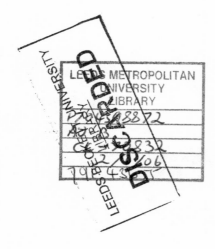

Contents

Acknowledgments

First, I would like to express my gratitude to all the contributors of this anthology. Their excitingly diverse approaches to exile and migration in contemporary cinema provide this book with its distinctive quality. The idea for this collection was first inspired by my work for the Annual Multicultural Film Festival at the University of Massachusetts, Amherst, which is organized each year by Catherine Portuges, Professor of Comparative Literature and Director of the Film Studies Program. I am deeply appreciative of her passionate advocacy for contemporary world cinema and her longtime support of all my endeavors. The editors, staff and readers at the University Press of Mississippi deserve special thanks. Seetha Srinivasan took a strong interest in this project from the beginning and guided the book to publication. Anne Stascavage gave excellent advice for editing and revision. The Press's reader commented generously and incisively on the essays. I also want to thank the students in my course, "Traveling Identities," for their enthusiasm and insightful perspectives on the topic of diaspora cinema, and my colleagues at Hampshire College for their support. Finally, this book is dedicated to Matthew P. Schmidt, my husband, who made time for some last-minute editing. His love and support make all things possible.

Introduction

Migrants must, of necessity, make a new imaginative
relationship with the world, because of the loss of familiar
habitats. And for the plural, metropolitan result of such
imaginings, the cinema, in which peculiar fusions have
always been legitimate . . . may well be the ideal location.

—from Salman Rushdie, *Imaginary Homelands* 125

The story of mass migrations (voluntary and forced) is
hardly a new feature of human history. But when it is
juxtaposed with the rapid flow of mass-mediated images,
scripts and sensation, we have a new order of instability
in the production of modern subjectivities. . . . These
[moving images] create diasporic public spheres,
phenomena that confound theories that depend on the
continued saliance of the nation-state as the key arbiter
of important social changes.

—from Arjun Appadurai, *Modernity at Large* 4

Opening Remarks

This volume of essays contributes to a relatively new and increasingly
significant subject in cinema criticism: exile, diaspora and immigration in
film from around the globe. Exile and diaspora film criticism calls attention
to a truly international genre of contemporary cinema, treating a wide range
of films that address, in a variety of national and transnational contexts, issues
and questions generated by a 'world on the move.' Indeed, the films represented in this study, and the critical and analytical thought brought to bear
on them by the anthology's contributors, could hardly be more pertinent

to the increasingly mobile and dispersed, yet complexly interconnected global culture we now share. This is the situation described so powerfully by postcolonial and diaspora writers and theorists of the 1990s, such as Salman Rushdie and Arjun Appadurai, who comment on the paramount role played by mass-mediated images—the cinema especially—in capturing what is perhaps modernity's great legacy—the sweeping mass migration and displacements of the twentieth century.

The essays in this book examine how contemporary cinema has imagined the experience of such migrations and displacement as well as the clash and fusion of different cultures and identities. The essays explore the ways in which cinema projects the many disjunctures and contradictions of exile and diaspora—the complicated meanings of "home," the exile's nostalgia for origins, the hopes and tragedies of border crossings, the difficulties of belonging to a strange society and of being a "stranger," the challenges of negotiating multiple cultural identities, and the conundrums of gender for the migrant, especially women's conciliation of cultural pasts and futures.

Reflecting a view of cinema as transcultural, the essays also address the ways in which films and filmmakers from particular nations locate themselves in a transnational media landscape. Recognizing that filmmakers participate in a global media marketplace dominated by Hollywood and the commercial demands of both investors and audiences, many of the films treated in this collection nonetheless attest to cinema's capacity to challenge political and cultural boundaries as they tell stories of the politically exiled and culturally displaced.

All the essays included here offer close textual readings of individual films, but taken together they demonstrate the wide range of critical approaches toward cinema in exile criticism, whether the focus is on internationally-known works such as *The Crying Game*, *Journey of Hope*, *Exotica*, *Chocolat* and *Lone Star*, or on lesser-known films that have often escaped critical or public attention, such as Seyhan Derin's *I'm My Mother's Daughter*, Lothar Warneke's *Blonder Tango*, Yamina Benguigui's *Mémoires d'immigrés, l'héritage maghrébin*, Mina Shum's *Double Happiness*, and Ruth Ozeki Lounsbury's *Halving the Bones*. The essays draw on different models of intercultural theory associated with anthropology, historiography, political economy, production and reception studies, feminism, travel writing and postcolonial criticism. This diversity is not accidental: exile and diaspora criticism benefits from an open and commodious theoretical and methodological discussion in order to best capture the complex, diverse and continually changing body of diaspora film. As Hamid Naficy, one of the major theorists of this category of film, cautions: "Attention to the specificity and situatedness of each displaced filmmaker, community or formation is an important safeguard against the temptation to engage in postmodern discursive tourism or the positing of an all-encompassing grand Exile or great Diaspora—or a homogeneous Accented Cinema" (*An Accented Cinema* 9). The particular zones of travel, motivations and circumstances of migration, of both filmmaker and his or her film subjects, constitute important historical and cultural frameworks for analysis. This anthology balances throughout a concern for cultural and national specificity with an exploration of the broader themes and issues at stake in this genre of cinema.

This introduction provides, first of all, a brief overview of some of the more significant theoretical frameworks and main concepts in exile and diaspora film criticism. A short discussion of Hanif Kureishi's *My Beautiful Laundrette* then follows in order to put into "cinematic practice" some of the theoretical considerations discussed in the overview. Made in 1985 for Channel Four, *My Beautiful Laundrette*, which concerns itself with issues of migration and cultural hybridity in Great Britain, is an especially interesting work in the history of diaspora cinema, having provoked considerable controversy over the politics of representation with its depiction of an economically opportunistic Pakistani middle class, a xenophobic white British working class, gay identities, and contemporary social unrest during the era of Thatcherism. Finally, a summary of the individual essays outlines their contributions to the overall focus of the anthology.

Some Theoretical Frameworks

Exile and diaspora film criticism draws on a broad variety of theories and critiques to analyze various aspects of transnationalism in cinema. Critics and scholars engage with postcolonial studies and postmodernist theories of fragmentation and dispersion, intercultural studies, critiques of globalization, ethnic studies, diaspora theory, critical ethnography and cultural geography. To put this broad critical horizon into perspective, it is important to realize the extent to which exile and diaspora criticism was shaped by the burgeoning and dynamic areas of postcolonial criticism, ethnic studies and Third World Cinema of the late 1980s and early 1990s which examined cultural dislocation, marginalized identities and the central role of diaspora in defining postcolonial subjectivities. Among the numerous theoretical and historical studies on diaspora and migration that have influenced film studies, I can only briefly mention here a few: Homi Bhabha's postcolonial critique of national narratives of cultural identity and of the complex, dialectical relationship between colonial center and periphery; Fredric Jameson's critique of the postmodernizing effects of global circuits of information and capital; Edward Said's work on culture and imperialism; Gloria Anzaldúa's manifesto on border consciousness and mestizo/a identities; Paul Gilroy's articulation of the black Atlantic as a historically significant transnational connection between dispersed African cultures in Europe, Africa and the Americas; James Clifford's expanded definition of diasporas as "nonexclusive practices of communities, politics and cultural difference;" Avtar Brah's diasporic space as the site "where multiple subject positions, of both dominant and minority groups, are juxtaposed, contested, proclaimed or disavowed," and theories of the Third Cinema, particularly the Latin American cinemas of liberation, by Teshome Gabriel and others.[1] There are many intersections between these theorists, all of whom attempt to come to terms with the increasing hybridity of cultural identities in the context of colonial, postcolonial and immigrant histories. While they differ in their emphasis on the importance of history, origins and cultural rootedness, many (but not all) adopt a postmodern view of shifting identities and cultural configurations in a state of "becoming."

Indeed, the issues and questions bearing on cultural identity in a global context addressed by these and other writers could not be more pertinent than they are today. At the turn of the twenty-first century, opportunities for international travel, modern technological advances and communication networks connect widely dispersed people across real and electronic spaces.

Yet groups of people and individuals separated by race, ethnicity, gender and class are pitted against each other in the defense of territory, power and dignity. Even as the rapid flow of global capital, goods, people, information and media such as film "deterritorializes" culture, creating increasingly hybrid communities and problematizing exclusive national traditions, entrenched narratives of history and identity continue to shape the politics, fears and perceptions of the present. Cinema plays an influential role in this truly global drama of cultural change.

Cultural anthropologist Arjun Appadurai, in his groundbreaking book *Modernity at Large: Cultural Dimensions of Globalization,* has undertaken an analysis of the disjunctions and contradictions generated by transnationalism. He argues that, in the era of globalization and mass mobility, media and migration are the two major influences or forces at work in shaping modern subjectivity and contemporary social change. By defining five interrelated but non-parallel dimensions of global cultural flows or interactions—of people, media, technology, capital and ideas/ideologies— Appadurai asserts that cultural productions and imagination can act as major transformative social forces beyond the strictures of national interests and identities. "The imagination is now central to all forms of agency, is itself a social fact, and is the key component of the new global order" (*Modernity at Large* 31).

Appadurai's analysis of global culture is echoed by scholars working in the specific area of migration and diaspora in the visual/media arts and film. Among the more seminal works are those of Ella Shohat and Robert Stam, Stuart Hall, Kobena Mercer, Nicholas Mirzoeff, Bishnupriya Ghosh and Bhaskar Sarkar, Laura Marks, and finally Hamid Naficy. Shohat and Stam's comprehensive and exhaustive coverage of colonial and postcolonial cinema and video art in *Unthinking Eurocentrism: Multiculturalism and the Media* moves the critical approach to world cinema from a Eurocentric to a "polycentric" perspective, showing how films from different cultural locations can be analyzed in relation to each other on the basis of their representations of social power, colonialism and race. Shohat and Stam examine how various dominant cinemas serve as the storytellers of national and imperial identities, but juxtapose them against them counter-cinemas that actively present strategies of resistance in visual culture.

Nicholas Mirzoeff has elaborated on this polycentric perspective in his anthology of essays, *Diaspora and Visual Culture: Representing Africans and Jews*. Taking seriously Shohat and Stam's call for a study of ethnicities- or diasporas-in-relation, Mirzoeff's anthology situates Jewish and African diaspora art in the context of their cultural origins and relation to their "host" country (such as the United States), and also explores the overlapping trajectories of African and Jewish displacements and exclusions in history and art. Mirzoeff coins the term "intervisuality" to designate the multiple connecting points and associations within the diasporic visual image, a useful concept for a comparative reading of different diasporas.

Postmodernist theory has, by and large, stressed a non-essentialist, decentered conception of cultural identity, critiquing the notion of a fixed, unified self. Current discussions of diaspora cultures by Mirzoeff, James Clifford, Avtar Brah, Rey Chow, and others are heavily influenced by postmodernism, claiming that diasporic nostalgia for origins and cultural authenticity reinforces static and past-oriented conceptions of culture. However, this claim tends to minimize the efforts by some diasporic filmmakers to retrieve often repressed cultural histories, to remedy the exclusion from dominant cinema of postcolonial realities, experiences, and perceptions— a central issue in both the Third World Cinema and in the works of immigrant directors and writers.

Stuart Hall, in the foundational essay, "Cultural Identity and Diaspora," juxtaposes the postmodern view of identity against the desire to authenticate one's cultural history in relation to the emerging diasporic Caribbean cinema. Hall writes that in some films cultural identity is conceived "in terms of one, shared culture, a sort of collective 'one true self,' hiding inside the many other, more superficial or artificially imposed 'selves,' which people with a shared history and ancestry hold in common" (393). In others, cultural identity does not rely on a discovery of a single, unified history, but rather takes account of the fact that identities are always in a state of becoming and are constantly producing and reproducing themselves through the "continuous play of history, culture and power." Hall favors the latter position and argues for cinematic representations that re-tell, not simply re-discover the past, and that recognize the ruptures and differences that develop from cultural change.

Hall does not cite specific examples of films that exemplify these two articulations of cultural identity. However, Martinique filmmaker Euzhan Palcy's 1985 *Sugar Cane Alley* is perhaps a fitting example of a film that seeks to authenticate cultural identity through the recovery of an unrepresented past. Palcy's coming-of-age story represents a strongly Afrocentric Caribbean black culture for the first time in Martinique cinema, chronicling the long history of slavery and oppression on Caribbean sugar cane plantations. In contrast, the more formally experimental and overtly oppositional films of the Sankofa Collective, including the work of black gay director Isaac Julien, do not focus on the return to a cultural past and heritage but instead explore the politics of contemporary black identities that emerge from intersecting African, Asian and Caribbean diasporas. Kobena Mercer's 1988 essay, "Diaspora Culture and the Dialogic Imagination," discusses the films of black British cinema and offers a critique of cultural identity that is similar to Hall's. For Mercer, black British cinema does not deal with "the expression of some lost origin or some uncontaminated essence in black film-language, but the adoption of a critical 'voice' that promotes consciousness of the collision of cultures and histories that constitute our very conditions of existence" (56). Much contemporary criticism of exile and diaspora film straddles these two theoretical and political positions. As several essays in this anthology reveal, particularly the ones by Durham, Wynne, Diaconescu-Blumenfeld and Knee, this issue opens up the field to a larger debate about the relationship between postcolonialism, diasporic identities and postmodernism.

More recent efforts that take up the challenge of defining diaspora and exile cinema and that identify some of its formal and conceptual innovations have come from Laura Marks and Hamid Naficy. Marks's *The Skin of the Film: Intercultural Cinema, Embodiment and the Senses* concentrates on experimental intercultural films and videos by minorities in the West during the 1980s and 1990s that challenge the representational conventions of narrative cinema. She examines in particular how experimental film styles capture the disorienting effects of dislocation and the negotiation of two or more cultural identities, and finds they often appeal to the full range of sensory experience—touch, smell, and taste in addition to sight and sound—in order to apprehend the exile's, immigrant's or a migrant culture's experiences and memories of place. Marks's contributions to exile and diaspora film studies are significant because of her application of theory to the textual specificities of film, suggesting the rewards of closely observing the texture of cinema itself—the uses of mise-en-scene, editing and narrative structures. One especially noteworthy concept (which is instrumental in my own reading of cultural memory in Ruth Ozeki Lounsbury's *Halving the Bones*) is "the transnational object," a term that refers to a material object which, because of its association in a given film with exile or immigration, comes to embody otherwise elusive cultural connections. For instance, small objects such as a wooden bird, a sari or a kachina doll in independent diasporic films are images "whose incommensurable pasts are the product not only of personal history but of intercultural displacement" (78).

Another innovative synthesis of diaspora theory and cinema is displayed in the 1995 essay, "The Cinema of Displacement: Towards a Politically Motivated Poetics." Offering a "poetics of the displaced imagination" in cinema, Bishnupriya Ghosh and Bhaskar Sarkar examine the "spatial turn" of diaspora criticism. Emphasizing spatial tropes that mark off and connect territories of home and foreign "host" countries in such films as *Perfumed Nightmare*, *Sammy and Rosie Get Laid*, *Close to Eden* and *Canticle of the Stones*, the authors draw upon on the theoretical work of Said, Anzaldúa, Chandra Mohanty and Naficy to identify a scale of different zones of displacement—symbolically represented in film by bridges, landscapes, "double spaces" that invoke more than one location, transitional places and shifting notions of "home."

The importance of transitional and transnational places and spaces featured in exile and diaspora films is most fully developed by Hamid Naficy. Beginning with *The Making of Exile Cultures: Iranian Television in Los Angeles* through *An Accented Cinema: Exilic and Diasporic Filmmaking*, Naficy has devised the concept of transnational cinema as "accented" and "interstitial," and argues that it distinguishes itself from dominant cinema through a variety of aesthetic, thematic and alternative production features. According to Naficy, transnational cinema employs "fragmented, multilingual, epistolary, self-reflexive, and critically juxtaposed narrative structure; amphibolic, doubled, crossed, and lost characters; subject matter and themes that involve journeying, historicity, identity, and displacement; dysphoric, euphoric, nostalgic, synaestetic, liminal, and politicized structures of feeling; inter-stitial and collective modes of production; and inscription of the biogra-phical, social, and cinematic (dis)location of the filmmakers" (*An Accented Cinema* 4). The advantage of Naficy's multipronged approach is that he is able to combine political, aesthetic, narrative, historical and production aspects of exile and diaspora cinema. His most recently published book, *An Accented Cinema* identifies exile and diaspora cinema as a loosely defined genre at the crossroads of social formations and cinematic practices. The most comprehensive treatment of exile diaspora cinema to date, *An Accented Cinema* provides a close reading of exile films in the context of larger patterns, pays attention to production modalities as well as the spa-tial and temporal disjunctions that become central tropes, such as themes of homelessness, journey and return, and the importance of history, nos-talgia and memory. Naficy's work is the culmination and synthesis of his earlier work on specific diaspora films, particularly Iranian and Middle Eastern cinema and media. Despite Naficy's attempt to identify a taxon-omy of tropes in exilic and diasporic cinema, he is careful not to insist on too rigid a definition of the genre, calling it a category of criticism rather than an established or cohesive cinema.

My Beautiful Laundrette: An Example of Diasporic Cinema by a Bicultural Director

The study of exile and diaspora cinema has emerged in large part from the urgency of contemporary world politics. At the very moment I sat down to write this introduction in July 2001, the violent confrontations between British Asian youth and police in the city of Bradford in the north of England, triggered by the xenophobic tauntings of white Britons associated with the right-wing National Front, exploded on the streets. The violence of the conflict reminded me that fierce nationalisms and the defense of national identities are alive and well in the twenty-first century.

Interestingly, in 1986, Pakistani British writer, playwright and filmmaker Hanif Kureishi published an essay on Bradford in *Granta*, addressing the very same tensions and racial hatreds that have flared up again fifteen years later. With its relatively large South Asian immigrant population and high rate of unemployment, Bradford "was a place I had to see for myself," wrote Kureishi, "because it seemed that so many important issues, of race, culture, nationalism, and education, were evident in an extremely concentrated way in this medium-sized city of 400,000 people, situated between the much larger cities of Manchester and Leeds. These were issues that related to the whole notion of what it was to be British and what that could mean in the future" (124). As he visited various constituencies and cross-sections of the population, both white and Asian, Kureishi discovered "diverse, disparate and strikingly various" communities. He met conservative, separatist groups among both white Britons and Pakistani immigrants, who ironically were more alike than different in defending their view of a culture as traditional and unchanging, even as the daily cultural practices in Bradford combined English rituals with "yoga practices, going to Indian restaurants, the music of Bob Marley, the novels of Salman Rushdie, Zen Buddhism, the Hare Krishna Temple, as well as the films of Sylvester Stallone, therapy, hamburgers, visits to gay bars, the dole office and the taking of drugs" (143).

In the previous year Kureishi and Stephen Frears had released their film *My Beautiful Laundrette*, which presents an ironic critique of the power relations between white England and the Pakistani immigrant community. The film focuses on the profoundly subversive, yet historically fraught homosexual bond between Johnny, a white working-class Briton and former National Front thug, and Omar, a Pakistani Briton, who despite all odds find themselves taking advantage of Thatcher's ruthless capitalism by refurbishing an old laundromat in South London. *My Beautiful Laundrette* represents Kureishi's more optimistic vision of a new hybrid, sexually and racially diverse community that survives the racism of white working-class London and the isolationist stance of the Pakistani immigrant enclave. Yet Kureishi never lets us forget that Omar's and Johnny's relationship is historically overdetermined, and like many human interactions, is based on asymmetrical power dynamics and self-interest as well as genuine affection.

One of the most interesting scenes in the film, from a visual and conceptual point of view, is the opening of the ritzy laundrette Powders, that Omar and Johnny have transformed from the seedy old laundromat Churchill with the help of a drug deal. The laundrette becomes an ironic utopian

paradise where characters act out their desires and fantasies, but it also represents what Bakhtin calls a "chronotrope," a moment materializing time
in space; it provides a fictional environment where historically specific
power constellations are made visible. This scene juxtaposes two generations of Pakistani immigrants and their white lovers, Omar's uncle Nassar
and his working-class mistress Rachel in the front room, and Omar and
Johnny in the back, separated by a one-way mirror. A third space outside
the laundrette is filled by the crowd waiting to be let in. The camera sets up
ironic parallels and differences between the pairs, fluidly moves between
these different spaces—"liquid windows" in Kenneth Kaleta's terms—to
articulate the ways in which groups and individuals see and don't see other
in the looking-glass they have created for themselves.[2]

Significantly, the grand opening is preceded by a scene in which Johnny
calls the laundrette the "crown jewel of South London"—Kureishi's ironic
and deliberate reference, of course, to India as the crown jewel of the British
Empire. In response to Johnny's remark, Omar remembers being brutally
harassed in the past by National Front skinheads, just as Johnny is about
to seduce him. Their intimacy and future co-existence is predicated on
confronting and acknowledging this violent colonial and neo-colonial history and re-evaluating their identities. At the end of the sequence, before
the laundrette's opening, Johnny comes over to the one-way mirror and
looks at himself: His face and Omar's overlap on the glass behind which
Omar is standing, remaining unseen to his partner on the other side. The
superimposition of their smiling faces has a particular political significance
and is perhaps the most striking visual image of Kureishi's filmic construction of a new British identity, one neither traditionally Pakistani nor
exclusively white British but both, altered and transformed by the changes
each character has wrought in each other. The shifting positioning of the
camera from Omar's to Johnny's point of view allows for complex spectator
identifications with both characters, even as the backroom space behind the
one-way mirror emphasizes that the different social spaces do not mingle
easily. In a different sense, the mirror scene also functions as a metaphor for
the screen in transnational cinema, the encounter between film text and
spectator that may create a third space of cultural meaning and identity.
Here, *My Beautiful Laundrette* offers—to use the term of Bishnupriya

Ghosh and Bhaskar Sarkar— a spatial "poetics of the displaced imagination," even as Kureishi at the end of the film shows that class conflicts, family quarrels and racial confrontations still cast a pall on his vision of a new, multicultural Britain (112).

My *Beautiful Laundrette* put Kureishi on the international map as one of the new British postcolonial writers and filmmakers; he received an Oscar nomination for best original screenplay and the film became an internationally acclaimed and distributed production. Yet the film also drew hostile responses from some segments of the Pakistani community. In his essay, "Bradford," Kureishi writes of a young Asian activist and local political star who called him a fascist and reactionary, presumably because he saw the screenwriter's refusal to show "authentic" and exclusively positive images of Pakistanis in Britain as reinforcing preexisting racist images and precluding South Asians from assuming positions of power.

My *Beautiful Laundrette* provides us with a powerful visual image of Rushdie's "peculiar fusions" in cinema and Appadurai's mass-mediated "diasporic imagination," one that invited multiple, sometimes contradictory readings. My *Beautiful Laundrette* is an early, provocative example, through by no means the only one, of cinema's exploration of complex histories, showing here how national identity is transformed through the incursion of the postcolonial past into the hybrid present. The film embodies many of the political challenges and possibilities of exile and diaspora film addressed in this volume of essays.

The Essays

This collection places a strong emphasis on migration in a European context. Europe differs from the United States in terms of its immigration policies and histories, its different conceptions of national identity, and its historical legacies of colonial relationships. Moreover, state-subsidized film production has underlined the role of cinema as a national storyteller in many European countries that have traditionally defined themselves in opposition to Hollywood. Yet films made in Switzerland, Germany, the former East Germany, Italy, France and Ireland that examine the roles of migrant identities in national cinemas today find themselves addressing the increasing hybridity of their own cultures through decolonization and immigration while producing films for a global market.

For immigrant filmmakers inside Europe who are documenting the displacements and cultural relocations of their families and communities, the complex politics of film production, reception and representation affects the nature of their work. This is no less true for larger European productions in which considerable financial investments are at stake. Outside of Europe the situation for making films with (im)migrant subjects is even more complex, with on the one hand the potential political problems facing filmmakers in various nations and on the other hand the commercial dominance of Hollywood at the global box office.

The anthology highlights the particularity of transnational contexts and trajectories—the specific mappings and histories of migrant journeys. Hence, the essays are arranged to reflect different perspectives on the similar geographical and cultural spaces represented in the individual films treated in the essays. For example, several essays that deal with the migration to and from Germany are grouped together, as are those that examine the border between United States and Latin America. This arrangement allows the essays to speak to each other in ways that confirm Nicholas Mirzoeff's view that "the diasporic visual image is necessarily intertextual" or "intervisual" (7). However, these connections are evocative rather than conclusive, and are meant to elicit comparisons between different depictions of the histories of displacement.

As suggested by the introductory quotations, the migrant, exile or refugee portrayed in film or literature thus provides a useful entry point for examining predetermined conceptions of self and nation. A central tension in many films about exile and migration occurs between the local and the global, national and transnational, the meanings of "here" and "there." Many contemporary cultural and postcolonial critics argue that the nation-state is a problematic model of belonging and identity in the age of globalization and the rapid transnational flow of goods, people, capital and media information technologies.[3] As Iain Chambers writes in *Migrancy Culture Identity*, "Considering the violent dispersal of people, cultures and lives, we are inevitably confronted with mixed histories, cultural mingling, composite languages and creole arts that are also central to *our* histories" (17).

The role of postcolonial and migrant history in the construction of national identity is directly or indirectly addressed in all of the essays. We therefore begin with Allen Meek's discussion of migrancy in "A Century of Exile: National Cinema and Transnational Mediascapes," which examines the figure of the migrant in the documentary film series on national cinemas, "The Century of Cinema," commissioned by the British Film Institute (BFI). Meek, in fact, looks closely at film representations of migrancy in two BFI segments, in director Stephen Frears' "Typically British" and Sam Neill's reflections on New Zealand cinema. Examining the complex articulation of national identities in two cinemas that often define themselves in opposition to the global hegemony of Hollywood, Meek poses the timely question that frames many discussions of national cinemas in an age of globalism and transnationalism: How should we understand the cinematic representation of migrants and migrancy in these BFI documentaries that, as Meek argues, are hard pressed to reconcile cultural specificity and ethnic diversity in British, New Zealand and other national cinemas, at a time when they are being increasingly integrated into transnational markets targeting a global audience? Meek contends that as migrancy becomes a more prominent metaphor for contemporary identity, it is also "quickly subsumed into the logic of image markets and the mobility of capital." The migrant thus becomes a multiple and contradictory figure in these BFI narratives of national cinemas.

The next cluster of four essays in the collection analyzes the articulation of migrant identity in German-speaking cinema: Angelica Fenner and Mine Eren focus on the representation of Turks who came to Germany in the post-war years as "guest workers," Barton Byg writes on Chilean exiles in the former East Germany, and David Coury on German expatriates in the United States coming to terms with their precarious post-war national identity and collective guilt, and the challenges of German reunification after 1989.

Fenner's "Traversing the Screen Politics of Migration: Xavier Koller's *Journey of Hope*" takes up the political dilemma addressed earlier by Allen Meek as she examines a film which, in its choice to portray generic Turkish peasants rather than Kurdish refugees migrating to Switzerland, tried to reconcile the political interests of two countries which appeal to an international audience. Fenner situates the 1990 Academy Award winning

Swiss-German-Turkish co-production within a current of European cinema apparent since the 1970s that treats the situation of migrant workers, particularly Turks, and is targeted to audiences within German-speaking countries. Fenner argues that *Journey of Hope* and related films largely represent a "cinema of appeasement" for German and Swiss audiences' ambivalence about immigration to Europe. The essay places *Journey of Hope* in its broader historical context and employs Foucault's theories of how spatial relations articulate power differentials to argue that *Journey of Hope* hails a superior, knowing Western European spectator and limits the migrant to the position of the abject, victimized Turkish subject.

Mine Eren's "Traveling Pictures from a Turkish Daughter: On Seyhan Derin's *Ben annemin kizivim/I'm My Mother's Daughter*" deals with the representation of Turkish immigrants from a different angle, or as she puts it, "from the margins" of German culture. Eren analyzes the autobiographical documentary work of Seyhan Derin, the first female Turkish director in Germany to visualize Turkish immigration. Through interviews with family members, archival film footage, fictional narratives, monologues, letters and various sound tracks—a bicultural Turkish German woman's retrieval of a lost history and fragmented family—Derin's *I'm My Mother's Daughter* recollects thirty years of Germany's Turkish immigration. Eren pays close attention to the testimonial narrative of the filmmaker's mother, countering prevalent negative stereotypes of Turkish women in German cinema as victimized, passive objects with her mother's complex life story and authoritative voice. The essay provides close readings of individual sequences to reveal Derin's dialectic intertwining of personal memory, fiction and history, a technique that succeeds in linking Derin's cultural outlook as a diasporic woman with the story of her mother's complex negotiations of Turkish and German cultures.

The former East Germany has not been widely discussed as a country of immigration and exile. Against the backdrop of the ideological contradictions and political maneuvering in the GDR's relationship with the Third World, Barton Byg provides an incisive analysis of Lothar Warneke's film *Blonder Tango*, based on the novel by the Chilean author Omar Saavedra Santis, who lived and worked in the GDR after the coup against the Allende government. Although socialist internationalism promoted an ideology of support for liberation struggles around the world and the GDR offered material help to leftist organization in the "Third World" countries, the presence of actual citizens of non-European cultures did not lead to multi-culturalism in the GDR. Combining a historical analysis of the GDR's political economy with a close reading of *Blonder Tango's* narrative, style and characters, Byg reveals the ways in which the East German realist filmmaker Warnecke's adaptation of Santis's novel exposes the historical and political barriers to multiculturalism and the extreme difficulty of inter-cultural understanding on a personal everyday level in the East Germany of the 1980s. Artistic understanding of Third World realities, argues Byg, is only possible by way of German "mourning work" (*Trauerarbeit*) over past political defeats and human tragedies obscured by contemporary real-ities and political ideologies.

In contrast to the cinematic focus on immigrants and exiles *within* German-speaking countries discussed in the three forementioned essays, David Coury addresses the vexed question of home and belonging in films from the late 1980s and 1990s that feature German exiles and expatriots in the United States, such as Percy Adlon's *Bagdad Café* and *Salmonberries*, Rosa von Praunheim's *Survival in New York* and Monika Treut's *My Father is Coming*. In "Servus Deutschland: Nostalgia for Home in Contemporary German Cinema," Coury discusses a generation of German filmmakers who, following in the footsteps of the New German Cinema of the 1960s and 1970s, re-examine the themes of *Heimat* (homeland) and German identity. The New German Cinema took as one of its central themes a coming to terms with the past (*Vergangenheitsbewältigung*), as German film-makers sought to define for their generation the question of German iden-tity and belonging in a homeland imbued with a fascist history. Coury argues that the later generation of German directors such as Adlon, von Praunheim and Treut often use the United States as a real and mytholo-gized space that functions ambiguously as a new place of belonging and a refuge from the ghosts of history after the fall of the Wall and in the era of German unification in the 1990s. Focusing on fictionalized German exiles in the United States, their films explore how the American West, Alaskan wilderness and New York City serve as alternative, albeit ambivalent homes and communities for Germans seeking to re-imagine their identities and work toward social change beyond the patriarchal and monocultural heritage of the German Fatherland.

German filmmakers are not alone in examining the traumas of their national history. Gianni Amelio's 1994 film *Lamerica* about contemporary Italy's relation to post-Communist Albania implicitly addresses the re-encounter of Italy to its own past—Mussolini's colonization of Albania, Italian immigration and poverty. Rodica Diaconescu-Blumenfeld's "The Desire of the Other: Balkan Dystopia in Western European Cinema" takes a critical look at the politics of representation in Amelio's film, with its harrowing depiction of the Albanian exodus in the early 1990s as the nation imploded in economic and political chaos. Diaconescu-Blumenfeld draws on postcolonial theory and its problematization of the representation of the other in order to illustrate how the Balkans function in European cinema as a dislocated identity and "mad" other. Specifically, she finds that *Lamerica*, which revives a neorealist Italian aesthetic and a Marxist humanist perspective, contains two contradictory discourses in relation to "Albanians-as-others." The film recognizes and affirms Albanians as subjects, giving them a voice and presence on the screen, while also providing a trenchant critique of contemporary capitalist Italy's amnesia about its own history as a colonizer. Yet, the Albanians in Amelio's film become primarily the "raw material" for an examination of the postmodern Western self, represented by an Italian protagonist who journeys back to Italy bereft of his traditional trappings of identity. By comparing *Lamerica*'s neorealist approach with more avant-garde works such as Pier Paolo Pasolini's *Notes for an African Orestes*, Chantal Akerman's *D'est: Bordering on Fiction* and Jean-Luc Godard's *Forever Mozart*, Diaconescu-Blumenfeld poses the question about how European filmmakers can critically examine their own "fictionalization" of the Balkans in cinema and address the reinscription of colonial images of the East.

The following two essays by Mark Ingram and Florence Martin and Carolyn Durham turn our attention to France's colonial history and relationship with its immigrants from the former North African colonies. Ingram's and Martin's essay "Voices Unveiled: *Mémoires d'immigrés. L'héritage maghrébin*" examines Yamina Benguigui's multigenerational documentary about Maghrebi immigration to France from the 1950s onwards. This essay also returns to the question of representation and point of view in diaspora cinema; it explores how Benguigui creates a "polyphonic" documentary that allows the "unheard voices" of first-generation North African immigrant workers, their wives and children, to be heard, voices that have not had a visible place in French public culture. Ingram and Martin reveal the ways in which the film portrays the negotiation of identity across cultural boundaries as an extremely complex passage between two worlds, genders and generations. They employ ethnographic concepts of "transnational cinema" as well as Evelyne Accad's theory of feminist humanism (*fémi-humanisme*) to consider the individual stories as part of a larger meta-narrative of North African immigration in France, and to reflect on how Benguigui's own tale as an immigrant daughter growing up with the myth of return "haunts" this representation of a collective history.

Claire Denis's autobiographical film *Chocolat*—the subject of Carolyn Durham's essay—visualizes the return journey of a young white French woman, allegorically named France, to the site of her childhood home in colonial Cameroon, now on the eve of independence. In "More Than Meets the Eye: Meandering Metaphor in Claire Denis's *Chocolat*," Durham sees the film as a "national allegory," employing Fredric Jameson's definition of texts that represent national histories and politics even when narrating apparently private stories. Paying close attention to the symbolic significance of naming, allusion and metaphor in the film, Durham unpacks the significant, yet overlooked reference in the film to the eighteenth-century Scottish explorer-travel writer Mungo Park. In the frame story of *Chocolat*, France's expatriate American black travel companion is called quite ironically Mungo Park. Reading *Chocolat* through its ironic references to Mungo Park's sentimental travel diaries and in relation to conventional narratives of European imperialism in which Africa becomes a setting for adventure and romance, foregrounds the film's critical presentation of colonialism and colonial power relations. She re-evaluates in particular the problematic interracial sexual encounter in *Chocolat* in light of its critique of the sentimental tropes of imperialism, the conventions of representation that "enable imperialism to write itself into reality/history."

Catherine Wynne's essay on *The Crying Game* considers Neil Jordan's film in the context of Irish colonial and postcolonial history and nationalist politics. Wynne establishes a historical connection between *The Crying Game*'s persistent and ambivalent transgression of gender and political borders in contemporary Northern Ireland and England and the rivalry among cross-dressed Irish agrarian secret societies of the nineteenth century. In doing so, she discloses how the film connects its dual drama of postcolonial Irish politics and gender identity to nineteenth-century British colonialism and Irish resistance. At issue is the film's contestation of the binary opposition between colonizer and colonized through its central protagonist, Fergus, whose journey from Belfast to London represents a complex exile into a postcolonial space of radical uncertainties, a carnivalesque space where both his gender and political identity are destabilized. Wynne expands and complicates Bakhtin's notion of the carnival as an oppositional space, exploring how *The Crying Game* invokes the ritualized performances of political opposition by nineteenth-century agrarian secret societies, and to what degree the film offers a challenge to established gender and political binaries and to what degree it re-instates prevailing notions of sexual and national identity.

A critical examination of the complexities of desire and border crossings in transnational cinema is also at the heart of Adam Knee's analysis of Atom Egoyan's *Exotica*, which moves us into a North American context. As an Egyptian-born Canadian filmmaker of Armenian descent, Egoyan has articulated the multifaceted interplay between cultural and national identities in much of his film work. Knee argues that Egoyan's 1994 film *Exotica* can be seen as his most fully realized examination of the permeability of personal and national borders in an era of globalization. The film's drama about a grieving widower's attachment to an "exotic" dancer and his chance acquaintance with a smuggler of exotic birds functions as a sophisticated allegory about Canada's status vis-à-vis the United States and the nature of transnational relations more generally—the incursion of the exotic into the local. Knee's essay explores how Egoyan effectively undermines simplistic binary oppositions between exploiter and exploited, cultural hegemonic forces and oppressed minorities. For Egoyan, whose own migration and ethnic history defy reduction to a stereotypical paradigm of immigrant identity, interpersonal and international relations always involve a complex process of negotiation between multiple, intertwined, often mutual desires.

The difficult challenge for migrants of mediating and negotiating their cultural identities is also addressed by my own essay, "Mediating Worlds/ Migrating Identities; Envisioning Home and Identity in Recent Asian American and Asian Canadian Women's Films." Focusing on three films by women directors made in the 1990s, the essay emphasizes the significance of their female-centered perspectives on Japanese and Chinese immigration. Kayo Hatta's historically-based feature film *Picture Bride*, Ruth Ozeki Lounsbury's auto-ethnography *Halving the Bones*, and Mina Shum's autobio-graphically inspired comedy-drama *Double Happiness* are analyzed in light of Lisa Lowe's critique of the "homogeneous, fixed and stable oriental object" and recent Asian American film scholars' multifaceted, globalized conception of Asian diaspora identities. All three films respond to the invisibility or the stereotyping of Asian American women in the media; each re-imagines and reinterprets the sedimented history of Asian migration to the US and Canada through a narrative intertwining of history and family memory, autobiogra-phy and fiction. Yet a comparative reading also reveals the very different cin-ematic and narrative approaches each film takes to the representation of the cultural memory of Asian migration and the negotiation of different cultural landscapes. *Picture Bride* recreates and complicates the history of "picture bride marriages" between Japanese women and male sojourners in Hawaii in the early part of twentieth century. Portraying the struggle of a Japanese pic-ture bride to reconcile her heritage to a new life in the U.S. territory, the film employs allusions to Japanese paintings of ghosts and the supernatural to articulate the sustained presence of Japanese culture in the protagonist's consciousness. *Halving the Bones* self-reflexively constructs immigrant his-tory and memory in three generations of Japanese American women through a non-linear, associative assemblage of family mementos, media images, and fabricated home movies. *Double Happiness*, a sharp-eyed social comedy, employs the trope of the "performance of ethnic identity" to highlight a young Chinese Canadian woman's mediation of the cultural spaces and tra-ditions both within her Chinese immigrant family and the larger social world of Vancouver.

The final two essays analyze two very different cinematic representations of migration between North and South America. Norman Holland's discus-sion of the 1933 Hollywood studio film, *Flying Down to Rio*, contextualizes it in relation to significant economic, political and technological changes occurring in the Americas in that time period. Using Ana Lopez's conception of Hollywood as an "ethnographer" translating Otherness for its audiences, Holland explores how *Flying Down to Rio* reflects FDR's Good Neighbor Policy toward Latin America through the celebration of a cross-border love affair between a rich Brazilian girl and a working-class American man flying to Rio de Janeiro. He shows how this genteel comedy's glamorization of the Latin star Dolores del Rio implicitly demanded that both the Latin American screen subject and the audience accept American values as the price for participating in Hollywood's spectacular vision of progress and modernity. Holland argues that later films from the 1980s and 1990s featuring Chicano characters and various Latin American migrants to the U.S. such as *La Bamba*, *The Perez Family* and *Lone Star*, create the possibility of new border romances and the ironic play of migrant identities. For Holland, *Lone Star*'s depiction of an interracial, incestuous relationship may signal "a desire to construct a bold, capacious and unencumbered Americas culture."

In "Forget the Alamo: Reading the Ethics of Style in John Sayles's *Lone Star*," Ken Womack and Todd Davis pick up on the central incest motif in *Lone Star*, with which Sayles metaphorically interweaves the multiethnic fabric of contemporary American life, a fabric strained by the past and present tensions between Chicanos, Anglos, African Americans and Native Americans in the border country of the American Southwest. Through an application of Gerard Genette's narrative principles and discourse theory and a close analysis of Sayles's elliptical editing, Womack and Davis demonstrate the moral impact of Sayles's visual style, his exploration of the ways in which our shared histories impinge on the ethical choices that confront Americans in the present. His particular use of flashbacks and flashforwards emphasizes how (mis-)perceptions and (mis-)understandings of the past have shaped the ethnic tensions that plague the border town's historical present. The frontier myth is here reinvoked through the film's classic focus on the sheriff, the power of state authority, and the inner workings of the law and politics in the border town. However, in Sayles's film the relationship between dominant and minority groups, between insider and outsider, between native and migrant, is more complicated than in most mythic Hollywood films; ethnic and racial identities in *Lone Star* assume distinctly pan-American permutations in the context of the history of border politics between Mexico and the United States.

Even as the arrangement of this anthology highlights the shifting yet interconnected spatial contexts and representations of exile and migration in the cinema, readers will discover other thought-provoking associations between essays in the collection. For example, Bartoner Byg's essay on the relations between the former GDR and Chile in *Blonder Tango* provides an interesting companion piece to Norman Holland's discussion of Hollywood's articulation of FDR's Good Neighbor Policy between the United States and South America during the 1930s in a film such as *Flying Down to Rio*. Both essays problematize how East German and U.S. foreign policies toward Latin America are treated in complex, sometimes contradictory and unresolved ways. Cross-generational relations between immigrants and their children in cinematic autobiographies are the focus of Eren's essay on *I'm My Mother's Daughter*, Mark Ingram's and Florence Martin's reading of *Mémoires d'immigrés, l'héritage maghrébin*, and Eva Rueschmann's discussion of *Halving the Bones* and *Double Happiness*. These essays also specifically address migration as a gendered experience, highlighting female subjectivities and daughters' retrieval of their mothers' or fathers' stories. Adam Knee, Catherine Wynne, Norman Holland, and Ken Womack and Todd Davis all comment on the possibilities, limits and consequences of border-crossing and border romances. The "ethics of representation" in relation to the migrant and the ethnic other is addressed from different critical perspectives by Angelica Fenner's reading of *Journey of Hope*, Rodica Blumenfeld's essay on *Lamerica* and Ken Womack's and Todd Davis's analysis of *Lone Star*. Hence, although the arrangement of the essays in this volume suggest particular connections between films and filmmakers in exile and diasporic cinema, readers are invited to make their own "intervisual" links between the films covered in this anthology.

Moving

Pictures,

Migrating

Identities

1. A Century of Exiles

National Cinemas and Transnational Mediascapes

—Allen Meek

It is often noted that what we call globalization today refers at once to unprecedented levels of mobility and displacement of peoples throughout the world and to the spread of telecommunications media that interconnect these dispersed peoples in diverse ways. For those who have been dislocated from the places, communities and nations which in the past have defined their social and cultural identities, representations of other people and other places have begun to play new and significant roles. Today both people and images are highly mobile. Moreover, the institutions of the nation state which have shaped the media representations of our social and political world—and thereby sought to locate us through a shared sense of time and place—are also rapidly changing.

The twentieth century was an age of massive human displacement and cinema can make its claim to be the medium *par excellence* of this central experience of modernity. It was the cinema which first provided a virtual "homeland" for the displaced urban masses in the great metropolitan centres

3

and industrial cities (Virilio 39). Cinema presented a transformation of the "imagined communities" of the nation based in print capitalism and thereby anticipated later global networks of electronic communication such as television and cyberspace. In the cinema we are always moving, in the sense of what Anne Friedberg has called the "mobilized virtual gaze" of modernity. Yet at the cinema diverse populations have also assembled and experienced new forms of community, sharing physical as well as virtual space.

The cinema both gathers together and disperses. How, then, should we understand the cinematic representation of migrants and migrancy at a time when national cinemas are being increasingly integrated into transnational modes of production and distribution? In attempt to address some of the issues this question raises, I want to discuss the figure of the migrant as it surfaces in some films from the series commissioned by the British Film Institute to mark the centenary of cinema, in particular Stephen Frears's film about English cinema, *Typically British* and Sam Neill and Judy Rymer's presentation of New Zealand film in *Cinema of Unease*. But before providing a more detailed discussion of these two films, I want first to situate them in the larger context of the *Century of Cinema* series. I won't pretend to do justice to the entire series in the limited space here, and indeed each individual film raises many complex questions about film and national culture. Instead I concentrate on two principal issues that seem to me to be at stake in these films overall: the construction of national cinema and the representation of migrancy (in terms of the mobility of both people and images).

A Century of Cinema

One of the fascinations of the *Century of Cinema* series is its global ambition to represent the diversity of cinema. As a result it's easy enough to gripe about all of the omissions and exclusions and "problematic" representations in the series. As series producer Colin MacCabe, faced with the massive task he had set himself, put it:

The solution came with the decision to abandon the quest for a total history, to opt instead for individual essays . . . and trust that from an incredible variety of approaches something of the complexity of the century of cinema would emerge. (22)

An interesting wager—but what strikes me about many of the resulting sixteen films of the *Century of Cinema* series is how often they present simplistic reactions to, rather than complex responses to, globalization. What I think we can see in the *Century of Cinema* are some clear examples of how economic and political pressures on media production support certain ways of negotiating a marketable identity but compromise critical reflection on the meaning of the nation and the role of media in our lives.

When considering the question of national cinemas today we note the deregulation of national broadcasting, the emergence of the multiplex cinema, the negotiation of the *niche* in the global market, the spread of satellite transmission and cable networks, the proliferation of digital communication technologies, etc. So why are so many of the *Century of Cinema* films framed by essentialist discourses about identity, in a period when both producers and consumers have been made aware as never before of the political economy of global media? After all, talk of globalization is hardly limited to academic criticism, and the multinational character of contemporary film is often plain for all to see.

For example, Jean-Luc Godard, in his *Twice Fifty Years of French Cinema*, poses an astute question about the centenary of cinema: are we celebrating the development of cinema or its commercial exploitation? But while the relations of film and capitalism are thus challenged, the notion of a French cinema is apparently not questioned: France, the birthplace of cinema, remains its homeland. The dark clouds of globalization gather on the horizons of the nation in Godard's film, as in several others. Not surprisingly, the first assumption which many of these films share is that national cinemas must be preserved, or perhaps rescued. This assumption is consistent with MacCabe's intentions:

> The national economies of the first part of the century had allowed many peoples to record their visions on celluloid. I was determined that the series would bear witness to this plurality of vision, to insist that the global culture must recognise local variety. (24)

In the face of Rupert Murdoch's globalism, MacCabe turns to the national as a site of difference.

But the *Century of Cinema* project is also inherently transnational in scope. MacCabe's attempts elsewhere to promote a "post-national European" cinema may help us to understand the particular construction of Western European cinemas in the series, especially the films on France and Germany. In this Western European media ecology, national traditions keep alive specific histories while repressing others. In Edgar Reitz's meditations on German cinema there is much said about the legacies of Nazism and the Holocaust, but almost nothing about Hollywood or the post-war presence of America. And Reitz goes much further than Godard in his assumptions about a national psyche and even a kitsch "essential German woman." Here the drive to preserve and promote European cinema inhibits historical understanding. A regressive assertion of national identity in these films explains why neither the French New Wave nor New German Cinema are discussed as complex negotiations of Hollywood as well as of national culture. Both films also ignore the various waves of emigration to Hollywood and the many extraordinary films that were the result—including, of course, *film noir*.

Godard's position is interesting here, as he takes the apparent "forgetting" of French cinema by today's audience as an opportunity to summon the ghosts of its great directors for their historic testimony. However, like any work of memory this conjuring of the past obscures other historical relationships: Hollywood is always the Evil Empire rather than the space of fantasy and transformation which it promised even Godard at other moments (think of Belmondo facing Bogart's image in the opening shots of *Breathless*). In the era of Quentin Tarantino and David Lynch there must be no European flirtation with American pulp. Here we see examples of how discourses of cultural imperialism can support a misrepresentation of the past. (On this point one should also mention Oshima's film about Japanese cinema which, like those on France and Germany, fails to address the history of American presence or the mass appeal of American pop culture.)

National cinemas stake their claims to distinctive identity in the face of the dominant Other of Hollywood. Putting a somewhat different slant on these matters, the film about Irish cinema gives a very candid account of both the Irish diaspora and the problems of sustaining a national industry in a global economy of image production. Here the Hollywood representation of Ireland is considered along with the national image constructed for export. One might say that this film did what *should* have been done in the case of New Zealand cinema. For this neo-colonialism of the image long experienced by the Irish is now becoming more familiar there, particularly with high-profile international co-productions productions like *The Piano* and *Lord of the Rings*. And many responses to *Cinema of Unease* in New Zealand saw Sam Neill's contribution to the series as reinforcing this neo-colonialism (see McDonald, and Martin and Edwards).

The situation becomes complicated further when we look at the presentation of Irish, Australian or New Zealand cinema with reference to postcolonial questions of identity. Here the ex-colonies confront their own ghosts, their own histories of imperialism and racism. Never mind surviving the impact of Hollywood, what about the cinema of indigenous peoples or migrant communities? How can these different claims for representation and recognition be reconciled with the demands of global marketing?

Transnational Mediascapes

In order to move toward a more useful understanding of these issues we need to move away from the frame of national cinema. To begin again with a more simple-minded question, then: why do people go to the movies anyway? Sometimes to see their own place, but more often to travel to some *elsewhere*. To paraphrase John Berger, the *Century of Cinema* is a century of departures and disappearances.

In his often-cited essay "Disjuncture and Difference in the Global Cultural Economy," Arjun Appadurai offers a definition of mediascapes. The first part of his definition relates to the political economy of media: ownership, control, distribution, modes of production and representation. The second part emphasises questions of identity. Appadurai further elaborates this dimension of the mediascape in the following passage:

> Mediascapes . . . tend to be image-centred, narrative-based accounts of strips of reality, and what they offer to those who experience and transform them is a series of elements . . . out of which scripts can be formed of imagined lives, their own as well as those of others living in other places. (*Modernity* 35)

For Appadurai the imagination is a "social process" of increasing importance for cultural identity in the contemporary world; indeed he calls it "the key component of the new global order" (31).

Mediascapes position human subjects in imaginary spaces which *may* support a shared sense of national identity or address "the need of the deterritorialized population for contact with its homeland" (Appadurai, *Modernity* 38). But where is this "homeland"? The "homeland" provided by the cinema may also be a virtual space of adventure and fantasy. In the West it is Hollywood which has most often provided this desired mix of the familiar and the exotic. So there are aspects of the "imagined community" of the cinema which may be profoundly at odds with any national imaginary.

Today national cultures are under increasing pressure to rearticulate their identities in the languages of global popular culture. Here the needs of groups with strong links to their immediate localities (most dramatically, indigenous peoples) and those of groups who look to a home located elsewhere, collide and converge. There is a sense in which technological media must always displace. If so, then it is different forms of exile and migrancy which define the politics of the mediascape.

On this note David Morley and Kevin Robins write that there is "still an obsessive and regressive 'desire to . . . fudge and forge a false unity based on faded images of the nation'" (Morley and Robins 31). It is this disjuncture, as Appadurai would put it, between transformations of the mediascape at the level of political economy and the formation of *imaginary landscapes*—offering both mobility and locatedness—that is at the heart of the question of the mediascape. Recent cinema, of course, abounds in such disjunctures: for example, in the image of "Englishness" produced in the films of Merchant-Ivory, an American and an Indian; or the English Queen *Elizabeth* played by an Australian (Cate Blanchett) and directed by an Indian (Shekhar Kapur).

There is a moment in Stephen Frears's *Typically British* (co-written by Charles Barr) when Frears, Michael Apted and Alan Parker, over afternoon tea in California, concur that Ken Loach is the finest director in postwar British cinema. Loach's critical realism seems exemplary in its commitment to the local, the regional and the socially disadvantaged. What they don't mention is that Loach's films are more often seen and acclaimed in

Western Europe than in Britain (Christie 71). Today the mode of representation constitutes only one dimension of our understanding of the mediascape.

Even Martin Scorsese's "personal journey" through American cinema pays tribute to the many emigre directors who are associated with the "dark side" of American film. The very notion of *film noir* has long designated a transitive space, a trans-Atlantic genre through which Europe flirts with American populism and America feigns European artiness. But the notion of emigre directors dissecting the alienation underlying American society is also a powerful myth. Thomas Elsaesser has argued that the experience of exile and immigration in Hollywood supported not only the supposed social criticism of *film noir* but lies at the very foundations of Hollywood as "a country of the mind" ("Ethnicity, Authenticity, and Exile" 121): a virtual world of fantasy, melodrama and adventure. This notion of cinema as an "elsewhere" is most interestingly explored in the episode from the *Century of Cinema* series on Polish cinema. Through interviews with the *viewers*, rather than the makers, of films we learn something of how the cinema becomes so deeply embedded in pleasure, memory, trauma, and desire: not just in terms of Hollywood as global escape route, but of cinema as a profound dimension of modern experience.

Cultural studies has drawn our attention to the ways in which subnational formations of class, gender and ethnicity have invented hybrid cultures through an imaginary relationship with American popular culture. According to neo-Gramscian applications of the notion of hegemony, this relationship has been often understood as a struggle over cultural meanings with America as a dominant influence rather than a totalising force. National cinema, then, has never been one thing in terms of its mode of representation nor meant one thing its different audiences. Appadurai describes a global cultural economy in which "the United States is . . . only one node of a complex transnational construction of imaginary landscapes" (*Modernity* 31). Whether one is speaking of the cultural institutions of the nation state, the global corporate interests of commercial media, or subcultural and minority identity formations, for Appadurai the imagination has become, in a new and urgent sense, a means by which social agency is negotiated. National cinemas address different audiences: both the citizens of the nation state and various international markets of cinema-goers and video-watchers. This latter group, of course, also includes all of those migrants who have left their original national territories but who continue to maintain communication links and cultural identifications with their home country.

On a more pessimistic note, Fredric Jameson has emphasised how the GATT talks were used by American lobbyists as an opportunity to dismantle national subsidies in the name of free trade—an intervention which "spells the death knell of national cinemas elsewhere, perhaps of all other national cinemas as distinct species" ("Notes" 61). Is Jameson's pronouncement here too absolute? And even if he is correct, what would it mean for national cinemas to disappear?

While the "cultural imperialism thesis" may be correct insofar as America clearly pursues economic and political power by means of distributing its mass culture, this argument must be counterpointed by the various ways that various cultural identities can actively negotiate an imaginary relationship with Hollywood as well as with different national cinemas. On the other hand, this negotiation can in turn be impacted by the role that the nation state plays in regulating and protecting their media markets and distinct economies of local and global resources. Cultural identities define themselves through mediascapes, but the elements out of which these imagined communities are formed are shaped by larger economic and political forces. If there is no diversity of nations or national institutions then there will surely be diminished opportunities to negotiate new identities or to formulate alternative positions or develop oppositional practices.

The particular institutional formations that support national cinemas have often been defined by their response to the multinational corporate power and cultural hegemony that Hollywood has come to embody (all of which is not deny that the nation state remains itself also a hegemonic formation). The problem located by Jameson is whether the very possibility of national cinemas including alternative modes of production to the Hollywood dominant is disappearing. If this is so what can be read in contemporary film texts that would enable us to better understand this historical development? The intention of the following discussion, then, is to read the figure of the migrant as s/he emerges in these different narratives about national cinema and performs different negotiations of transnationalism within the global cultural economy.

Typically British

Stephen Frears's history of British cinema is organised primarily around a narrative of migration: of British filmmakers to Hollywood. In Los Angeles, Frears discusses the dilemmas of being British with directors Michael Apted and Alan Parker, both of whom have pursued successful careers in Hollywood. The conversation turns at several moments to consider directors like Ken Loach and Mike Leigh who have remained committed, throughout the 1980s and 1990s, to making films that document social and political change in England. While all of these directors share a common origin in the British film and television industries of the 1960s and 1970s, a clear narrative emerges of a defining choice between indigenous and expatriate filmmaking in the later period.

Frears himself occupies something of a middle position between the apparent alternatives of commercial imperative and politicized localism. Making his reputation through the success of films like *My Beautiful Laundrette* and *Sammy and Rosie Get Laid* for Channel Four, Frears achieved a third possibility through a locally-produced drama, focused on interethnic and transnational encounters, that attracted a surprising amount of international interest. This in between-ness that defines Frears position performs a complex symbolic function in his narrative about British cinema.

In *Typically British*, Frears begins with what are presented as the absurd, archaic, but nevertheless endearing characteristics of English society and culture: public school, drinking tea, the hegemony of the middle class, and patriotism. Two qualifications of this nostalgic evocation are thus, from the outset, put aside. The first is that "Englishness" has often alienated the British mass audience which has historically preferred American films, television, and popular culture. The other theme that is strikingly absent from Frears's account is imperialism, and this repressed history of imperialism could be said to return in *Typically British* in the representation of the Indian immigrant community in the films Frears made scripted by Hanif Kureishi. In these films we witness what Edward Said has called the "voyage in" of the former subjects of empire who reappear as the new migrant identities inhabiting the metropolitan centre. The British Empire missed its chance—later exploited by the USA—to pursue global hegemony through the enormously powerful new medium of film. The decline of Britain's imperial power, however, also supports a certain national nostalgia that colours *Typically British* and the British film industry generally but is never considered by Frears in these larger historical contexts.

Migrancy, then, performs a complex function in defining national cinema in *Typically British*. The migration of English directors to Hollywood dramatises a perpetual crisis in the national film industry; the imperial voyage out is replayed in the British export industry for costume drama (for example, in *A Passage to India*); while the presence of new immigrant groups in Britain has helped to promote internationally a certain image of British cosmopolitanism (this process is somewhat clearer in the popular music industry). One avenue of film production for Britain's Channel Four embodies this cosmopolitan tendency. However, the role of cinema in dramatising localised political struggles—including those of immigrant communities and ethnic minorities—has in some respects been subverted through the internationalising of film production and distribution. *My Beautiful Laundrette* and *Sammy and Rosie Get Laid*, for example, are films about the impact of Thatcherism on ethnic, gender and class conflict which can also be consumed internationally in terms of an essentially depoliticised "multiculturalism" or "quality" arts and entertainment.

In the 1980s and 90s the transnational productions for *Film on Four* have probably constituted the nearest contemporary equivalent of the transatlantic art house movies (made by European *auteurs* but featuring American star actors) that achieved a certain commercial success in the 1960s and 70s. John Caughie has reminded us of the particular infrastructures of British film and television—based in the Reithian ethic of public service and Grierson's theories of documentary realism—which support what has now become a fully transnational cinema. While Loach and Leigh have become the survivors and contemporary masters of those British traditions of critical realism, their films now circulate through the channels of public television and international film festivals alongside those of Merchant-Ivory, Krzysztof Kieslowski, Wim Wenders and others. Transnationalism and migrancy are common themes in all of these films, not only because they seek to represent real social and cultural changes but also because they address the multi-national audience that composes their various markets.

As Caughie points out, the shift from the original public service context of British realism, which addressed a national audience with a very limited choice of films or, later, of television channels, to the niche marketing of *Film on Four*, late night movies, international film festivals, and video, has also transformed the role of critical realism as an effective mode of address. Without a specific national public sphere in which to intervene, films like Loach's *Ladybird, Ladybird* or Leigh's *Secrets and Lies* (both of which feature migrant characters and diasporic cultures) become characterised by particular forms of cultural consumption rather than political struggle. Caughie notes:

> what the international market values in national specificities are precisely those qualities which transcend the local and make it universal: humanity, character, and, in particular, character in adversity. What is more difficult to sell on the international market are the material social conditions which produce the adversity. (221)

These dramas of migrancy are themselves migrant texts. We must acknowledge Appadurai's point that there is no way that the meaning of any media text can be fixed to any one social or cultural context, but that the text forms a site where different negotiations of the global and local will inevitably take place. However, the possible meanings of these imaginary landscapes do have significant institutional contexts as well as cultural and ideological parameters. One must, in a sense, weigh the critical impulse, whose social and political meanings must always in some sense be localised, against an indentificatory impulse which can potentially recompose the meaning of any image or narrative in what may be radically different social and historical contexts. Both impulses are necessary for cinema to communicate politically, but only the second may be necessary for it to survive commercially.

Frontier and Exile

To pay attention to representations of migrants and migrancy, then, may provide a useful focus on the cinematic negotiation of identity or, conversely, may blur one's sense of historical locatedness. Nevertheless, it remains our critical responsibility to challenge the forms of ideological containment which unquestioned assumptions about national cinema can impose. In this spirit, Hamid Naficy has proposed a genre of "independent transnational cinema" in order to address the ways in which film studies paradigms like genre, auteurism, and national cinema can overdetermine our understanding of cinema history. Slipping across borderlines, the cultural productions and historical experiences of exiles, emigres, refugees, and expatriates, challenge us to understand films in terms of "intertextual, cross cultural, and transnational struggles over meanings and identities" ("Phobic Spaces" 121). In contrast to this transnational imaginary, the mythology of the American frontier continues to be evoked as a means of assimilating dissonant, exilic voices into Hollywood's multinational imperial imaginary.

For example, Martin Scorsese's film for the *Century of Cinema* series, while it pays tribute to many emigre directors (he mentions Tournier, Ophuls, Lang, Wilder, Ulmer, and Sirk), also tends to fix those innovators to an image of the director as "outlaw hero" which is thoroughly imbued with mainstream American myth (see Ray). Anthony Heilbut has written of the European political exiles in America that the myth of the frontiersman "suggested that Americans lacked a firm locus of self, while the refugees, with no space at all to manoeuvre, knew only too well who and what they were" (49). In Scorsese's narrative the director/hero is the individual confronting the mass conformity of corporate America, but this heroism sits uneasily with Scorsese's exclusion from his discussion most of American film after about 1970. For it is post-Vietnam American film that most disturbingly reveals the dark side of frontier mythology at a global level (Scorsese's own *Taxi Driver* is itself an interesting displacement of the Vietnam legacy onto a *noir* drama of urban alienation). Like *Typically British*, then, Scorsese's narrative about American cinema tends to repress narratives about imperialism and global hegemony and to subsume the figure of the exile or migrant into a mythology of national identity.

This mixing of exilic and frontierist mythologies also informs the film about New Zealand cinema from the BFI series, *Cinema of Unease*, in which an immigrant and expatriate (and Hollywood star), Sam Neill, gives an account of New Zealand cinema by way of his own life story and transnational experience. Neill speaks of two kinds of exile. The first is the kind experienced by the colonisers of New Zealand, nurtured on feelings of nostalgia for the home country and inferiority to the home culture. So New Zealanders attended schools modelled on English schools, read textbooks produced in England, and in their leisure time watched English movies. The second exile is experienced more recently by New Zealanders who have developed a sense of their own national identity but are now displaced in various parts of the world and "dream of home." In both cases the sense of identity is closely related to physical displacement along with a desire for international recognition.

Cinema of Unease is about "coming of age," which in the white settler ("pakeha") culture of New Zealand usually means defining one's own identity by leaving home and establishing a sense of individual independence. Neill's ongoing sense of estrangement organises his narrative: as a child in the 1950s his family immigrated from the UK and he currently lives and works as an expatriate. The nostalgia for home that he experiences at different moments in his life becomes for him a way to understand the imaginative power of the cinema. Today many New Zealanders travel widely and, in an increasingly globalized and deregulated economy, work overseas—including many New Zealand film directors. In this light Neill's wistful question, "What I want to know is: what do they dream of when they dream of home?" that closes his reflections of New Zealand filmmakers, may have a broad resonance. However, more uncomfortable questions arise in response to Neill's narrative: why does his discussion of the indigenous Maori people of New Zealand have to wait until he has outlined the cultural-economic break with Britain in the 1970s? The relationship of Maori and pakeha is the central theme of the few feature films made in New Zealand before this time (see Blythe). As Naficy reminds us:

> If internal exile were to be defined as "isolation, alienation, deprivation of means of production and communication, exclusion from public life" then many intellectuals, women, artists, religious and political figures, and even entire communities have suffered from it within their own countries. ("Phobic Spaces" 123)

The question of uses of cinema in New Zealand by its indigenous people, as well as the positions of various immigrant and minority groups in that country, puts the issue of exile into another perspective that is either marginalised or ignored in *Cinema of Unease*. So while migrancy is also a central theme in this film from the BFI series, it is again a depoliticized migrancy that has a certain promotional function in the international media marketplace.

Conclusions

Why do the films in the *Century of Cinema* series so often reproduce myths of identity which are blatantly contradicted by the technologies and political economy of the media in which they are represented? We can see in these films different negotiations of economic and political change. On one hand they abound with expressions of what Freud called "ideologies of the superego": attachments and identifications which have outlived the social structures which formed them (Easthope 216). This would account for the rather mournful atmosphere of many of the films for the series. Something has been lost. On the other hand these films clearly seek to symbolise these losses, to mourn cinematic identifications, while looking for new, and possibly progressive, narratives of identity.

In this matter I think MacCabe's premise for the BFI series was obstructive. By assuming the category of the national as the basis of difference in the global media economy, the series inhibits a working-over of the different identifications—local, national and transnational, traditional and modern—which shape the production and reception of cinema today. Ultimately I think we need a cinema, supported by nation states, which present us with imaginary landscapes in which we are able to recognise and reflect on these different identifications. In the age of transnational mediascapes, this might even be seen as a significant measure by which to evaluate any so-called national cinema.

It is in response to these shifting contexts of identity that Jameson has commented on the new relation of (what classical Marxism called) base and superstructure in the current stage of globalization. Jameson notes that while in the cultural sphere one might welcome the apparent emergence of new hybrid identities and forms of cultural difference, in the economic sphere globalization tends to subsume difference into ever enlarging and penetrating modes of homogenising power and control ("Notes" 56–57). The shift in media studies away from marxist categories like ideology and cultural imperialism toward debates about postmodernity and globalization needs itself to be understood with reference to economic restructuring over the past twenty years. For Jameson postmodern culture has become fully instrumental in the circulation of capital through the codes and economies of electronic information. But while cultural studies sought to formulate a politics of consumption and identity and sometimes lost sight of political economic realities at a global level (John Fiske's work has become emblematic of this slippage), influential marxist positions on cultural imperialism (see Schiller)—which Jameson tends to uncritically repeat in his recent essay on globalization—often provide no theorization of cultural transformation in any positive sense.

Because the issue of migrancy and transnationalism, as I have tried to demonstrate, clearly circulates between both economic and cultural registers it also offers a significant opportunity to ask how we can begin to sketch a "cognitive map" that can describe these shifting registers. What makes the debates I have briefly outlined above so important is that they prompt us to formulate an understanding of culture and identity that is supported by a more adequate account of economic and political forces. As migrancy becomes a more prominent metaphor of contemporary identity it is quickly subsumed into the logic of image markets and the mobility of capital. While human displacement has increasing urgency in defining social and political experience, it has also become part of the *lingua franca* of postmodern culture in contemporary capitalism. In these films commissioned by the BFI to "celebrate diversity" in a century of cinema, national identity is articulated through the image of the migrant and by way of the migrant image.

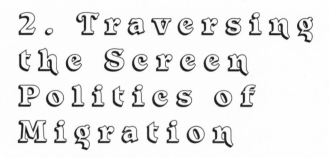

2. Traversing the Screen Politics of Migration

Xavier Koller's *Journey of Hope*

—*Angelica Fenner*

Introduction

When Xavier Koller's Swiss-Turkish co-production, *Journey of Hope*, garnered an Oscar for Best Foreign Language Film at the 1990 Academy Awards, no one was more astonished than the director himself.[1] Although a previous film of his, *The Black Tanner*, had been submitted by the Swiss Film Board as an Oscar-nominee in 1987, Koller was virtually unknown to U.S. film audiences. This most recent production had moreover received only minimal previous public exposure in the U.S. and stood in competition against four other nominees which had benefited from commercial runs in theaters nationwide. Since many viewers and critics had surmised the French historical romance *Cyrano de Bergerac* to be the most formidable contestant, the announcement of Koller's film as prize winner (snatched as it were, from under *Cyrano*'s nose) was initially greeted by stunned silence followed by a smattering of polite applause in the Academy halls. In France, perhaps not uncharacteristically, the jury decision nearly resulted in national disaster, with the French film industry convinced that the selections had been rigged and complaining vociferously of an international conspiracy. Daniel Toscan du Plantier, head of Unifrance and promoter of French films, complained in the *New York Times* that the award went to an "obscure low-budget movie from a country without cinema" (Bernstein 16). Meanwhile, in Koller's homeland, film critics seemed to embrace the film without reservation, although its reception was clouded within both left- and right-wing groups in Switzerland variously triggered by its inflammatory topic. The director himself speculated that state funds for publicity may have been minimized because of the film's critical stance towards Swiss immigration policies.[2]

This abbreviated synopsis of the early reception of *Journey of Hope* evinces the inevitable vagaries that characterize the trajectory traced by any film from the level of financing and production to that of distribution, exhibition and reception. Indeed, the attempt to retrospectively decipher a justificatory logic at work in the aleatory processes that fatefully target a group of films as recipients of the coveted Academy Award is fraught with conjecture. One may assess a given film's theme, its cast, its production and publicity budgets, the profile of the producer and director, the political and social climate into which it was released—factors which operate in complex tandem, mutually enhancing or undermining one another. However, in the instance of *Journey of Hope*, its distinction as Oscar prizewinner fortuitously coincided with a critical juncture in history, offering lingering testimony of the capacity for the filmic medium to become a crucible for contemporary political debates. The fall of the Berlin Wall in 1990 precipitated a decade of accelerated transitions, unhinging a world polarized for nearly half a century by the Cold War. Public attention shifted to a more ambivalent preoccupation with reconfiguring the political topography of Europe amidst contestations as to the parameters that constitute its limits and the permeability of those borders. Disputes in the Mid-East leading to the Gulf War, as well as tribalized warfares in Eastern Europe, represent only a few segments in the long concatenation of violent ruptures that triggered tides of veritable *Völkerwanderungen*. These mass migrations drew those seeking political or economic asylum from economically impoverished and war torn areas into the more affluent nations of not only geographically proximate Northern Europe but also Canada, the United States, Latin America and Australia.

Koller's film is loosely based upon the true circumstances of a Kurdish family that sought to illegally migrate from rural Anatolia to Switzerland via Italy; it traces the tragic circumstances of their hapless journey into the Alps and subsequent delivery into the hands of Swiss immigration authorities. Within the fictional plot Koller did not actually code the family as Kurdish, having been warned that if word of an even circumstantially Kurdish thematic leaked out during shooting in Turkey (in part, on location in the original village), the lives of cast and crew could be endangered. He later reasoned that the ethnicity of the family was ultimately immaterial, for Turkish and Kurdish migrants suffered similar experiences in their migrations northward. Thusly billed as a film about Turkish peasants who temporarily leave their village to earn Western currency abroad, its thematic nevertheless became metonymically linked in the western media with the plight of ethnically persecuted Kurds fleeing for their lives and with displaced populations in the war zone of Iraq, herein revealing how imprecise understanding remains in many industrialized democratic nations of the diverse circumstances that impel global migration today. When Koller began work on the film in 1989, the Kurdish topic had not yet gained international media attention; however, the situation of desperate Iraqi Kurds crossing Turkey's eastern borders surfaced fortuitously close to the time of the Academy Awards, causing a number of critics to expound upon the timeliness and relevance of Koller's "intervention." Other critics alluded to the Academy Award as a placative gesture intended to appease the conscience of the U.S. public in the aftermath of the Gulf War, which had intensified havoc Middle East and further displaced already persecuted populations. Once *Journey of Hope* had been released onto the international distribution circuit following the Academy Awards, it arguably functioned as a spectatorial experience offering viewers worldwide an opportunity

*Haydar (Necmettin Cobanoglu), Mehmet Ali (Emin Sivas),
and Meryem (Nur Surer) in* Journey of Hope. *Courtesy of
Jerry Ohlinger's Movie Materials Store.*

for a fleeting moral catharsis, in its original Greek sense of a discharge of
emotions (here, most particularly that of moral indignation and diffuse
guilt) with regard to a more widespread phenomenon most viewers felt
helpless to remedy.

Tracing the Genealogy of the Migrant Film

By locating *Journey of Hope* within a broader film historical context, by
analyzing spectatorial identifications at work in its media reception and by

Xavier Koller, director of Journey of Hope. *Courtesy of Jerry Ohlinger's Movie Materials Store.*

pursuing a close reading of some of the work's narrative tropes, this essay strives to unpack some of the politics at work in the visual representation of migration. When Koller himself points out: "This theme of migration is very old and many movies have been made about it" (Kermode 21), he is referring to a specifically European context of representing migration, one which I would hasten to distinguish from the context of *immigration*, a thematic more properly attributable to U.S. cinema, which has historically captivated its audiences with the myth of the American melting pot. The representation of migration within European cinema has historically focused upon the impermanence of the migratory experience, utilizing a neo-realist aesthetic or even ethnographic approach to limn the immediate sociological predicament of cultural and familial displacement. Although Koller adopted the title of his work from an Italian film of the 1950s, Pietro Germi's *Il cammino della speranza*, which portrays the travails of a Sicilian worker in Milan, I would argue that his film more properly owes its debts to a nationally specific genealogy of West German films that explore social and economic questions accompanying the influx of migrant labour from southern Europe since the late 1950s. These "films of migration," as I shall rhetorically refer to them, could be said to constitute a subcategory of a genre loosely known as the "problem film," which has existed in one form or another since at least the Weimar era, where *Aufklärungsfilme* or educational films sought to educate the public about various social issues such as physical hygiene, sexual propriety, the need for welfare reform, and so forth. The propitious expansion of state subsidization of filmmaking beginning in the late 1960s helped revive production of this type of film during the halcyon era of the New German Cinema, when script content evincing social relevancy was preferentially perceived as constituting a worthy investment of state monies.[3]

As its label implies, the West German *Problemfilm* adapts the feature film format with a heavy dose of documentary realism to bring to public attention a variety of social concerns (ecological decline, single mothers, racism, corrupt politics, child labor). For better or worse, these films have often been driven by a commitment to social justice wedded to an overly pedantic directorial imagination exhibiting a torpid fixation with tragedy and victimization. In the instance of this subcategory of "the migrant film," the politics of representation furthermore become closely aligned with the discourse of ethnography with regard to the problematic of, "Who is speaking for whom?" Some of the most prominent directors of the New German Cinema have addressed the topic of migration in their work and garnered international accolades for conjoining innovative aesthetics with socially relevant thematics: Rainer Werner Fassbinder's *Fear Eats the Soul*, about the relationship between a Moroccan migrant and a German cleaning woman, garnered an international prize at Cannes in 1974, while Werner Schroeter's *Wolfsburg oder Palermo*, about a Sicilian laborer at the German VW plant, won the coveted Golden Bear at the Berlinale in 1980. However, even the most innovative films seeking to give voice to the experiences of foreign labourers have not been immune from the hazards of unwittingly reinscribing the latter's marginalization, by reflecting more about the director's own perception of the cultural other or alternately making the subject in question into a vehicle for venting a more personal directorial critique of society.[4] Indeed, it is not a little ironic that many directors founded their careers on the critical acclaim of films displaying this propensity.

Koller's visibility in the public eye was secured following his Academy Award and paving the way for his entry into the Hollywood arena with another project similarly implicated in speaking for others, namely, the 1994 Disney production of *Squanto: A Warrior's Tale*. Within this genealogy of films it is worth noting, however, that several West German feminist filmmakers of the 1970s and 80s, conditioned by their own marginalized status within the film industry to interrogate inherited narrative strategies, engaged in a greater degree of self-reflexivity at the level of enunciation. Consider, for example, the experiments with flashbacks and dialogic voice-over in Helma Sanders-Brahms's *Shirin's Hochzeit* (1976) and Jeanine Meerapfel's *Die Kümmeltürkin* (1984) and *La Amiga—Meine Freundin* (1987).

It would be tempting to postulate this disparate assemblage of films by vastly divergent directors as constituting something akin to a distinct genre, "the migrant film" or "migration film," by dint of their common thematic focus, consistently pessimistic narrative trajectory, and syntax of binarisms (e.g. urban/rural, oriental/occidental, native/other, hegemonic/subaltern, oppressor/victim, etc). However, not only do these individual works deserve to be read within the context of their individual aesthetic and political agendas, there would be a potential redoubling at work in ghettoizing a body of films themselves preoccupied with the politics of marginalized identities. Scholarly discussion in the field of genre criticism seems, moreover, fraught with irreconcilable contentions which Rick Altman sums up in the crucial questions, "What is a genre? Which films are genre films? How do we know to which genre they belong?" ("A Semantic/Syntactic Approach" 6). The parameters defining a genre are by no means static; they are subject to changes in cultural attitudes, innovations introduced by influential new films, the economics of the industry, and so forth.[5] Consider, for example, the transformations undergone within the Hollywood Western, from its early beginnings, in which the hero represented an agent of law and order on the western frontier territory, to its contemporary transmutations, in which the protagonist may be a renegade outlaw or even professional killer and the entire setting potentially transplanted onto the equally harsh and unyielding terrain of an urban ghetto.

Since the invocation of the genre discussion would ultimately serve to unduly overdetermine the topic of migration in German film, one might instead posit a body of films as comprising something approximating an identifiable "discursive practice" in the Foucauldian sense of invoking certain discourses within a specific institutional environment where relations of power play a central and defining role.[6] It is therefore not merely the thematic of migration that is a unifying factor, but the fact that representations of cultural difference within the visual field of cinema history have been focalized through a certain ethnographic gaze, one that transforms difference into alterity or more often, subalternity and herein effects a form of knowledge production closely wedded to particular relations of institutional power. The nexus of power/knowledge need by no means be understood as some invidious force latent within particular practices; Foucault's methodology of exteriority neutrally situates it at the very surface of discourse.[7] In the instance of "migration films" it is evident in the moral indignation and compassion (itself symptomatic of extant power differentials) which inspired diverse directors to shoot films about the situation of foreign workers and illegal aliens with the Enlightenment-based goal of enhancing among hegemonic audiences political and cultural understanding of a particular minority population, i.e. producing/disseminating knowledge about them.

This practice gains greater historical specificity when considered in the light of a highly politicized cinema, the New German Cinema, which found itself trapped between the directorial ambitions of social and cultural intervention and interrogation of the fascist legacy, on the one hand, and the retroactive appropriation of these artifacts on the international distribution circuit and by cultural ambassadors of the State such as Internationes and the Goethe Institute. Under the latter's patronage they came to constitute part of a national cinema offering testimony to the revived status of the Federal Republic as *Kulturnation*. The institutional context of state subsidization of film production necessarily also informed the discourse of "migrant films," insofar as it necessitated the submission of film scripts to Film Subsidy boards or television networks before approval for financing could be granted. While many filmmakers have understandably criticized this structure as a form of pre-production censorship, there is a sense in which this practice merely articulates more literally the manner in which filmic discourses are inherently "subjected," in the sense that they assume coherent form not *despite* restrictive systems but rather as the unavoidable result of being made to serve the interests of those institutions wielding power.[8] The notion of a cinema critical of state policy (in this instance, films that criticize the assumed temporary resident status of migrants or reveal institutionalized discrimination towards them) need not be incommensurable with the notion of state subsidization when one furthermore comes to recognize that the orientalist and ethnographic discourses unwittingly invoked in so many films functioned to maintain migrant workers at arm's length through their benevolent exoticization, romanticization, or abjection. In a certain respect, financial and ideological approbation of these films served to underscore the state's noble generosity towards its artists while also evincing that public sentiment toward immigration and the defining parameters of German citizenship was not in earnest danger of being swayed by such filmic interventions; indeed, they could even serve to collectively purgate social anxieties.

The Politics of Film Production in the New Europe

Although *Journey of Hope* was not a West German but rather a Swiss production, I would argue that its discursive practice was informed through isomorphic ideological and institutional constraints that situate it within this same genealogy. Koller's film stands as a product of an era in which European co-productions have increasingly become the norm following the establishment in 1988 of Eurimages, a crucial support fund under the umbrella of the Council of Europe, whose subscribing members include not only the EC nations but also the countries of Scandinavia, Poland, Switzerland, Austria, Turkey, and Hungary, among others. Eurimages represents one of a variety of initiatives by means of which the European Community has sought to revivify national film industries plagued by dwindling state resources and meager audience turnout. Modest domestic productions lacked that budget and the star casting to compete against multi-million dollar Hollywood blockbusters flooding European movie theaters.[9] Through a consolidation of financial resources among subscribing

European members, a sizable fund was established with which to invest greater amounts of money in a few promising scripts likely to secure a broad niche at the box office; beneficiaries of this approach include Koller's 2.3 million dollar production, as well as Volker Schlöndorff's *Voyager* (1991) and Jaco Van Dormael's *Toto the Hero* (1992). There are a number of conflicting ambitions bound into this enterprise, as into any number of pan-European initiatives such as the EC's MEDIA program, which provides loans and support for small producers. It is not as crass as merely wishing to produce a counter-Hollywood, although certainly there is a keen desire for consolidated European media interests to become 'global players' alongside the media giants of the U.S. and Japan in an era in which the latter are pushing for "free circulation" of (primarily their own) products and media programs on a global scale. There is also a significant cultural dimension bound with establishing mutual cooperation among European peoples and nations and increasing consciousness of commonalities as well as respect for differences. As British social geographers David Morley and Kevin Robins (1995) summate the challenge, it is about "the reimagination of community and identity in Europe" (178). Such an ideological mission faces the antinomy of reconciling values, interests and identities at regional, national *and* European levels. For the screening board of Eurimages or of other supranational agencies of the European Commission granting approval and funding to film scripts, it entails navigating some impossible middle ground. They seek filmic content that emulates purportedly common European values or highlights specific issues deemed worthy of public attention while simultaneously promising financial success at the box office. In effect, the ideal film will address some sort of composite pan-European interlocutor/ consumer who will, however impossibly, feel addressed, compelled and entertained on individual cultural terms by the content of the films promoted.

Arguably, then, Koller's film project was operating under constraints imposed by the not necessarily complementary political interests of the nations of Switzerland and Turkey, while also seeking to hail an international audience less invested in the interests of either country and more likely to be moved by a "universal" and concomitantly depoliticized message. To outline the unenviable ideological terrain the film must therefore negotiate: it cannot risk offending the Swiss or severely undermining the nation's honor by presenting immigration policy in too harsh a light. At the same time, it seeks to inform the public about the economic situation of rural Turkish citizens who seek to work abroad, without representing Turkey as an insolvent nation unable to provide sufficient employment for its citizens. The expedient elision of the Kurdish question is a further example of the accommodations that occur at the level of character development, film plot, script dialogue, conspiring to create a film whose enunciation ultimately remains ambivalent towards its protagonists.[10]

The Narratology of the Migrant Film

A close chronological reading of the film's narrative trajectory, in tandem with an assessment of how aspects of its plot were received in Swiss, German and U.S. media may bring these ambivalencies to the foreground. The film opens upon a village celebration for a Kurdish man about to embark upon the northward journey in search of employment in Switzerland. We are offered glimpses of ritualistic preparations involved in such festivities, scenes clearly included to heighten the non-Turkish viewer's sense of cultural voyeurism towards a region not only geographically remote but ostensibly accessible only through the mediating eye of the participant-observer camera. In a visual citation already captured on countless miles of archival ethnographic footage, we bear witness to the slaughter of a sheep, which metaphorically foreshadows the victimization of the film's protagonists while also heightening the overall idealization of the villagers as bearing a less mediated relationship to their means of production. Indeed, the setting seems almost prelapsarean, as constituted through social relations informed by mutual interdependence rather than purely by monetary exchange. Haydar, a Kurdish farmer with seven children, has just received a postcard from a relative in Switzerland encouraging him to join him in a land "where butter would flow from the udders of your goats." As he contemplates his options in the ensuing days, his reluctance to leave his homeland is conveyed through the longing with which he silently gazes out upon the fields of his property, implying a fealty to the rugged and unyielding terrain which the land itself seems to reciprocate. When he nevertheless resolves to make the journey to Switzerland together with his wife, Meryem, and to

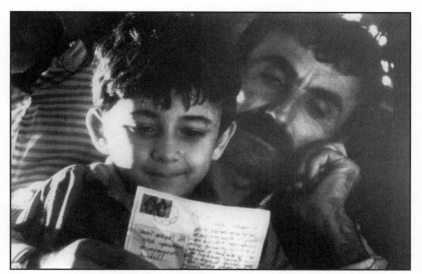

The promise of a better life? Mehmet Ali (Emin Sivas) looks at the coveted postcard from Switzerland with his father Haydar (Necmettin Cobanoglu) in Journey of Hope. *Courtesy of Jerry Ohlinger's Movie Materials Store.*

temporarily leave the children with relatives, his father questions his choice, demanding, "Are we lacking anything here? Even grass comes out with its roots. Once you've sold everything, you'll be without roots, a nothing." Koller's script here lapses into what anthropologist Arjun Appadurai (1988) has referred to as "the spacial incarceration of the native," a prevalent tendency to naturalize cultural and spatial divisions in the representation of cultural alterity. While bearing a poetic appeal, naturalistic metaphors in this instance effectively mask the harsher economic and political realities which impel migration. The story itself will unfold in the manner of an allegorical tale, Haydar's motivation to move to Switzerland herein assuming the contours of a biblical (or, more appropriately, Koranic) temptation. He is depicted as coveting Western affluence, for which he is prepared to forfeit community solidarity and the fundamental sustenance which the agrarian mode of production has ensured his family. The film seems to innocently reinforce the folly of his investiture, one which unravels the material coordinates of his life as he sells his land to one neighbor and the sheep and oxen to another. Subsequently, the camera documents his impulsive purchase of a bag of Swiss chocolate for the children (a sort of guilty bribe, since they will have to stay behind with relatives), capturing a shot of his face through a display window as he peers at glittering gold wares from which he selects a bracelet and necklace for his wife and his oldest daughter. His wife Meryem's emphatic resistance to his plan right up until the night prior to their common departure for Istanbul, together with the recurring strains of ominous extra-diegetic music, seem to portend that this is to be a hapless journey of vain hopes.

At the level of character development, I would argue that the film fails to present us with protagonists whose motives we can respect and justify and this is one of the fundamental ways in which its enunciation hails a hegemonic viewership easily prone to believing that Haydar and Meryem (and by association, all refugees) do not really have sufficiently compelling grounds for leaving their homeland and would be better off staying where they are. Although we may sympathize with the Kurdish couple, their motives are insufficiently developed within the sketchy plot and herein establish one of many deterrents to identification. A cursory glance at a number of film reviews corroborates the prevalence of this spectatorial reaction, as Tom Charity in the journal *Sight and Sound* writes, "Haydar's life in a remote Turkish village is initially pictured in such idyllic terms that it's clear he should not leave it. . . . In part, this is the tragedy of a foolish man" (5). Meanwhile, in *The San Francisco Chronicle* we read, ". . . existence on their sunny farm seems happily bucolic, but it's not good enough for 35-year old Haydar, who dreams of a more rewarding future for their youngsters" (Stone E3). And in London's *Independent*, film scholar Sheila Johnston sums up the plot as ". . . a Turkish peasant dreams of quick riches in Switzerland and stakes his farm and his fortune on the roll of the dice" ("The Long and Winding Road" 16).

What also remains ambiguous is the extent to which Haydar and his wife are aware of the auspices under which they will enter Switzerland, i.e. whether they know that they have been issued false identification documents and are undertaking a very risky venture, or have been duped into believing that their entry has been legally arranged. The eerie music track that accompanies the overdone characterization of the smugglers who arrange their transport in exchange for an exorbitant fee sets up a situation in which the viewership is, in any case, privileged to greater knowledge than the protagonists. This superior positioning makes it too easy for the viewer to begin to fault the poor peasants for not exercising better judgment. The villainous typecasting of the smugglers, when coupled with the submissive positioning of their overly trusting customers, establishes a simplistic playing field comprised by victims and unscrupulous shakedown artists; if there is anyone in the film we despise by the film's end, it is these predatory traffickers in human cargo. Jay Carr in *The Boston Globe* hails the film's efficacy in restoring a moral universe, writing, "Already, the airing of the family's story has had one result: the man who fleeced would-be immigrants is now on Interpol's wanted list" (B6). Such placative reassurances offer the public an immediate sense of closure while touching upon what are merely secondary symptoms of global refugee flows likely to continue unabated.

The screen time which the script robs from a more proper assessment of the local cultural, political and economic circumstances impelling migration is then reallocated to documenting an unrelenting concatenation of harrowing events to which the family (and the viewer) are subjected during their northward odyssey. A great deal of media attention dwelled upon the fact that Koller's plot was inspired by a newspaper account of a Kurdish family trapped in a blizzard while traversing the Alps in October 1988. According to the director, he even visited the family in Anatolia, although they initially refused any contact and were wary of any publicity. (It is their original house which appears in the opening sequence of the film.) This aura of authenticity seems to have captured the public imagination, herein raising Koller's film from the status of feature film to the level of an authentic reenactment and assigning this cultural artifact greater truth value and political clout. However, Koller did not merely represent the facts of one family's experience, he undertook a zealous metaphorical condensation of all the possible abuses that could occur on the migratory journey, including episodes recounted by illegal migrants in other contexts. With regard to the scriptwriting process, he recalls:

I also came across the case of a wife who was raped by a sailor. I had a similar scene in the original script, but then I thought: it's not possible. First of all, it would have been so brutal, and second, the hero would have lost face. He wouldn't be able to continue his journey. It's a climax but it comes too early and leads in a different direction. I realized that the audience would be too exhausted at the end of the film to go over the mountain; they would switch off. So I smoothed it down. (Johnston, "Incredible Journey" 19)

Such comments betray the degree of calculation that goes into plot development, involving finely tuned manipulations of the viewer's emotions in the service of ideological interests. It is not the deviation from the original story that I am contesting, of course, it is the condensation of tragic events in an excessive ploy for sympathy which I would submit is similarly integral to the discursive practices prevalent in West German "migrant films." Koller cuts to the heart of his strategy when he remarks, "My intention was to deal emotionally with the events rather than the arguments surrounding the (immigrant) problem. Hardly ever do you experience the people, the drama behind the issue" (Lipper 10).

Certainly, emotionality has played a central role in debates about global migration and has been the driving force behind many progressive initiatives to accommodate economic and political refugees. Koller's original impulse to shoot *Journey of Hope* was similarly grounded in a strong visceral response to media reports. En route to Paris to work on his next film at the time, he recollects how the story haunted him, "Everybody felt guilty. It hit them emotionally very strong. The way I felt guilty all of a sudden" (Lipper 10). His response, reprinted in the international press, effectively became synecdotal for the feeling of helpless empathy experienced by citizens worldwide, while his ensuing filmic intervention served to collectively discharge the accompanying guilt. Yet, as I have tried to demonstrate earlier through a discussion of character profiles and the ambiguous plot developments, pathos does not necessarily and automatically inspire viewers to embrace a protagonist's plight. If anything, the litany of abuses which the refugees encounter in Koller's film are documented by the camera with an exaggerated vehemence that seems more likely to induce disbelief and disavowal. The scenario is very reminiscent of both the motivations and the reception that accompanied an earlier West German product of this same genealogy, namely Günther Walraff's *Ganz Unten*. This is a documentary study released in 1985 (and later made into a feature film) by a West German journalist who went undercover as a migrant worker using the Turkish

pseudonym "Ali" to reveal appalling working conditions among foreign
workers illegally employed in the chemical and pharmaceutical industries.
Highly contested for both his subversive research methods and the sensa-
tionalistic publication of his findings, Walraff's work exhibits strategies of
representation reminiscent of Koller's film. As Anna Kuhn summarizes,

> *Ganz Unten* illustrates the pitfalls confronting even sympathetic members
> of a hegemonic culture when they try to (re)present and/or plead a minority
> cause. In order to test the tolerance of his compatriots, Wallraff consciously
> pandered to prevalent clichés about foreigners. His Ali is a naive, somewhat
> slow-witted soul, whose bastardized *Ausländerdeutsch* (foreigner's German)
> conforms to prejudicial notions that Turks are basically stupid and/or uneducated
> and cannot speak anything approximating cultivated German. Thus, instead of
> exposing a system of representations that generate and support negative images of
> the other, *Ganz Unten* helps perpetuate them. By cloning the victim, *Ganz Unten*
> calls for identification with the underdog. In the double sense of *Mitleid*, it allows
> German readers to both empathize with and feel sorry for the *Gastarbeiter* they
> are oppressing daily. It thereby arguably permits them to placate their consciences
> and to feel superior at the same time. (192)

In her review of the book, Turkish-German author Aysel Özakin also
astutely captured the dynamics of identification set into motion among
German readers of such reportages about foreign workers, polemically asking, "whether pity isn't the most elegant expression of scorn and contempt" (qtd. in Kuhn 192).

The Confessing Turk

What precisely is achieved through Xavier Koller's unrelentingly grim
revisitation of the traumatic events of one Kurdish family, a documentation virtually assuming the form of a *Stationendrama*, so heavily overdetermined is it by the allegorical qualities of crucifixion, betrayal and remorse?
To unpack this drama in its literal and figurative dimensions, I would turn,
once again, to Foucault and to his exegesis on the confession as one of the
central rituals employed in western societies for the production of truth
since the Middle Ages. Tracing the decline in accusatory procedures in
criminal justice and the abandonment of tests of guilt and the concomitant

rise of methods of interrogation and inquest, he points to the evolution of the word *avowal* as emblematic of this development: "from being a guarantee of the status, identity, and value granted to one person by another, it came to signify someone's acknowledgment of his own actions and thoughts" (*The History of Sexuality* 58). He maintains that we have become "a singularly confessing society," one in which confession has become aligned with not just the production of, but even liberation of truth, seen to be harbored within the inner sanctum of consciousness and the individual soul. Confession is seen to free us, while power exerts a repression and reduces us to silence. However, Foucault's discursive reversal endeavors to point forth the manner in which "the obligation to confess is now relayed through so many different points, is so deeply ingrained in us, that we no longer perceive it as the effect of a power that constrains us" or recognize this "production of truth" as thoroughly imbued with relations of power (*The History of Sexuality* 60).

While *Journey of Hope* may appear to be engaged in an analogous sort of investigation of the etiology of illegal migration coupled with a cautious disclosure of the purported heartlessness of immigration quotas—an interpretation which places the Swiss director in the heroicized role of renegade in relation to domestic politics—the onus of confession really rests upon the Turkish actors who dramatize their own subjection in its twofold sense: in effect, compelled to articulate their status as tropes of/in western society dwelling under the sign of the abject Turkish/Kurdish migrant. For the confession, as Foucault understands it,

> is a ritual of discourse in which the speaking subject is also the subject
> of the statement; it is also a ritual that unfolds within a power relationship,
> for one does not confess without the presence (or virtual presence) of a partner
> who is not simply the interlocutor but the authority who requires the
> confession, prescribes and appreciates it and intervenes in order to judge,
> punish, forgive, console, and reconcile; a ritual in which the truth is
> corroborated by the obstacles and resistances it has had to surmount in order
> to be formulated; and finally, a ritual in which the expression alone,
> independently of its external consequences, produces intrinsic modifications
> in the person who articulates it: it exonerates, redeems, and purifies him;
> it unburdens him of his wrongs, liberates him, and promises him salvation.
> (*The History of Sexuality* 62)

Arguably, the interlocutor of the confessing Turkish migrant is not just the film director Koller but, by synechdochal extension, the broader international public which bears witness in movie theaters worldwide. It is surely evident that in this drama, "the agency of domination does not reside in the one who speaks (for it is he who is constrained), but in the one who listens and says nothing; not in the one who knows and answers, but in the one who questions and is not supposed to know" (*The History of Sexuality* 62). When one film reviewer writes that the film "is centrally concerned not with migrants, but with the reactions which migrants inspire in their host countries," he inadvertently touches upon the mutuality inhering in this confession of misguided migratory endeavors, one which also "subjects" the hegemonic viewership, albeit under entirely different terms involving their reinstatement as empathetic and moral citizens of the world (Kermode 21). Koller has further remarked, "My goal was to give the audience an experience of who these people are, and how it feels to get close to them. I wanted the audience to ask themselves: 'How am I affected by these people? How do I relate to them?' and I wanted to talk to them through their hearts rather than by arguments" (Kermode 21). His comments broach this broader hermeneutical structure, which Foucault has pointed out as constituted in two stages, "present but incomplete, blind to itself, in the one who spoke, it could only reach completion in the one who assimilated and recorded it" (*The History of Sexuality* 66).

A late sequence in the film dramatizes this confessional scenario with heightened, indeed, excessive pathos. Haydar and Meryem both survive the midnight trek across the Alps during a blizzard, stumbling into a Swiss spa village in separate contingents. Haydar has just come from the doctor's office where his son's death from exposure was confirmed, and is delivered to the hotel where the bedraggled refugees have been temporarily quartered. From beyond the glass doors of the sanitarium, the camera silently follows Haydar intent upon breaking the news of their son's death as he approaches his wife bundled in blankets in a lawn chair next to the pool. The silent tension that builds as we view Haydar leaning over his wife is broken when Meryem's scream of grief pierces across the glass barrier, extorting from her a sempiternal truth towards which the entire narrative seems to have been hurtling, namely the ontological victimhood of the Turkish (Kurdish) people.

This tableau of absolute abjection is rendered complete when Swiss officials in uniform promptly swarm forward (exhibiting an implausible degree
of insensitivity) to draw Haydar away to police headquarters. It is little
wonder that the Turkish members of Koller's film crew together with Feride
Cicekoglu, co-author of Koller's screenplay and a widely esteemed oppositional writer in Turkey, ultimately denounced the film on the grounds that
the final product presented a distorted image that would only perpetuate
the manichean universe already so firmly entrenched in asylum politics
and in the representation of Turkish migrants (Bloemertz 16).

The final scene of the film, a prison visitation between the Swiss truck
driver, Ramser and Haydar, iterates the hermeneutical structure which so
evidently informed the production process, the narrative content and its
enunciation. On Ramser's focalization within the film script, Koller has
commented, "I wanted to put one of our characters into the film early to
experience what is happening. He represents people from the West."
Ramser had offered Haydar and Meryem a ride from Milano to Switzerland
against payment of DM 300. Originally intent only upon earning some fast
cash, he developed an affection for the family as they spent hours packed
together in the cab of his truck, trying to communicate despite the evident
linguistic impasse. The young Mehmet Ali assumes a mediating role, his
youthful innocence endearing him to the Swiss father of four children. Of
this relationship, Koller remarks, "By experiencing the innocence of the
[Kurdish] child, he comes away with a different perspective" (Lipper 10).
Problematic, however, is the manner in which the child becomes a synec-
doche for the putative naiveté of Turkish migrants generally, stumbling
forth into the world ill-prepared for the predatory hazards they encounter
and linguistically hampered from articulating their subjectivity. When
Ramser parks at a truck stop in the morning to eat breakfast with his illegal passengers, a photographer offers to take a snapshot in exchange for a
few Swiss Francs. Ramser poses for Mehmet Ali, raising his hands behind
his head and ghoulishly sticking out his tongue. In its obscenity, the gaze
of mockery that rolls out of the instamatic camera moments later effectively anticipates the intersubjective impasse which will haunt the final
encounter between Ramser and Haydar in the prison cell. Upon hearing
from Haydar that Mehmet Ali's body is to be returned to Turkey "to give

us new strength there," Ramser haltingly offers financial assistance for the funeral. Gazing numbly across the glass pane dividing them, Haydar murmurs in Turkish, his interpreter explaining to Ramser, "I would have liked to be your friend." Not only does this wistful remark come across as an enfeebled reproach, the use of the past subjunctive also reduces aporetic Turkish-European relations to some already irretrievable past.

Conclusion: The Foucauldian Mirror

It is this predisposition towards delimiting (other) cultures as occupying a discrete space and a discrete temporality (one generally trapped in the past) that situates *Journey of Hope* within a broader cinematic genealogy perpetuating particular assumptions about the phenomenon of global diaspora. However, where Koller's work does touch upon a very important if neglected dimension of migration is in his cinematographic acknowledgment of the powerful role of the imagination in spatializing territorial limits. Central to the politics of migration is the discourse of space; indeed space as an organizing principle could be said to constitute the epistemological limit of migration policy, susceptible to seeking unproblematic linkages between identity and place. Several sequences in *Journey of Hope* serve to foreground the imaginary foundations, that is to say, the visual stimuli perhaps most evident in contemporary media, which have motivated so many migrations and which underpin our understanding of demarcated spaces generally. As Appadurai points out in *Modernity at Large*,

the images, scripts, models and narratives that come through mass mediation (in its realistic and fictional modes) that makes the difference between migration today and in the past. Those who wish to move, those who have moved, those who wish to return, and those who choose to stay rarely formulate their plans outside the sphere of radio and television, cassettes and videos, newsprint and telephone. (6)

We need only recall the postcard image of the Alpine landscape, first received by Haydar in Turkey and then clutched by Mehmet Ali throughout the family's road trip northward, functioning as what Appadurai refers to as a "mobile text" that assists in the construction of imagined selves and imagined worlds within ongoing global deterritorialization. Switzerland is

posited within the gaze of the rural Turkish peasant as a utopian site, invested
with the aspiration for prosperity and a life less defined by physical hardship.
Simultaneously, this Swiss 'mirror' of projection functions heterotopically
insofar as it impels painful choices with very concrete and irreversible
consequences for the family in question.[11] The fragility of this imaginary
relation and its tenuous negotiation between the realm of representation
and the realm of the phenomenological are comically foregrounded when
Mehmet Ali brings the postcard to the family goat to nibble on in the
belief that it will subsequently produce butter as the cousin in Switzerland
ebulliently claimed.

The manner in which this imaginary screen functions not only as a site
of projection but also of division and exclusion is vividly captured in a late
sequence after the refugees have traversed the Alps. They stumble upon a
public building and tap desperately upon the spotless glass pane of a Swiss
spa in whose reflection we simultaneously glimpse a corpulent man in goggles surfacing within a heated swimming pool. His struggle to remove the
goggles at the pool's edge and determine the nature of the disturbance at
the window recalls the perceptual difficulties involved in discerning the
import and urgency of ongoing migratory flows, and the resistance which
those in a position of privilege have often brought to bear upon the drama.
The glass window at once metaphoricizes the territorial struggles of the
nation-state via the indoor/outdoor division, while also literalizing the
mirroring process at stake, in which the glass window not only reflects but
becomes the site of traversal between liminal spaces whose fateful inscription as utopian, heterotopian, or dystopian is directly dependent upon differentials of power, privilege and citizenship. Indeed, Koller's film itself
could be said to occupy this selfsame imaginary space of the mirror, an
instrument of reflection and of projection, negotiating between the dual
sites of the hegemonic and the subaltern, between Switzerland and Turkey,
between directorial ambitions and heterogeneous spectatorial identifications, and, finally, between cultural cooptation and political intervention.

3. Traveling Pictures from a Turkish Daughter

Seyhan Derin's *Ben annemin kiziyim—I'm My Mother's Daughter*

—Mine Eren

In an exemplary analysis of contemporary women's writing in Turkey, Saliha Parker suggests that this literature recollects a past, a lost memory, by telling stories from and about women down the generations (291). According to Parker, this trend is grounded in a self-critique among women writers who question Western feminism and its relationship to Turkish culture, as well as its influence on female socialization and identification. By reconstructing their pasts and preserving images of women that have been erased from their collective memory, trivialized, and built over, these women authors attempt to 'unearth,' literally and metaphorically, ". . . an indigenous and rather mysterious 'knowledge' of womanhood that is now 'lost' and must be retrieved" (Parker 290). Turkish author Latife Tekin, for example, emphasizes the importance of reconstructing women's lives:

> I keep thinking that when I go back to my childhood I remember my mother and aunts as the subjects of strange, narrowly framed photographs. These women used to scatter about into rooms in whispers, bury their money-boxes deep in trunks, wore lonely expressions in the back-rooms but changed them when they were in a crowd, and moved back and forth with incredible speed between this world and their other one. It seems to me quite important to understand what in fact they experienced, and how. One can always start with oneself to reach out for this lost knowledge; maybe there is no other place to start but there. (qtd. in Parker 291)

Within this context, it is intriguing that in the last two decades a proliferation of autobiographical expression in literature by women and minorities within a transnational framework has emerged, at a time when postmodernist discourses announced the 'death of the author' and the end of humanism.[1] In response to this paradoxical development of women's writing, feminist critics, as, for instance, bell hooks, have pointed out that many women and minorities want to formulate a notion of subjectivity, agency, and collective identity as women before they start to deconstruct them ("Postmodern Blackness").

It is perhaps no accident, then, that the shift to an emphasis of identity and history occurs simultaneously within the framework of a "borderless cinema."[2] In light of this, I would like to draw attention to the documentary film *I'm My Mother's Daughter* (*Ben annemin kiziyim*)[3] by Seyhan Derin, a graduate of the Academy for Television and Film in Munich who belongs to a very young generation of bicultural German filmmakers. Seyhan Derin was born in Turkey and emigrated in 1972 with her parents to Germany and has lived there since. She has produced many short films and one feature.[4] In fact, *I'm My Mother's Daughter*, which premiered in 1996 at the Berlinale and has won four major international awards, is the first documentary by a minority woman that recapitulates the theme of migration in German cinema. This documentary is the result of an exchange program between the Munich film school and the Ministry of Culture in Turkey based on the project to give an account of three generations of women. It establishes from the point of view of Durkadin Derin, the mother of the filmmaker, a relation between German history and biography that the German filmmaker Jutta Brückner had accomplished before in her film *Years of Hunger* (1980).[5]

The work of Seyhan Derin belongs to a new wave of films that has been emerging from Germany's cinema landscape since the mid 1990s. Interestingly with this boom of films there has also arisen the need for classification and categorization. Film critics define this cinema as "New German Film" or "German-Turkish Cinema" because they recognize in these films a new genre through which a young generation of filmmakers from Turkey tells stories that have thematically not yet been told in German cinema (see Kulaoglu). Also important, however, is the emergence of a culturally diverse group of "women behind the camera" in recent years.[6] What is offered to the viewer by this "alternative" cinema, or what I will call "Post-*Wende* Cinema," are images and spaces that counter the vision of homogenous society that prevails in German cinema.[7] In this view, Seyhan Derin's *I'm My Mother's Daughter* does not only call into question the idea of a coherent national identity within the context of increasing globalization and transnational movements. Derin's documentary, I argue, suggests a filmmaking beyond national boundaries and is a reconciliation of cultures and generations. In *I'm My Mother's Daughter* spaces melt into one another, the transitions between Germany and Turkey, and vice versa, are all continuous, there is no break or chasm between the two geographies.

In this paper, I will examine the representation of gender in *I'm My Mother's Daughter* and how Derin's filmmaking differs from the audiences' expectations of the portrayal of (Turkish) immigrant women. However, it is not only the misrepresentation of women from Turkey and the trivialized images about them in German public and aesthetic discourse that I would like to explore in Derin's film (see Göktürk; Karpf, Kiesel and Visarius; Gökberk). Derin, I will argue, "unearths" her mother's story to reclaim, in Latife Tekin's words, a "lost knowledge" about her past. Through my discussion, I will also emphasize how Derin's autobiographical film suggests a female subjectivity on history and diasporic experience within which origin is constructed as a significant factor of identity (Petty 8). It is not surprising, therefore, that through the presentation of Derin's journey and arrival at her *Heimat*, the rural village *Caycuma*, *I'm My Mother's Daughter* opens up a space for a rhetoric of origin, a center, as Sheila Petty suggests for the borderless cinema of black diaspora, "in which to anchor identity construction" (10).[8]

Before I sketch out the structure and move to a closer analysis of the film, I would like to refer to some cinematic narratives that have offered a female perspective on the relation between migration, history, and identity. The Hollywood production *The Joy Luck Club* (1993), adapted from Amy Tan's 1989 best-selling novel, is the best-known example of this type of cinematic treatment. Here, it is the memory and tales of mothers who are all first generation immigrants from China which establish ethnic continuity. Another remarkable narrative is offered by the work of African-American filmmaker Julie Dash, who over a period of ten years collected historical documents for her independent film *Daughters of the Dust* (1991), which is a memory and "celebration of black experience in America and its African roots" (Walker 284).

In European cinema, on the other hand, *I'm My Mother's Daughter* and *Memories of Immigrants* (*Mémoires d'immigrés*) (1997) by filmmaker Yamina Benguigui, who lent expression to the Maghrebi voices in France, are the earliest documentaries to recapitulate diasporic experiences from the margins. Both accounts challenge, through archival material and oral stories of immigrants, the collective memory of the country of immigration, or, as Azade Seyhan puts it, "[w]hat was lost, forgotten, erased, or occluded, is recovered in figurative discourse" (76). More importantly, however, it is not coincidence that both films were released at a time when fiery debates on multiculturalism, confrontational politics and animosities against foreigners were raging. It might be argued that both works present cinematic oral histories of three generations of immigrants to call into question the idea of a coherent national identity within the context of increasing globalization and transnational migration. Derin, for instance, realizes this through her voice-over at the beginning of her documentary reciting her father's words "We all hope for a better life, you said" (Fig. 1), which recalls the economic miracle in postwar Germany and its immigration history.

This observation brings us back to the beginning and structure of *I'm My Mother's Daughter*. In fact, the multi-layered character and complexity

Figure 1

of Derin's narration, which combines oral memory, documentation and fiction, makes it difficult to map all themes employed in the film. The complexity is first seen in the opening sequences, which are also cinematically the most captivating and therefore deserve closer analysis. Here, the inner reality of the filmmaker is visually articulated. Derin expresses, in her reflections about the past, her desire to declare her emotions of regret, anger, denial and acceptance as a daughter. A lyrical cinematography opens the narration, as the rush of ocean waves and a cut to a black-and-white passport photograph are projected onto the screen. The opening sequence presents a woman and four children, three of the faces crossed out, affixed with a seal that reads "ungültig" (invalid) (Fig. 2). Portrayed through a close-up, Seyhan Derin as a child and her mother are captured. The next sequence shows the filmmaker in her apartment in Germany, where she looks at family pictures with her niece. Through their dialogue, the spectator is introduced to the names of family members and siblings and told which of them are married and which are not. As the film progresses, the

Figure 2

theme of marriage becomes a central motif that is interwoven in Derin's narrative. Like *Years of Hunger*, Derin's film probes the presentation of a "gender-specific framework," in Barbara Kosta's words, for women's socialization ("Representing Female Sexuality" 244).

Derin's niece also finds a handwritten letter that she attempts to read. The text, written in the language of her mother (that she is not able to speak), begins with the Turkish words "Sevgili babacigim" (My beloved Father). While Derin's voice-over recites the letter, the story of her family comes alive, especially that of her father's, who belongs to the first generation of Turkish immigrants, the so-called *Gastarbeiter* (guestworkers). The close-up and juxtaposition of several photographs reproduces her family and especially her father in his youth and take the spectator back in Derin's memory. Derin's narrative recapitulates how migration caused the metamorphosis of her family's situation into one of isolation and fragmentation, a reality that shaped her diasporic consciousness. The narrative reveals many details about the family's past. We are told that the father, as many fathers did at that time, went first to Germany and left the family behind in Turkey. Derin's mother, taking all her children with her, emigrates from Turkey when Derin is five years old. When, ten years later, Derin's father wants the family to return to Turkey, the sisters run away from home to their older sister Nefise, who is married to a German. Thereafter, the parents don't have contact with them. Alienation arises in the family when, after a court trial, Seyhan and her sister Bilhan are placed in a boarding school by the German state. During this time, no contact exists between the parents and the children. In fact, the dialogues between the filmmaker and her mother in *I'm My Mother's Daughter* are the first attempt after this long separation to deal with the past. To speak publicly about family problems becomes a challenge for the filmmaker throughout the making of this film.

Supported through the daughter's fragmentary narration, the intimate portrait of her family unveils itself in less than three minutes' viewing time, framed by a voice-over that reiterates emotions of anger and grief. However, while the daughter offers all of this detail, she also explains how her father was paralyzed in an accident in a German coalmine. *I'm My Mother's Daughter*, simultaneously, reveals that the dream of a better life that her father had as a young man and that has brought him, like many other immigrants, into a "foreign" country, has become, because of his fateful injury, an illusion. In her lamenting voice, criticisms as well as emotions of despair and pain are interwoven, especially when Derin compares her family's past with its present and future.

Before a letter addressed to her mother is presented, the narration is followed by a sequence in black-and-white footage that is shown shortly after the prologue and varied three times during *I'm My Mother's Daughter*. Here, Derin visualizes a silent and fictional story of a girl who is on a train. Striking is the arrangement of nondiegetic sound and mise-en-scene as the sound and image are affirmatively combined, a method far more evocative than the previous monologue. As the story is rendered, a fade-in of a girl's close-up is seen. Iris masking closes down to isolate the girl's face as if framed in a photograph. The spectator, who is left in a moment of uncertainty, soon recognizes the window in the door of an empty train compartment behind

Figure 3

which the girl stands (Fig. 3). The rhythm of the nondiegetic sound supports the idea of a moving train. The shot then cuts to an image of a tunnel and a person, from whom the train distances itself gradually. The next point-of-view shot presents again the girl, who this time stares out of the window in the direction of the spectator and sees men and women waiting in a public space of a train station. Here, Derin's montage of archival film footage in this sequence that shows images of people leaving a train connects to a historical moment, namely the arrival of the first guestworkers in Germany. The revelation is accompanied by close-ups of undressed men's bodies whose arm movements are supported by the rhythm of the nondiegetic sound. With this, Derin reminds us of and circulates images of immigrants and their mandatory physical examination after their arrival in Germany.

From an arrangement of this archival shot with the point-of-view shot of the girl, the narration brings us back to the train compartment and presents the hands of the girl, who wants to open the locked door. As the film progresses, the idea of the confinement of the girl within this space is rendered so that the train appears to us as an impersonal and gigantic machine. The audience bears witness to her experience and reconstructs equally her feelings of loss and anxiety as the next shot illustrates a small house on a hill that the girl looks at and wants to go back to. Followed by this train sequence is a long shot of a dreamlike landscape, a device to create a sense of being far away in the mise-en-scene. As soon as a transition to color occurs, we find ourselves in front of a saturated panoramic image but also feel relieved from the claustrophobic portrayal that the black-and-white footage supported by the bold black film frame and controlled exposure previously evoked.

Symbolically, the train sequence can be described as a melodrama of a girl who was forcefully separated from her *Heimat* (Fig. 3). The brilliance of this sequence lies in the fact that Derin's portrayal of displacement allows us to relive the emotions of a girl and immigrant. Her narrative moves from presenting images mechanically to a clear description of the emotions around those images. At the same time, the crosscutting of personal memory and history suggest a female subjectivity as Derin reconstructs the theme of migration from her perspective within this fictional narrative. It might also be argued, building on Anton Kaes' discussion of Walter Ruttmann's *Berlin. Die Sinfonie einer Grosstadt* (*Berlin. Symphony of a Great City*, 1927), that Derin's opening scene, like the train sequence offered in Ruttmann's film, not only offers "glimpses of nomadic life," but also illustrates the urban experience of the arriving migrants (Kaes, "Leaving Home" 191).[9] This amounts to saying that the images combined with the story of Derin's family, who migrated from a rural area to the peripheries of German metropolises, suggest the existence of center and periphery relations that shape our contemporary world. In this sense, Derin's narration articulates the history of people in a locality, here, the rural village *Caycuma*, where Derin was born and from which her family emigrated in the 1970s, near the major city of Zonguldak in the Black sea region of northeast Turkey that is known for its tea and hazelnut plantations. This is simply because the director is mostly interested in problematizing the power relations between different locations and its consequences in the lives of women.

The dissolve to the following scene manipulates time as the saturation of the landscape image takes us back to the present. While the voice-over explains now her motive in undertaking this project (that she names a journey), extreme long shots introduce us to this "small" world, where it seems as if time has come to a standstill. Focused on the dialogues between mother and daughter, the narration follows Derin on her journey to recollect the past through her mother's storytelling. We also become witnesses to various interviews that the filmmaker then has with other family members and women, both in Turkey and Germany. This technique enables us to see Durkadin Derin's biography in relation to the social, political, and historical realities of her life. In a key scene after this train sequence, the voice-over addresses the following letter to the mother:

My beloved mother,

I don't ever remember having written to you and if I have, I never sent off the letter like so many letters that I wrote to father. I know little about you. My knowledge of our family history is made up of images and facts of my father's family. That doesn't surprise me, as Turkish tradition presents the male line as the more important. Thus my childhood is characterized by my father's tenderly-spoken sentence, "you are the daughter of your father." Today, I myself an adult woman, I have set out on a journey and want to know who my mother really is. She who for most of the time was overshadowed by my father and caught up in traditions, which I could not accept as valid for me. A journey, not only in a world between Germany and Turkey, a journey of which I do not know the destination.[10]

Derin makes her mother's biography her theme from the beginning. But to give an intimate portrayal of one's mother, the biography of an "Anatolian" woman that does not allow the voyeuristic look that prior filmmakers have employed in German cinema,[11] is quite a challenge in itself. The images these filmmakers created are cinematic constructions and have, unfortunately, generally shaped our picture about Turkish immigrant women. Is it at all possible to both avoid a discourse of victimization and represent the experiences of minority women for a Western audience in a way that does not reproduce and perpetuate an ethnocentric view? What if the filmmaker is aware that her own perception is also shaped by these Eurocentric images and faces this dilemma? What strategies need to be employed to construct an image of a rural woman who is *not* "caught between tradition and modernisation?" (Spivak, "Can the Subaltern speak?" 306). Representation yes, so to speak, but how to formulate it cinematically in a new way?

I mean these remarks to sketch out the problematic of embarking on such a film project. Prior filmmakers in German cinema principally explored the situation of Turkish women in Germany in relation to patriarchy and constructed images of women based on a universal value matrix (see Göktürk). This monolithic discursive practice represents Turkish women as a homogeneous mass characterized by their experience of oppression—what Chandra Talpade Mohanty has termed the "Third World difference." Also, these films set an example of the problem presented when filmmakers claim the right to represent the "other" (Turkish) women who they believe cannot speak for themselves (see Göktürk; Karpf, Kiesel and Visarius; Gökberk). Here, Gayatri Spivak's criticism in "Can the subaltern speak?" regarding Julia Kristeva's work *About Chinese Women* proves as relevant. Spivak shows skepticism towards the representational system in the Western culture and demonstrates how in Kristeva's article the "gendered subaltern" dissolves. Spivak argues that Chinese women become objects of Kristeva's theoretical analysis since they never represent or speak for themselves and are only "heard" through Kristeva's own presentation.

In *I'm My Mother's Daughter*, the filmmaker remodels the encounter with the "Other" (woman) by giving, literally, voice and narrative authority to her. It is this dialogical approach that foregrounds Durkadin Derin's testimonial narrative. Significantly, the film's beginning brings us to the house and village that were presented before, from a distance, in the train sequence. Their visit to this house, in which the filmmaker was born and where her family used to live before migration, signals the actual beginning of Durkadin Derin's biography. While close-ups mostly concentrate on the mother, her remembrance takes us back to the past. The amalgamation of her oral story with cuts to the debris in this deserted house oscillates images from a "lost" history in our minds. Stylistically, it is as if the camera picks up on these forgotten items like relics of another time. The interweaving of oral narrative and mechanically-rendered images touches on such events in Durkadin Derin's life-story as childhood, life as a young woman, marriage, childbirth and her work as a peasant woman. At the same time, much of her narrative, taken during interviews in Germany, depicts her diasporic experience. Speaking in regional dialect, Durkadin Derin conveys her thoughts and beliefs in regard to her life and work experience in German culture. In the following statement, she recalls how the German village looked thirty years ago:

Mother: Germany wasn't like it is for me now at that time. It was quite like Turkey.
Seyhan: How do you mean?
Mother: It wasn't as well looked after as today, not as clean, the streets weren't as good, these days there's asphalt everywhere. Do you still know what Ludweiler was like? It was like a village.

In fact, Derin focuses on the memory of her mother and grandmother, but also of women who live in *Caycuma*, which in effect creates many layers of narration in *I'm My Mother's Daughter*. There is no synchronization in the German language or a voice-over to give a translation of these stories in order to grant authenticity and a more powerful moment to them. In other words, testimonial narratives reach the spectator untouched and are orally not transformed into the dominant language. As each oral history combines with others in the film, we find ourselves confronted with spoken Turkish language and themes such as childbirth, illness, marriage, work, loss of physical strength, aging, and also superstition, gossip and rumor.[12] As a result, the village *Caycuma* serves Derin as a resource to understand both the morality of denial and self-sacrifice that controls the women of her mother's generation and the hierarchical world in which they have lived for generations. While capturing the unequal gender relations in this locality, the filmmaker avoids a discourse of victimization by showing women who use silence as an act of resistance. This female consciousness is best expressed in an interview with Derin's grandmother and her routine answer: "I don't know. You must know best." What at first glance seem to be attitudes and gestures women have internalized are, as the documentary unveils, means of survival in reality. This altered understanding is expressed in a letter by Derin, who could not accept for herself for a long time the hard work and persistence that characterize her mother's life.

In this letter, Derin attributes the dilemma in living, what W. E. B. DuBois has called a "double consciousness." "Not recognizing themselves in the reflections of cultural representation," so argues Susan Stanford Friedman in her seminal essay "Women's Autobiographical Selves: Theory and Practice," "women develop a dual consciousness—the self as culturally

Figure 4

defined and the self as different from cultural prescription" (Friedman 39).[13]
A shot that demonstrates the diffusion in the self-image and the perception of women and their bodies on the visual level is developed in Figure 4.
Reacting against the hegemonic deployment of images of the (rural) woman
in dominant culture, the filmmaker challenges them by reconstructing an
"alternative" image about her. At the same time, one can argue, Derin's
journey to *Caycuma* and the presentation of female life-stories are an
attempt to redefine her own origin. This gesture is first enacted through
the film title.

The invisibility and silence of women are conveyed specifically in language. Derin makes us aware about this fact and the symbolism in language
through the twist upon the idiomatic Turkish expression "babasi'nin oglu"
(his father's son) that stresses the resemblances within the male line in the
traditional Turkish family. There is no equivalent expression for women in
oral speech. The title demonstrates, as have poststructuralist theories, that
the concept of identity is a societal and cultural construction, which leads

to the marginalization of women in culture. At the same time, Derin's film title exemplifies that the representation of women is not inherent in language. Derin's purposeful alteration of the original, male-centered expression to "I'm the Daughter of My Mother" invents a language and creates a cinematic space where women (including herself) *can* be represented and made into carriers of meaning.

On the other hand, *I'm My Mother's Daughter* reinforces the question of female socialization. As Barbara Kosta argues within this context, "[s]ince most mothers have been traditionally complicit with patriarchal ideology, they too have programmed their daughters for psychological identification with the female role of passivity, submission, and silence" ("Representing Female Sexuality" 246). Thus the thematization of marriage and its impact on the daughter becomes a reference point for Derin. The filmmaker realizes this in her use of two traditional folk songs, one in its original and the second in an updated modern version, to create a reference to women's reality in past and present. These texts reinforce the experience of entrapment and isolation from a female perspective. In the vocalization of the first lyrical text, presented in regional orality, the lamenting voice of a mother who wants to ease her daughter's fear about marriage can be identified:

My bride is weeping hot tears, she says, "I'm not going," and shakes her head.
Do not weep, my bride, your last night before the wedding should be blessed.
Your wedding celebration should be happy.

The use of visual symbolism while this text is presented suggests the idea that marriage confines women to imprisonment. The film's aesthetic distinguishes here two subsequent scenes: the first represents a blue saturated night scenery in which a moon is depicted. The next scene mirrors the same moon within a window frame when the word wedding is voiced. In reality, this mythical text evokes the Turkish tradition of the *kina gecesi*, which literally translates as "the night of henna," the day before the wedding, at which women gather in the house of the bride. It is a symbolic farewell to the daughter whose hands are colored with henna and for whom women weep with songs, a means to express their wishes of courage and strength. The film reveals how women, in taking the power of words, find a way to break silence and establish collective identity. Derin, who is interested in visualizing the perspective of the bride, identifies with her situation and rebels against the institution of marriage by showing its social and cultural constraints on a woman's life in the image of the framed moon. In other words, the filmmaker de-mystifies the idea of marriage being *the* only ruling metaphor in a woman's life, an idea that has been mediated by generations of time and space. In another key scene, Derin also records a lyrical negation illustrated from the perspective of a daughter who conveys her resistance to the "faith" of women and the culturally imposed restraints on their lives and identities. In this text, the female voice expresses her alienation and regrets being born as a woman:

> In the forest, I carry wood, see, what has become of me because of you, in the fields a maid slogging away, in the house a willing spouse. A child in my belly, six at the hem of my skirts, your mother's chatter gets me down. As if the cares of the world weren't enough, you want, when at last there's a bit of peace, your way with me, too. Oh, violins should play, I want to blow in a horn, and even if they explode, my parents-in-law, I want to have my fling at last. Oh, you fine hands, you are becoming cracked and fat. I've had enough of you, oh, if only I were still in my father's house, oh, you unjust world, why have you conspired against me? I had a doll made of material, a whole bundle full of dreams, my time as a girl was much too short, I'd like to have my mother back again.[14]

I'm My Mother's Daughter takes also into account the intervention of public and political discourses with the private space. This is uncovered when the filmmaker takes us back to the roots of female emancipation in Turkey. Here we are presented with archival footage, which presents women in the period before and after the emergence of a Turkish nation-state. As Sirin Tekeli stresses within this context, "when national struggle for independence began, . . . [women] participated in a number of activities outside their traditional roles" (143). In particular, Derin demonstrates, through crosscutting of ideological film material, the influence of Kemalism on Turkish society and culture in the context of the modernization of women.[15] The filmmaker also presents cultural images, as Brückner did for the German context, that shaped women's consciousness and served as role models for female identification (Kosta, "Representing Female Sexuality" 244). To illustrate the failure of the emancipation process, Derin compares images of the past and present, urban and rural spaces. In speaking of the present, the filmmaker underscores her point in including images of working women, carrying heavy bundles of wood or buckets of water. However, by drawing on this fact, *I'm My Mother's Daughter* does not reinforce generalizations or binary oppositions between genders, but rather points to the existence of power relations that structure the socio-economic organization in this locality.

However, we should certainly not read Derin's documentary as one battling against confining images and categories. Aesthetically speaking, *I'm My Mother's Daughter* offers a "triangulation of vision," as Derin takes three roles within her film, namely as woman filmmaker, actor and spectator (O'Sickey and Zadow). It is Derin's look that circulates throughout the film and that weaves autobiographical and biographical images at the same time to reconcile through her mother's memory the disruption between past and present in her memory. While the viewer is sometimes bound to puzzle over the multi-layered narrative, Derin's documentary composes an alternative way of thinking about the experiences of women in diasporas. Durkadin Derin's autobiographical narrative in *I'm My Mother's Daughter* presents life as a constant test of survival. Derin's images suggest a portrayal that counters beliefs in the dominant culture, as the following observation of a German viewer, mentioned by Seyhan Derin during an interview, exemplifies: "Now, after I have seen your film, I won't pass by a woman with a headscarf without taking notice of her. Up till now, these women had no personality for me. But after I have met your mother, I know that this is not true."[16]

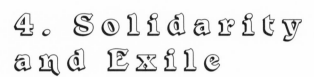

4. Solidarity and Exile

Blonder Tango and the East German Fantasy of the Third World

—Barton Byg

Since the early 1990s, neo-Nazi activity and attacks on perceived "foreigners" in reunited Germany have frequently made international headlines. Right wing extremism in the five new German states that made up the German Democratic Republic (1949–1990) represents something very new to the region, however, with striking historical contradictions. Twin pillars of that former socialist country's identity and claim to international legitimacy were anti-fascism and solidarity with "Third World" peoples in their struggles against colonialism, imperialism and racism.

It would be facile to explain this situation with generalizations about German racism and socialist hypocrisy, but the position of the GDR in regard to the Third World does provide food for thought about national identities, exile and border crossing, and the role of German and "socialist" history in public conceptions of homeland and identity. That the ideological claims of the GDR relied on both nationalist feeling and consumerist

55

attitudes to the legitimacy of the state may help explain the link between anti-foreigner activity and anti-state feelings in the post-unification era.

Recent publications in English have dealt with the role of Third World culture and the legacy of colonialism in contemporary Germany, two of which provide important reference points for this essay. Arlene Teraoka's *East, West, and Others: The Third World in Postwar German Literature* traces the limits of solidarity imposed by the abstract conceptualization of the Third World that persists in German culture. *The Imperialist Imagination: German Colonialism and Its Legacy* (edited by Sara Friedrichsmeyer, Sara Lennox and Susanne Zantop) explores why Germany in the post–World War II period exhibited amnesia about its colonial past. The major concern was to put the Nazi era to rest and rebuild; fantasies of brotherhood with the Third World reflected mainly a wish to return to a lost German innocence.[1] Although treated to a degree by these works, the relation of the former German Democratic Republic to the Third World merits much more examination on its own.

The East German film *Blonder Tango* (*Blonde Tango*, 1986), written by Omar Saavedra Santis and directed by Lothar Warneke, is a very late work in a long tradition of cultural representations of German–Third World interactions.[2] Since it comes near the end of the GDR's history, it provides a look back at what one Latin American country meant in the imagination of GDR artists and intellectuals—and a wider public as well. On the other hand, as a film set in the East and as one of extremely few works written by a non-German and with a non-German protagonist, it provides an unusual perspective on the complex interaction between German culture and the supposed "other." As such the film shows how the limits of solidarity look from the non-European point of view—limitations imposed by exile, political failure, cultural barriers and the structuring constraints of fiction itself.

The story of Rogelio, a young Chilean exile who chooses to move to East Germany in the 1970s, *Blonder Tango* is a powerful and moving exploration of the condition of exile—the exiled person's real and imagined relation to a remembered homeland and the real and imagined challenges of becoming integrated into a foreign culture. In the following, I will first place the film in the context of the history of the GDR's official relations to the Third World, and the function of this ideologically based position

Blonder Tango. *Cinematographer: Thomas Plenert. Courtesy of DEFA Film Library.*

in the self-understanding of the GDR itself. Then I will examine the film's contribution to an understanding of this history—at a time when the Gorbachev era in the Soviet Union was heralding dramatic rethinking of socialism's conceptions of democracy and its own past.

The GDR's relation to the Third World falls into two historical phases, before and after three key events in the early 1970s: the transition to the regime of Erich Honecker, the normalization of relations between the GDR and the FRG (the Federal Republic of Germany, or what was then West Germany), and the admission of the two German states to the United Nations. This period, from 1971 to 1973, also happens to coincide with most of the short-lived socialist Chilean government of President Salvador Allende. Thus, one of the GDR's most optimistic times in its history has a resonance with Latin America.

This is an exception in many ways, however. For the most part, Latin America played a rather small part in the GDR's relations with the Third World, and such relations in general served European political purposes more than the needs of the countries involved. Before 1972, relations with the Third World constituted what Lamm and Kupper have called a GDR version of the Hallstein Doctrine (54–55). Under the Hallstein Doctrine of West German foreign policy, the FRG threatened to break off relations with any country which formally recognized the GDR as a state. By cultivating relations with Third World states not firmly in the Western ideological camp, the GDR was mainly attempting to discredit the West German policy. And, most importantly, any success in the international arena helped legitimize the East German government for its own people (ibid.; Barnett 95–96).

It is striking that the GDR had such an active interaction with the Third World—the most in the socialist bloc outside the USSR.[3] At the same time, the country was never one of immigration, only exile. The foreign population was so insignificant that the *Book of Lists* in the 1980s listed the GDR and North Korea as the two most ethnically homogeneous countries in the world. Foreign exchange students and work brigades were generally isolated and definitely expected to return home; exceptions were possible but their experiences were often difficult. Unified Germany's policy to repatriate temporary workers the GDR had brought from Vietnam and Mozambique provides continued evidence of this lack of integration.

Both the documents published by the GDR and recent scholarship by political scientists attest to the fact that GDR concern with the Third World, even after 1972, concentrated far more on Africa, the Middle East and Asia than on Latin America.[4] The purpose of such interaction, for the most part, was dedicated to German and European political strategy. It was not the pure result of altruism, dedication to the cause of socialism, belief in the importance of Third World liberation struggles to socialist progress, or even the view that GDR material interests or GDR society benefitted from interaction with the Third World. Both the GDR's own pronouncements on the subject and more recent sources make it extremely clear that GDR officials did not see relationships with Third World countries as exchanges among political or ideological equals. There is never any mention of learning anything for socialist practice either internally or internationally from anyone outside the GDR or the USSR. On the contrary, where a political goal was evident in relations with a Third World country, it was dedicated to the training and support of Marxist-Leninist party cadres to the exclusion of any other model. Variant indigenous practices or neo-Marxist concepts were condemned by the GDR as revisionist, and Third World movements toward democratic socialism or a "Third Way" between the Cold War camps were rejected as a danger to the Leninist Party model. The European model was one which was already known, not something about which discussion with Third World colleagues was desired.[5] Even with Cuba, the level of interaction was quite circumscribed (Baske 51), so that a widespread impact on the GDR from the physical presence of out-siders cannot be assumed despite the official pronouncements of solidarity.

But in all this, the most significant fact is that the goals of the GDR in Third World relations were mainly to shore up its own legitimacy, especially vis à vis West Germany, and to reduce what Thomas Barnett has labeled its "leverage deficit" with Moscow. Regarding the internal legitimacy of the SED government and its connection to foreign relations, it is helpful to recall the four avenues Barnett identifies by which East European socialist governments might attain legitimacy: ideology, dictatorial coercion, nation-alism, and economic performance. Aside from coercion, all three shed an interesting light on the GDR's relations to the Third World and the role of culture (and such films as *Blonder Tango*) in this arena.

Since the population preferred their government earn legitimacy by economic performance or at least by appealing to nationalism, the GDR's strategy for state legitimacy was based on a compromise that Barnett calls "consumeristic authoritarianism." Here ideology plays a key role in miti-gating the contradictions inherent in these two terms. Cultural produc-tions reflective of the GDR's society and history relate directly to this ideological task, and *Blonder Tango* provides an ideal illustration.

Ideology is present everywhere in the film, and it reveals over and over again the importance of two interrelated aspects of ideology in regard to GDR legitimacy: the anti-fascist basis of the GDR and the equation of its rival West Germany with Nazism and the continuation of such barbarism in the form of Western imperialism. The Third World was consistently pre-sented by the GDR as the victim of such Western evils, from the Congo and South Africa to Vietnam and Pinochet's Chile. Since the purpose of this ideology was mainly to distinguish the GDR from the FRG, however, GDR ideology stressed West German support for such institutions as apartheid in South Africa, for instance, while underplaying the more neutral phenomenon of far vaster trade relations between the Third World and the FRG than with the GDR. The fact that the principal goal was distancing from the West Germans, not the cause of combatting racism and colonialism, is underscored by the lack of East-West cooperation on such issues. *Blonder Tango* subtly but explicitly brackets out such a possibility by having its main character enter East Germany by way of a French-speaking office of Amnesty International. A reminder of the presence of Amnesty International in West Germany, and the prohibition of such voluntary citizens' groups in the GDR, is thus avoided.

Here, ideology, nationalism and consumerism overlap. The contradictions in practical, political and economic terms virtually require feats of fiction (in the realm of history and ideology) to sustain them. Barnett succinctly outlines the GDR's situation: In the first instance, the GDR's consumer economy was always fragile and lagged behind the West Germans', so distinction from the West in ideological terms (through a contrasting Third World policy) was crucial to solidify USSR support so necessary to the economy. The West Germans' more successful economy and superior position regarding the Third World could at the same time be seen as a moral justification for the GDR's inferior consumer economy: after all, the FRG was only successful through imperialism (equated with Nazism). As Barnett puts it, "Wherever possible, West Germany's worst aspects could be highlighted in the South and used to explain its higher standard of living (e.g. through imperialism and neo-colonialist exploitation)" (147). After 1972, however, this stance, too, becomes a contradiction: improved trade relations with West Germany soon became a principal pillar of the GDR's consumer economy. On the other hand, the USSR made economic overtures to West Germany that threatened to ignore the GDR. Thus, the radical discrediting of the West as an alternative in the population's mind had to take place principally in the realm of ideology, since both trade relations and consumerism suggested more acceptance of Western norms. The key to maintaining distance from the West (*Abgrenzung*) was ideology, and the Third World was the ideological battleground (Barnett 6, 34–35).

Barnett sums up of the GDR's need for an active Third World presence to resolve the contradictions in its own domestic legitimacy and in its relations to the FRG and the USSR. Thus the South offered East Berlin a chance to demonstrate simultaneously that a divided Germany was still in the Soviet bloc's best interests and that, European similarities notwithstanding, the "revolutionary" Germany remained in direct conflict with the "imperialist" Germany abroad. Furthermore, the state-building activity in the South offered a positive outlet for the German nationalism suppressed by the policy of *Abgrenzung*. In sum, the South offered Honecker several channels through which to mitigate his regime's lack of legitimacy both at home and throughout the world (151).

In the context of the above, *Blonder Tango* provides an excellent example of the role culture played in the GDR's attempt to distinguish itself from the West and depict itself as an agent on a par with both the FRG and the USSR in Third World relations as well. By downplaying other European, international socialist or even Soviet activities in the Third World, and by treating the Third World itself as an undifferentiated abstraction, the GDR's image was enhanced. As Barnett puts it, the whole point of the GDR's conceptualization of the Third World was to create it in its own image (152–53).

The fact that Chile's political symbolism is out of proportion to its relatively minor role in GDR foreign relations is thus consistent with the GDR's reliance on ideology for its legitimation. One could almost say that the timing, brevity and intensity of the identification with Chile on the part of both the GDR leadership and a wide portion of the population contributed to the symbolic power of this identification once President Allende was assassinated and his government overthown by the Pinochet coup. Teraoka describes the massive outpouring of sentiment about Chile in the 1970s, resulting in widespread cultural production dealing with Chile and other Latin American countries and a massive protest campaign which managed to assemble the signatures of 15 million citizens (in a country of only 17 million!). Solidarity with Chile became, in official pronouncements, almost synonymous with the self-definition of the GDR. At the Seventh Writers' Congress in 1973 the author Volker Braun spoke out against counterrevolution "on all borders of our potential Chiles" (cited in Teraoka 84). Treating Chile as an abstraction for the Third World, linking it with Western imperialism as a continuation of fascism, and asserting the need for borders (i.e. the Berlin Wall against the FRG)—all this harnesses Chile as a bulwark for GDR legitimacy.[6]

For the purpose of this essay, then, it is a conscious choice to use the phrase Third World and treat such a broad category of countries, ethnic and political groups as a unity vis à vis East Germany or Europe. This after all reflects the mainstream thinking regarding Europe and the Third World to this day, and *Blonder Tango* participates in the GDR's perpetuation of this dichotomy.

Treating the Third World as an undifferentiated abstraction can be seen in the first instance as the result of the European and Intra-German concerns discussed above. The GDR was interested in differentiating itself from the FRG through solidarity with the oppressed "other" in general, but dialogue with, or influence from, that "other" was another matter. In ideological terms, the GDR had no need to "learn from" Third World movements because it was a place where socialism had already been achieved (either as the heirs of Marx and Engels or as the beneficiaries of liberation by the USSR from the Nazis). But depictions of the Third World also needed to remain abstract for domestic political purposes as well. The solidarity with the Third World was meant to affirm the position of the SED's government, not introduce alternative models to its policies. Thus, it would not be in their interest for depictions of the Third World to dwell on political tactics or procedures (parliamentary elections and governing with opposition parties intact, for instance), since such discussions were out of the question in the GDR.

The story of *Blonder Tango* is as complicated in its narrative structure as the GDR's relations to the Third World. It uses a complex layering of fantasy and flashback very rare in East German cinema. In simplest terms, the story follows a period of several months in the life of a Chilean exile in East Berlin. The narrative consists of three separate complexes that only overlap in the main character. Most of the screen time is devoted to the love triangle in the theater where Rogelio works, with his friends, fellow foreigners and an elderly neighbor providing related dramatic interest. The framing story of the film is Rogelio's desperate visit to the Baltic coast, where he is taken in by an old German man named Stephan—a former anti-Nazi exile and Spanish Civil War veteran. Rogelio's life in Chile is largely told in flashback, through his daydreams or the images conjured up by the letters he exchanges with his mother. It is the dissembling quality of these letters, along with Rogelio's romantic disappointments, which bring the narrative strands to a single conclusion.

Thus *Blonder Tango* dwells on Rogelio's Chile and exile in very limited terms, to the exclusion of obvious questions one might raise. The first is the role of the Soviet Union in defeating Nazism and instituting socialism in the GDR—or any role in contemporary GDR life for that matter. The abstract solidarity with Chile and other Third World countries tacitly rewrites history to imply that the GDR itself was the result of an indigenous movement.

The most explicit anti-fascist claim the film makes is during a scene in which Rogelio travels to the Chilean consulate in West Berlin to apply for permission to return to Chile. The freedom to travel to West Berlin is of course another thing that pointedly separates Rogelio from East German citizens, but he only once makes use of this mobility (based on a decision of "the committee" that all political exiles there should test the Chilean government's invitation for them to return, as a gesture of reconciliation). In the end, Rogelio is not allowed to return to Chile, but while in West Berlin he confronts a group of young punks in the subway, one of whom is wearing the German iron cross. GDR dramaturgy would not resort to the inflammatory sensationalism of a swastika or SS insignia (forbidden in both German states), but Rogelio is so outraged by the iron cross that he starts shouting "Auschwitz" and attempts to tear it off the young man. As in the film's displacement of the Western office of Amnesty International into the French language, Rogelio is suddenly inarticulate in German in West Berlin, simply repeating his aggressive muttering of "Auschwitz." After the ensuing fist fight, Rogelio and the punks end up in the police station where they are all given the minimum fine for public unruliness.

But it is in conversation with the police officer levying the fine where the film most explicitly links up with the GDR's and the DEFA studio's anti-fascist tradition. Rogelio recovers his articulateness when the officer tells him the punks thought that "*Auschwitz* is an insult in Turkish or something," to which Rogelio replies, "*Auschwitz* is an insult in any language."[7]

The ensuing conversation quotes at times almost verbatim from Konrad Wolf's groundbreaking film *I was 19*, his semi-autobiographical narrative of returning from exile in the USSR with the advancing Red Army in 1945. His Red Army comrade and friend, Vadim (a Jew from Kiev who loves German culture), confronts a landscape architect near the Sachsenhausen concentration camp about his ability to live in Nazi Germany.[8] The architect gives a long disquisition on the philosophical origins of German obedience, and basically argues that one government is like another. The officer who lets Rogelio off with a 20 Mark fine makes similar points on the lack of real difference between East and West Germany, and repeats the statement of the architect in Nazi Germany: "How refreshing it is to speak with an intelligent person for once." To this subtle equation of the intellectual complacency of West Germany with Nazi Germany, Rogelio adds a specific assertion of the superiority of the GDR: "There, wearing an iron cross would get a lot more than a 20 Mark fine." Thus, the GDR's legitimation and contrast to the FRG is upheld by the "authentic" representative of Third World liberation, and the Chilean fills in for the anti-fascist credentials of Vadim—the Soviet, Red Army officer and Jew.

This rather tendentious link to the anti-fascist legacy of the GDR is balanced however by the more broadly based connections the film makes to the struggles of the twentieth century, which take on a much more melancholy and poetic tone. For the most part, the anti-fascist past of the GDR—and Germany's Nazi past—are only recalled by the elderly characters in the film, with whom Rogelio has a special relationship. While the elderly characters in *Blonder Tango* represent the GDR's anchoring in the battle against Nazism, at the same time they reveal its fragility. In all these instances, the representatives of true anti-fascist struggles are social outsiders.

Stephan, for instance, is the old man who finds Rogelio freezing at the Baltic shore and brings him inside where they eventually exchange their life stories. He is the only German character who understands Rogelio's Spanish, and by implication he is the only one who understands Rogelio at all. Like Rogelio, Stephan has fought fascism (in the Spanish brigades) and has lived in exile (in Mexico). Like Rogelio he fell in love in exile but Stephan felt (or was) forced to abandon his lover and return to Germany, never to regain contact with her. The two men bond because both of their political histories belong to the past. Indeed, Rogelio's desperate journey is on the fifth anniversary of his exile, and the film is made over a dozen years after the Pinochet takover. Both men's lives are marked by victimization, loss, futile but principled solidarity, and longing. The only personal relic of Stephan's exile and anti-fascist past is a picture of his lover Eleanora, which he gives to Rogelio. The stories Rogelio tells Stephan about Chile, as with the letters from his mother, also depict only fear, victimization and dignified gestures of solidarity but never direct political activity or resistance of any kind. The only exception is one letter's description of a protest demonstration in which Rogelio's mother is injured on her hand, explaining why subsequent letters are in the handwriting of another family member.

So a history of exile and political resistance make both Stephan and Rogelio outsiders in GDR society, which is implicitly a critique of the political stagnation and chauvinism we have been exploring. When Stephan is scolded by his local bartender for speaking Spanish with Rogelio in a pub, he replies with the film's philosophical message: "Wir brauchen auch die fremden Augen, um uns anders zu sehen" (We need foreign eyes, too, to see ourselves in a different way). Beyond the merely melancholy depiction of just how non-revolutionary GDR society was, already a taboo in official media in any case, this is at least a suggestion of a critical view of the GDR from the point of view of revolutionary outsiders. But the focus is still concerned with the self, since the object is clearly to reflect on German history and the legacy of Nazism rather than on the defeat of socialism in Chile. The loss and self-denial Stephan conveys in his story he also links to an explicit shame that the country of Goethe and Bach could also have produced Guernica.[9]

The other elderly character in Rogelio's experience is Frau Hube, a woman who lives next door to him in Berlin. She is drawn to speak to him because of the music he plays on his record player, the tenor Joseph Schmidt singing "Ein Lied geht um die Welt" (A Song Goes round the World)."[10] This song and the old woman weave together many of the affective strands of the film, both on a symbolic and narrative level. In the first place, Schmidt singing "Ein Lied geht um die Welt" is the principal musical theme of both the beginning and the ending of the film. In each instance it dominates extra-diagetically the image on the screen: the waves crashing on the shore. At the outset of the film, it is clear it is the freezing Baltic Sea to which Rogelio is exposed. But at the end, after an image where only a bit of ice is visible, a second shot of waves on the shore and rocks bathed in a warmer light suggests that this might be the coast of Chile and not Germany. And at the conclusion, Salvador Allende's voice is blended with the song. Thus the only documentary element from Chilean socialism, an exhortation of the people to grasp their power to harness social forces and shape history, is blended at the film's conclusion with a "universal human-ist" expression from a Jewish exile from Nazism.

The immensely popular Schmidt song and its implicit reminder of Germany in 1933 plays specific narrative roles in the film as well. In a coun-terpoint to Stephan's gift of his Mexican lover's photograph to Rogelio, Rogelio gives the Schmidt record to Frau Hube after she tells of seeing his spellbinding performance in person, and that her husband had been jealous of her adulation of the singing star. Her husband and two sons had all died in the War, so her narrative connects the losses of the past with romantic longings Rogelio shares. For Rogelio, too, the record is a connection to the past: it is the only thing mentioned in the film that he still has from his late father.

But when Rogelio attempts to use the record to express his unfulfilled longings in the GDR, things do not work out. At the theater where Rogelio works as a spotlight operator, he has become infatuated with a shallow and vain blonde singer, Cornelia. Cornelia is played by Karin Düwel, who at the time was being cultivated as a romantic lead with "star" quality in the GDR. She is at best amused by Rogelio's advances, and after standing him up entirely on their first date, she does go out with him and they spend the night together. After that, she gives him a gentle but firm brush-off and it is clear that they are finished, despite Rogelio's persistence. Telling, however, is the fact that she has no receptiveness to Schmidt's music when Regelio plays it for her. She says that it reminds her of an old-people's home.

By contrast, Luise is another co-worker of Rogelio's who is falling in love with him. He is not physically attracted to her, however, and one is tempted to read some symbolism into the casting here. In addition to wear-ing glasses, being more earnest and having darker hair, Luise is played by

Johanna Schall, the granddaughter of Bertolt Brecht. As such she is a political and theatrical counterpoint to the film-star Düwel.

Before we examine the implications of Luise's unrequited love for Rogelio and the humiliating charade he conducts with her, let us look at one more context for Rogelio's alienation from GDR society. Not only is Rogelio frustrated in his romantic pursuit of Cornelia, he is quite isolated in general. His boss cannot pronounce his name and constantly threatens to fire him for daydreaming, smoking or sleeping on the job, or for missing work after a binge of drinking and depression. Aside from this, however, Rogelio has little contact to German men. His best friend is a Hungarian, Zandor, who has plans to return home, and the film shows us only one male Chilean friend. This friend is married to a German woman, who, like all the German characters except the old man Stephan, does not speak Spanish.

This isolation and the dialogues with Zandor serve to underline the abstraction of Rogelio's situation into a metaphor for all Third World experience in the GDR. This is consistent with the German tendency to lump even southeast Europe into the Third World as a generalized "otherness," even in expressions of solidarity. The "exotic" southern and eastern-European is a relatively common trope in GDR film. Often this revolves around food, and numerous children of exiles refer to their expertise in cuisine as something that distinguishes them from the stubborn meat-and-potatoes tastes of the indigenous GDR population. In Günter Reisch's comedy of GDR development *Anton der Zauberer* (*Anton the Magician*, 1978), the main character enjoys the spicy and imaginative cooking of his Hungarian colleague as they share schemes for manipulating socialism's shortage-prone planned economies. In *Blonder Tango*, the Hungarian Zandor jokes with his friend Rogelio that he and the Latino are pretty much the same to the Germans. "Prosit, Columbian," "Prosit, Bolivian," they toast each other, using anything but their true nationalities as nicknames. And Zandor quips, "To them South America is just a bigger Hungary, Equadorian." The German lack of internationalism finally returns to a food metaphor, as Zandor observes, "Where the sauerkraut ends, there *terra incognita* begins." Food is also related to coldness and sexual frustration. In one of the scenes of Rogelio's frustrated love for Cornelia, he cooks an elaborate dinner for her, to which she never comes. And in one of their argument scenes, Rogelio shouts at Luise about the coldness of the country and the awful food that he'll eat cold, too.

Interestingly, the sensual side of the "East European Third World" is most often confined to Hungary in GDR film, and one suspects that this is a displacement from the equally proximate but politically threatening Poland. After all, the West German and Social Democrat author Günter Grass linked Latin American liberation theology with the Catholic working class reform represented by the Solidarity movement in Poland (Grass 39). Such a recognition of non-Leninist potential even in the GDR's eastern neighbors is exactly what could not be explicitly depicted in the 1980s, and Allende's Chile provided a distant, stable and historical alternative.

It is a fair question then, to ask what the film *Blonder Tango* is really about. Clearly it is not about Chileans in Germany, because of the great lengths it goes to bracket out any but the merest suggestions of an exile community there. But is the film in the end only about the GDR? Much of my analysis so far might imply this, since the GDR's anti-fascist legacy, its distinction from West Germany, its *abstract* but not nuanced interaction with the Third World are all indeed the basic context for the film. But the film's narrative complications take it well beyond these bases in cliché and ideology.

To trace its originality it might help to recall just how much the film brackets out in isolating Rogelio as it does. On the one hand, its narrative and characters self-consciously deal with clichés about southern, non-German culture. Rogelio accuses Luise of being too rational while she retorts that he is too sentimental—but it is he who does not respond to her affection. This, by the way, is only one of many reversals of the stereotypes common in German literature about the Third World. Another is the commonplace that the Third World is simple and natural while Europe is the land of artifice and deceit (Teraoka 98). Rogelio even calls this the German maxim: "Don't do anything simply when complicated will serve." Yet nothing could be more complicated than the narrative of deception on which the film itself is based.

Here we turn again to the biographical basis of the film. As we have noted, Rogelio is seen not as an intellectual but as a relatively lowly worker. He is isolated from most other exiles in the GDR and from other

Chileans except his family, and he is totally without contact to the West. This places the film's superficial structure squarely in the realm of West German *Gastarbeiter* narratives, which conventionally depict the pitiable fates of isolated males of low status (Friedrichsmeyer et al. 4). Yet both the author and the lead of the film are exceptions to this condition. Aside from their roles as intellectuals and cultural producers active in the GDR, the narrative's basis on deceitful letters connects it to, yet renders invisible, another "real" exile experience: The narrative of *Blonder Tango* bears a striking similarity in its use of deception and assumed identity to Antonio Skàrmeta's novel *Ardiente paciencia* (*Burning Patience*), which was recently filmed as the internationally acclaimed *Il Postino* (Michael Radford, *The Postman*, 1994). But Skàrmeta's novel had already appeared in translation in West Germany where its author, too, was living in exile. It was even filmed before *Blonder Tango* (and long before *Il Postino*) as a 1983 Chilean production directed by the author himself, and broadcast on West German television. Furthermore, unlike Rogelio, the Chileans involved in this film were indeed in contact with compatriots in the West, and the lead actor Alejandro Quintana Contreras had even directed Skàrmeta's *Burning Patience* on the West Berlin stage (Kersten 273).

This biographical displacement and obfuscation adds significance to the fiction of deception that is already at the core of *Blonder Tango*. The audience is led at the beginning to believe that the deception which drives the plot, both comically and tragically, is rather straightforward: with each disappointment in exile, Rogelio has written exaggerated letters home claiming that the opposite is true. He says his boss loves him and often invites him to dinner. When Cornelia rebuffs him, he writes that he is engaged to be married. Hearing how his family in Chile rejoices at this, he compounds the deceit by writing that he is about to become a father. In Chile the rejoicing again increases: photos are raffled off and debates break out over names for the baby.

On the serious side, Rogelio takes advantage of Luise's friendship to support his deception, convincing her to pose in a wedding dress for a photo to send. All this results in our presumption at the beginning of the film that it is Rogelio's unhappiness in exile (and in love) that propels his self-destructive flight to the frozen Baltic coast. As the flashbacks unfold, however, it becomes clear that these are not merely Rogelio's trivial attempts to reassure the relatives at home that he is all right. This would be trivial, after all, because no matter how well he does as an exile it would still be preferable for him to go home.

The deeper and more complex deception, and the one more closely related to Skàrmeta's theme, is the revelation near the end of the film that the letters from Rogelio's mother were also a deception on his family's part. In truth, she had actually died one and a half years before the conclusion of the narrative, indeed, probably before Regelio's own deceptions began. So while he was deceiving them that his exile was a happy one, they were deceiving him that he had a mother (or perhaps a motherland) to return to.

The bitter irony of this is implied in retrospect by several scenes in the film. The death of old Frau Hube next door is one example, Rogelio's fantasies are another. In one of the few scenes with Chilean rather than European music, Rogelio imagines a trio playing in a park with a fountain. His mother then enters this beautiful space and it becomes clear that she has come to visit her husband's grave nearby. Finally, Rogelio imagines her dancing in the park to this music with his father—which we can recall at the film's end as a foreshadowing that indeed both his parents are dead.

But with this re-casting of the location of the film into the permanence of exile, it takes on another connection to Skàrmeta's story. What is a political poet like Pablo Neruda to do under house arrest after all, if not to help another man pursue his love? At the conclusion of *Blonder Tango* we are confronted with images of Rogelio taking leave—in terms of plot he takes leave of Stephan and returns to Berlin (not to Chile). One could speculate about whether he will return to Luise. In his fantasy, in the last scene of the theater, he had taken leave of his memories and fantasies of his family. While standing alone on the theater stage pretending to sing Joseph Schmidt's "Ein Lied geht um die Welt" while the record blares, all his friends, relatives and associates pass before him as in a dream of parting. They all urge him to "Sing, Rogelio."

This is juxtaposed with the rather mundane final images of Rogelio in the film, sitting on the bus taking him away from the Baltic, watching the locals get on one by one, while his uncle's letter reveals in voice-over that his mother has been dead all along. The retrospective re-evaluation of the plot enacted by this suggests that his exile might be permanent, and that his fantasy of happiness might be more like the real give-and-take he has had with Luise. As his friend had told him when asked how it was to be married to a German woman, "Mal geht's, mal nicht" (Sometimes it works, sometimes it doesn't).

For both the GDR audience and the Chilean author, the battle of Chile is a memory that is confined to the realm of memory. Yet it could have had a utopian force as a critique of the political limitations of the 1980s. After all, there is a plenitude of pleasure in the film's images of Pinochet's Chile that far outshines the bleakness of Honecker's GDR. But it is the limitations of the here and now in which Rogelio and the audience are placed. Still, the film does not end with the concrete image of Rogelio on the bus, but with the utopian suggestiveness of images of the seashore and the voices of Joseph Schmidt and Salvador Allende. The film's last words, as warning or utopian promise, are death and eternity.

If it is a lie that Rogelio can still hope to return from exile, the revelation of the lie could motivate him to engage with the here and now. Here is another link to the cinematic canon of the anti-fascist film, which was not lost on a reviewer moved to connect sympathy for the exile with sympathy for the Jewish victims of Nazi Germany (Voss). But the motivation for this connection is not a sentimental but a critical work, Jurek Becker's *Jacob the Liar*. Although *Jacob the Liar*, like *Blonder Tango*, seems to conform to the GDR ideology of solidarity and anti-fascism, both narratives convey a critical aspect as well. Both raise the possibility that the anti-fascist resistance struggle, evoked in memory, may itself be a fiction. And both works suggest that the issue is not so much the memory of resistance in the past but the potential of resistance in the present. After all, Stephan insists to Rogelio that they both have to tell the truth about what they've been through, to which Rogelio replies with the rhetorical question which would not be foreign to Becker's Jacob the Liar, "And where might that lead?"

5. Servus Deutschland

Nostalgia for Heimat in Contemporary West German Cinema[1]

—David N. Coury

The question of German identity has changed markedly in the post–Berlin Wall era and at the turn of the millennium, as broader societal recognition of the presence of diverse minority cultures in the Federal Republic has brought about a more inclusive notion of what it means to be "German." Consequently and in recognition of this fact, German filmmakers have in the 1980s and the 1990s increasingly problematized the situation of minorities in Germany and the role they play in shaping German identity, as well as how exiles have transformed their newly given geopolitical space to compensate for the missing "Heimat" or homeland. While "minority" film-makers have added a sorely lacking bi-cultural perspective to these same issues,[2] a number of German directors in the late 1980s and 1990s turned to the experiences of German exiles to re-focus, question, and broaden their view of Germany and its cultural identity. Exile is by nature inexorably con-nected to and necessitates the concept of homeland, be it a real or imagined one. As Hamid Naficy has demonstrated in his collection of essays, *Home, Exile, Homeland,* to be exiled is not restricted to being relocated to another geographical or territorial space; exile can be voluntary, internal or external, imagined or real, but in each case necessitated by the inability to inhabit or peacefully coexist in one's homeland. In the post-WWII era, this discourse has been central to debates surrounding questions of German identity and the nature of "Heimat," the traditional German designation for a sense of home and belonging, tied very much to the geopolitical space that is Germany.[3] Not only were many individuals and groups forced into exile from Germany during the National Socialist period, but many Germans in the post-war era (in both the East and the West and especially those of the following generations) have found themselves in both internal and external exile due to their inability to form ties to their homeland for social or political reasons. This "love-hate" relationship became a central theme of the New German Cinema (NGC) from the 1960s through the 1980s, as filmmakers such as Alexander Kluge, Rainer Werner Fassbinder, Werner Herzog, Wim Wenders, Margarethe von Trotta and others sought to define what it means to be German, addressing questions of collective guilt, patriotism and nationalism in the wake of fascism and the Holocaust for their generation.[4] Beginning in the late 1980s and continuing through the period of reunification, a number of filmmakers chose to explore ideas of "Heimat" and German identity through the fictionalized experience of exiles and expatriates who seek to create and then inhabit new communities which they can call home.[5] This article will focus on Percy Adlon's *Bagdad Café* (1987) and *Salmonberries* (1991), as well as Rosa von Praunheim's *Survival in New York* (*Überleben in New York,* 1989) and Monika Treut's *My Father is Coming* (1991), discussing how these films problematize the central tension that exists between an imagined and/or adopted homeland and the exile's self-conception as a German, a polarity which itself reveals much about German identity and culture at the end of the twentieth century.

Toward a Multicultural Germany

In the 1998 federal elections, the question of Germany's antiquated citizenship laws developed into a central theme of the campaign and discussion carried over into debates in the public sphere regarding federal law, justice and national identity. At the root of the problem was the issue of immigrants and foreign workers who had in many cases been living in the Federal Republic for some 30 years and whose children were born in Germany but who were denied citizenship due to the remnants of nineteenth-century *jus sanguis* laws embedded in the constitution. While the conservative Christian Democrats were adverse to changing this statute, claiming that it would result in a flood of migration into the European state with already the most liberal immigration laws, Social Democrats argued that besides being unjust, failure to change the law was a failure to recognize the reality that Germany is and long has been an immigrant and multicultural state, an *Einwanderungsland* much like the United States.[6] Along this nexus arose a new debate, corollary to the first, in which not only the articles of Germany's Basic Law (*Grundgesetz*) would be called into question, but so too its national identity. Whereas artists and intellectuals on the left had long worked toward and maintained a diverse conception of German society and identity and while cultural critics had been examining and awarding works by Turkish-German, Afro-German, Jewish, and Muslim writers who had chosen Germany as their homeland or German as their lingua franca, Germany's political system had failed to make this jump and legally redefine the notion of what it means to be "German."

But while cultural critics had recognized and debated these issues long before they became a divisive campaign topic, German cinema, especially feature films, has been a bit slower to deal thematically with these very same issues.[7] Although the New German Filmmakers were concerned with outsiders and non-hegemonic discourses and, as John Davidson has argued, even used these discourses to construct a vision of Germany as the "other" in attempting to come to terms with Germany's past, few films of the time explored the diverse nature of Germany's cultural identity, an issue which for the left was crucial in solving the "German question" by normalizing a society which had historically been hostile to notions of otherness (8). Save for several politically oriented films (like those of Christian Ziewer and Peter Lillenthal which sought to draw attention to the plight of political refugees in Germany in the 1970s and 80s), New German Filmmakers were concerned more with probing and (re)establishing their own personal German identity and that of the first post-war generation.

While this identity was inclusive of gender, class and sexual orientation, little attention was paid to cultural minorities or exiles and the incorporation of their experiences into a larger German national identity and especially how Germany was viewed from the outside. Davidson argues that the NGC developed in a state of "neocolonialism" in which the West was continually vying to re-establish its previous domination.[8] Central to this process is the notion of the development of national and cultural identities, both on the part of the colonizer as well as of the colonized, and with this came an emphasis on the creation and recognition of a national cinema, an idea once anathema to the left. Moreover, he establishes, the NGC constructed itself and its conveyance of German identity as a minority discourse through its "fetishization" of its fascist past. As such, a dominant theme in the NGC from the 60s through the 80s was coming to terms with the past, a *Vergangenheitsbewältigung*, in which succeeding postwar generations questioned not only their parents' role and complicity in National Socialism but also to what degree they could identify themselves with notions of "Germanness" and German identity. For many, the mere fact that they were born German and into a country with such a past made it impossible to feel any strong ties to or feelings of pride in their country.

"Heimat" and the Trauma of Separation

Critical attention and debate on these topics intensified when in 1984, Edgar Reitz released his monumental eleven-part television series, *Heimat*. The film (as well as its sequel) focused on one family in a small, rural German town from 1919–1980 and explored the effects of various social and historical occurrences on the town and its inhabitants as well as their changing affinity toward the town, the region and Germany as a whole. While the "Heimat" film as a genre was certainly not new (it developed in the 1950s as a non-political, sentimental genre which filmmakers of the 1960s and 1970s rejected in a wave of so-called "anti-Heimat" films), Reitz' film renewed interest in "Heimat" within Germany, capitalizing on debates among the German left.[9] These discussions first arose in response to both the growing environmental movement in the 1980s and then to growing anti-Americanism spurred by the deployment of cruise missiles on German soil. Consequently, filmmakers began to explore German identity anew but this time from a much more multicultural perspective, whereby they sought to analyze Germany both from the inside and outside, using the experiences of German immigrants and migrants alike to construct a more inclusive and hence more realistic image of Germany.

In his 1985 article "'Heimat' and the German Left," Michael Geisler argues that the political and cultural left has long suffered from a trauma due to its inability to identify with Germany as a homeland or "Heimat." Historically, this break arose from a sense of isolation and ostracism on the part of the liberal and radical left, a situation which began in the nineteenth century in the wake of rising German nationalism and the failed revolution of 1848 and then reached its zenith in the twentieth century with the rise of fascism. Geisler goes so far as to claim that "the story of the German left has been a story of exile, external and internal" which has "permanently traumatized relations between the German left and the country they expected to call 'home'" (30). This led to the paradoxical situation in which leftists born in Germany felt exiled from their native homeland; on the one hand there was the natural desire for belonging, evident in the ties to one's native culture, while there existed on the other hand an abhorrence of all things "German" as well as of any social or political identification with Germany. The only solution was to distance oneself from the native culture, a sort of self-imposed exile, which resulted in a necessary "Trauerarbeit" or act of mourning, an important step in coming to terms with past.[10]

While the act of mourning surrounding the Holocaust and vis-à-vis questions of German historicity have been discussed and analyzed in great detail by political and cultural historians, I would argue that the mourning and/or melancholia arising from the trauma of exile necessitated by the forced separation from the "Heimat," results in a nostalgia for a reconciliation between the dichotomy of homeland and "Deutschland." This mourning and nostalgia is thematized in certain films of the 1980s and 1990s particularly through the experience of emigrants who seek and desire a sense of belonging in a culture or society open to and inclusive of the other, a facet which often they see—in a mirroring of the intellectual left—as absent in German society. Indeed, this connection is inherent in the term "nostalgia," which is itself a neo-Greek translation of the nineteenth-century German concept "Heimweh," a designation for a painful (*algos, weh*) longing for a return home (*nostos, heim*).[11] It is exactly this pain of separation from one's home country (or the abstraction of this idea) which Freud, in his treatise on the subject, has defined as "Trauer" or "mourning": "Mourning (Trauer) is regularly the reaction to the loss of a loved person, or to the loss of some abstraction which has taken the place of one, such as one's country, liberty, an ideal, and so on" (239–60).[12] Oftentimes filmmakers use idealized and utopian spaces in juxtaposition to Germany as a means of exploring identity through the "other." Interestingly, America, both real and mythologized, is most often used in these films as a trope for exploring ideas of constructing societies in which the individual's conflict with Germany can be played out in a space either devoid of history or one historically open to issues of otherness. Moreover, America serves to polemicize the relationship emigrants have to Germany and in doing so, it reflects the construct of an idealized society in which the issues surrounding the trauma of separation from the German "Heimat" can be probed and ultimately resolved.

The term "Heimat," though, much like the similar word "Vaterland," has a particularly masculine connotation, one that refers not only to the geographical land of one's father but also to the patriarchal heritage. In this regard, these films also represent a decidedly oedipal urge to dismantle the male oriented "Heimat" in favor of more tolerant, balanced communities in which the repression and oppression of the patriarchy is diminished. In all four films, the exiled protagonists are women who have left their husbands and/or fathers behind and who thus associate *Deutsch*land with the *Vater*land. The oedipal complex is completed, in fact, in that by the conclusion of each film, each protagonist in these four very different films has established a new relationship, be it platonic or sexual, with another woman, oftentimes an exile or displaced person. The desire to reject the patriarchal "Heimat" is articulated especially well in Adlon's *Bagdad Café* which posits the creation of a matriarchal community as the solution to the various problems of the film's two protagonists. Here individuals of various races and ethnic and economic backgrounds can live in harmony.

Utopian and Dystopian Desires

Bagdad Café, originally released in Germany in 1987 under the title *Out of Rosenheim* and the first of a number of films in the 1980s and 1990s to deal with German exiles, tells the story of Bavarian hausfrau Jasmin Münchgstettner, who during a vacation in the American West leaves her husband in the middle of the desert to find inevitably not only independence but a sense of family and belonging ("Heimat") amongst an odd assortment of people populating the Bagdad Café. While the film serves in many ways to reinforce a certain idealized myth of America—the land of opportunity where anything and everything is possible, in which people of all groups and nationalities can come together to construct a sense of home and belonging—it also serves to ridicule certain American stereotypes of Germany, namely Lederhosen-wearing Bavarians obsessed with orderliness. While such a view of America is generally viewed by philosophers and cultural critics as a founding myth of this country (and one not representing the reality of American society), the desire for such a utopian society played an important role in the works of many post-WWII German writers and filmmakers (especially those of Wim Wenders), who suffering from the trauma of identity, sought refuge in American culture and the dream of constructing a new "Heimat." Moreover, the American model is at the heart of the German left's conception of a multi-cultural and multi-racial Germany. Adlon, aware of this tradition in the NGC, is able to transform many of the stereotypes of the America myth—as well as the many German stereotypes—by constructing what Davidson has termed the "international community of the West" in which equality is established between the German outsider and neglected housewife (Jasmin), the African-American store owner (Brenda) and the other outcasts at the café (92). The trauma of exile and the nostalgia for the homeland is then reconciled in the end via the creation of a new "Heimat" that offers home, shelter and a sense of belonging in the utopian space that is the mythical West. As the West is a locale devoid of history (at least from the Western, colonialist perspective which is clearly the reference point here), Jasmin and Brenda (the African-American store owner who in the middle of the Mojave desert is herself displaced) not only overcome their sense of otherness but also establish a new sense of community devoid of the cultural and socio-political problems that accompany the space which they have left. The fairy tale nature of the story, and especially the ending, underscore the utopian nature of this community, as does the magic act which Jasmin performs for the customers. After Jasmin is deported, she longs to return to Bagdad and eventually does, as she is apparently unable to find a sense of belonging with her husband in her homeland. With Brenda, who has similarly kicked out her husband, Jasmin is able to assume control of her life and, through the variety act, find a means of self-expression.

David J. Levin has argued that from the perspective of racial community formation, the variety act at the conclusion of film is regressive, in that it posits the dominance of the German through the marginalization of the African-American (117–28). Indeed, Jasmin has taken center stage (both figuratively and literally in the magic act) and as Levin has quite astutely pointed out, Brenda and her children assume the secondary role of entertainers in a manner common in entertainment films of the 1940s.[13] However from a gender perspective, it is the men who have been jettisoned and marginalized and the women who have seized control of the café and their lives. There is not a magical return of the nuclear family, as Levin argues, but of a matriarchal family whereby a new, prosperous community is formed by Jasmin and Brenda. While the "orderly German" has assumed a central role in this community, it is almost as if ethnicity has supplanted the patriarchy. Jasmin has rejected her German homeland in favor of this mythical community in the American desert.

The impetus for the film, as Davidson recounts, had its origins in two ideas both dealing with conceptions of re-negotiated space and community (93f.). The first involved a re-working of the road movie, a genre popular among NGC directors for its innate sense of displacement and exile, as well as for the quest to find meaning and belonging. While driving with his wife in the desert, Adlon came upon an unusual light in the sky that he followed to a town which no longer existed and was listed on the map only as "Bagdad." The idea then struck him to have his muse, Marianne

Sägebrecht, encounter a "black" person in such a landscape, whereby both question the identity and motives of the other in a typical Western show-down. Ultimately, in this same mythologized tradition, both would come to an understanding and acceptance of the other, whereby in the end they work together to construct a community, in this case, given the clear racial implications, a newly formed exile community offering a sense of harmony and tolerance which their respective homelands lack. This idea is, as Ingeborg Majer O'Sickey has argued, a common theme in Adlon's works, namely one positing that "as citizens within multicultural societies, we find ourselves in the curious position of wishing to assert our allegiance to parti-cular groups (be they cultural, national, or ethnic), while at the same time we feel obligated to break down or at least question established and normative categories of national, cultural, and individual identity" (408). Whereas at first both Brenda and Jasmin feel a need to assert allegiance to their particular cultural identity (albeit expressed rather superficially and stereotypically—the German desire for cleanliness and orderliness, and the American notion of extreme individuality), they slowly come to re-negotiate these concepts of self and other, leading to the creation of a community which supports, tolerates and even blends such normative categories.[14]

The second story Adlon relates as to the genesis of the film is more autobiographical in nature. Adlon tells of his uncle Louis, who left Germany for the States in the 1920s to learn the hotel trade. Later this uncle returned to Germany as a media correspondent, but he never again felt a sense of belonging in his former homeland: "he was always a young man cut off from place," Adlon remembers (Davidson 94). Adlon's uncle is in many ways symbolic of the exiled German in the post-war era who suffers from the trauma of uprootedness from his/her homeland. Not surprisingly Adlon had intended to make a film chronicling his uncle's life, when he stumbled on the idea for *Bagdad Café*. Through the fictional film, Adlon was able to reconcile what his uncle could not: namely, the identification with the land of exile through the creation of a tolerant, liberal community which furthers the growth and understanding of the other.

Thus in *Bagdad Café*, exile does not lead to mourning or nostalgia, but to freedom and independence via a self-constructed (albeit mythical) commu-nity which fosters tolerance and self-actualization. Indeed self-actualization, as Geisler has shown with regard to Reitz' *Heimat*, is a central part of the new "Heimat" movement of the 1980s as much as identity, shelter and the acceptance of being part of an "in-group" (45)—all things which Jasmin inevitably finds at the conclusion of the film. Geisler argues further that the creation and construction of "Heimat" in the post-war era is necessarily a work-in-progress, as it exists as a construct only in the future (48). Reitz, Geisler notes, argues that "Heimat" (or perhaps better, the *desire* for "Heimat") only becomes a utopian notion when compared with empirical reality. As a work-in-progress, though, "Heimat" becomes an impetus for social change or a means of self-actualization, whereby the exiled individual is enabled to come to terms with his/her identity conflict so as either to return to the homeland or else establish meaningful ties to a new community (thus relinquishing any desire for the "Heimat" of one's youth). This dilemma forms the central theme in Adlon's 1991 film *Salmonberries*.

Unlike *Bagdad Café*, Adlon's *Salmonberries* does not offer such an easy (and idealistic) solution to the trauma of exile. Like *Bagdad Café*, though, *Salmonberries* is set in the U.S., but this time in northern Alaska, in an even more harsh setting than the American West, but one nevertheless still tinged with ties to Germany. The film, which together with Adlon's other successes *Sugarbaby* (1986) and *Rosalie goes Shopping* (1990) forms a trilogy, is perhaps the most complex and interesting of Adlon's films due to the multiple layers of identity formation which are probed in the narrative. As O'Sickey has noted, *Salmonberries* is "one of the first cinematic treatments of the so-called 'German Question' following the unification of Germany" (407). Adlon expands upon the "German Question" that was central to the films of the NGC, though, by exploring how East Germans had to come to terms with the legacy of forty years of communist rule. This issue is problematized in the film through the relationship that Roswitha, one of the two lead characters, has toward her exiled homeland of East Germany. In 1970, Roswitha and her husband had attempted to flee East Berlin. Betrayed by her brother to the authorities, Roswitha's husband was shot and killed during their escape. Afterwards Roswitha moved to a remote village in Northern Alaska ironically named "Kotzebue," a town named after its founder, the explorer Otto von Kotzebue, the son of eighteenth-century German playwright August von Kotzebue whose dramatic assassination by a radical university student in 1819 is recounted in the film via a series of drawings and a voice-over explaining how the town came into being. The choice of setting and the connection the town's nomenclature imbues to Germany and its liberal tradition is very appropriate, for it not only situates the film in the tradition of the love-hate relationship to "Heimat," but it also foreshadows the protagonists' search in the film's diagesis for their own origins and identities. Moreover, the fact that August von Kotzebue lived over half of his adult life in exile subtextually establishes this theme as a central focus of the film. Further references at the outset of the film to *Madame Bovary* similarly set up the film to be concerned not only with "fables of identity" (as O'Sickey has termed it), but also with the dissatisfaction with these created fables, a problem from which Emma Bovary suffered tremendously.

The second protagonist in the film experiences a similar estrangement from her homeland: as a young unemployed miner of half Amero-Eskimo, half Euro-American descent ironically named Kotzebue, herself, or Kotz for short (played with an intentional sense of androgyny by singer k.d. lang), this figure plays with and explores issues of gender and sexual identity and serves as a foil and future romantic interest for Roswitha. Like Roswitha, Kotz too suffers from a dissatisfaction with her own fragmented identity and the rejection she endures from the others, a suffering which leads almost to the point of self-loathing.[15] Whereas Roswitha attempts to suppress and deny her history and identity to avoid the trauma of separation from her homeland (as well as the pain of familial betrayal and the loss of her husband), Kotz actively searches for her own history as a basis to help create and stabilize her own identity. In the process she forces Roswitha to confront her past by undertaking a trip to Germany in order to reconcile her issues with the past. O'Sickey maintains that both women share an important "structuring principle": namely that "the identities of both characters are constituted in and by historical trauma. Kotz's trauma derives from her father's role as a colonizer and exploiter of the Inupiaq people; Roswitha's historical trauma is the division of East and West Germany" (415). As an indication of her distress, Roswitha plays certain games of repetition, which Freud has characterized as signs of traumatic suffering.[16] I would argue, however, that Roswitha's suffering stems not from the trauma of the geopolitical division of East and West Germany (she shows no signs of interest in politics or in discussing the fall of the Berlin Wall, an event which enters the film's narrative through news reports on television playing in the background of her apartment), rather from the pain of separation from her homeland, her "Heimat," her inability to come to terms with the past and the loss of a stable and supportive community. Having come to the frozen tundra of the Alaskan north, Roswitha chose the most remote and icy landscape so as to remove herself from the pain of her past and any reminders of her past life. Her mourning is evident in her demeanor and the bitterness she shows toward Kotz and other members of the community, a temperament bordering on self-torment. Having lost both her husband and her homeland, Roswitha clearly exhibits signs of a *pathological* mourning, a state which Freud has characterized as a sign of melancholia. For Freud, this state is brought about in reaction to the loss of a loved object and manifests itself in "a profoundly painful dejection, cessation of interest in the outside world, loss of the capacity to love, inhibition of all activity and a lowering of the self-regarding feelings" (244), all symptoms from which Roswitha suffers. The complex relationship to her lost homeland has thus advanced her trauma to a state of melancholia. Kotz subconsciously recognizes Roswitha's melancholia and attempts to bring her out of this state, by engaging her in a dialogue about her past; by criticizing her anti-social behavior and disinterest in the outside world; by undertaking a trip to Berlin with her; and by initiating a sexual relationship with Roswitha despite the latter's continual assertions that she is unable to love.

While the initial rupture in Roswitha's self-imposed exile, as O'Sickey argues, does indeed come from historical determinants, it is only the forced reconciliation with her past and her re-encounter with Berlin and her brother, her homeland and community, which enables Roswitha to come to terms with her traumatic melancholia. While the fracturing of Germany has been resolved via re-unification, the split between rejecting "Germany" yet being drawn toward one's homeland (from which Roswitha has suffered) cannot be so easily resolved. Although in the end she rejects her brother's attempts at reconciliation and returns to Alaska, the questions of her sexual desires created by her encounters with Kotz lead to further instability of her identity. But Roswitha is not alone in her suffering; Kotz too is plagued by similar issues of exile and separation. In a rather comical scene in an East German bar, Kotz mounts a pinball machine and exhorts: "I understand you! I'm Eskimo" implying that she can empathize with their plight, for like them, she too has lost her homeland through colonization (one Marxist, the other capitalist) and further, like them she too suffers from the ambiguity resulting from the trauma of identification with one's homeland: thus the "German Question" is presented in the East German realm but verbalized by an Amero-Eskimo.

Unlike Jasmin in *Out of Rosenheim*, Kotz and Roswitha do not find a utopian space in which they can work toward establishing ties and bonds to a newly adopted homeland. Instead, both are left with difficult questions (and in some cases answers) as to their identities. In this way, Adlon seems to be saying first that the "German Question" in the East will not be so easily resolved as some politicians at the time had hoped and second, that national identity only forms a part of our complex overall identity. What Roswitha has begun, though, through her coming to terms with the past is the beginning of a process of self-actualization, which is the true point of departure for negotiating a space which can be called home (see Geisler 48, n. 44). Her period of exile has led her to confront many different facets of her identity—ones which involve issues of social, racial, economic and sexual identity as well as national and historical—and she must now explore these elements so as to determine the nature of the space and the type of community to which she would choose to belong. Returning to Germany might be as equally difficult as staying in Alaska, for the historical trauma which she encountered cannot be healed so easily.

American Idylls

America has long served as a space of utopian freedom for immigrants both historically and cinematically. While NGC filmmakers in the 1960s and 1970s sought their own cultural identity in the post-war era in American pop and youth culture, filmmakers of the 1980s and 1990s have at times been more critical and skeptical of American culture and its politics. However the personal freedom that America can afford, especially to those seeking the anonymity of the urban metropolis to establish a new identity, is a theme that forms the basis for two important films by two of Germany's most visible gay and lesbian filmmakers, Rosa von Praunheim's *Survival in New York* and Monika Treut's *My Father is Coming*. Both films are constructed around the facet that the extreme nature of American society, together with the personal liberty afforded individuals by a city like New York, allows immigrants to distance themselves from the identity they associate with their homeland and to develop and explore their true personality and identity in a foreign land. In these two films the characters exhibit neither mourning, melancholia nor a longing for the homeland, for they are able to create communities and explore subcultures which reflect the alternative lifestyles they have chosen. In this way these films take up the classic portrayal of the immigrant's search for personal freedom, but instead of seeking religious or political freedom, these figures are in search of communities which support their sexual identity and lifestyle choices.

While both films are thematically concerned more with sexual freedom and lifestyle choices, Treut's *My Father is Coming* establishes an interesting dialog with issues surrounding the conflict with "Heimat" and the separation from one's homeland. Vicki, the exiled protagonist left her home in the conservative Bavarian provinces to live in New York City. Although she is a struggling, out of work actress, she has found a group of people who share a similar lifestyle and explore issues of their own gender and sexuality, from bondage and S&M to performance artistry using the body as a means of expressing personal freedom. While Vicki is able to live in relative freedom in this community, her world is suddenly confronted with her past when her father, a stereotypical, conservative Bavarian, announces his pending visit to New York. Vicki is afraid that he will discover that she is not the happliy married successful actress that she had claimed to be, so she begins arranging a fictitious world in which she is happily married and well off. His visit sets up a confrontation between past and present, between the conservatism of Vicki's Bavarian "Heimat" and the liberalism of the utopian exile community, as well as—in somewhat cliched fashion—between the "Old World" and the "New World," but here exhibited in the somewhat different sense of community formation. The film sets up this dialectic in the title, in which the dominance of the patriarchal homeland (father) threatens to invade the space and freedom of the exiled daughter who has attempted to break from the restrictive bonds of the past and the conservatism of the "Heimat." Treut's film, however, moves in its own idyllic world, for when the father arrives in New York, he is indeed confronted by an array of people and sites which overwhelm and challenge his view and understanding of the world, but rather than address this conflict directly, Treut chooses the whimsical path of having the father seduced by the freedom and licentiousness of New York's subcultures. Instead of being shocked and admonishing his daughter for her lifestyle and for breaking from the moral strictures of her "Heimat," he himself falls in love with a sex goddess (played by Annie Sprinkle) and begins to explore this hitherto unknown world on his own. When in the end he finally confronts Vicki, it is only to express understanding for her lifestyle and to express his support for her attempt to find happiness in a community and space which allow her this freedom. In this way, the film is structured more like a fairy-tale (with requisite happy end) than as an exploration of the conflicts between the freedom of the exiled community and the desire for homeland and "Heimat." Nevertheless, the film engages an important conflict of exile communities, namely the tension between the desire for the homeland and the freedom of the chosen or created space which affords the potential for self-actualization.

This same issue of self-actualization is the primary focus of Rosa von Praunheim's documentary *Survival in New York*, which focuses on three young German women, Claudia, Anna and Uli, who for various reasons came to New York and despite many obstacles and difficulties have opted to stay.[17] Together, these two films in many ways underscore Geisler's contention that the desire to find a space away from the German homeland in order to achieve one's full potential is indeed a defining element of the new Heimat discourses of the 1980s. In his memoirs, von Praunheim writes that *Survival in New York* is to date his most successful film, both commercially and artistically, in part because it had so much to do with issues in his own personal life, that of a gay director who spends half of his time in the U.S. and half in Berlin, thus attempting to bridge the tension between home and exile (von Praunheim 356). Unlike von Praunheim, though, all three of the protagonists in his film have opted to stay in New York primarily because the city fascinates and affords them the potential and possibility to develop their own identity in ways not possible in their homeland. Claudia, whom von Praunheim describes as the "intellectual" of the three (355), grew up in a middle-class family in the largely Catholic city of Cologne. In the film she recounts that as a leftist, she at first rejected America as a racist, imperialist, superficial consumer society. Upon arriving, however, she became fascinated by the quotidian nature of the city's extremes ("Alltäglichkeit der Extremen"). For her, her sojourn in New York became a permanent journey of self-discovery, which has allowed her to discover and acknowledge her sexual orientation as well as to overcome her intro-vertedness. Moreover, despite earlier financial difficulties and being bru-tally raped in her own apartment, she states at the end of the film that she has "angst" to return to Germany, for she can see more, learn more and experience more in New York than anywhere else. In New York, she feels, she is confronted with "truths about herself" and is unable to live a lie; per-haps most importantly, though, in New York she feels at home, "zu Hause," for it is "her city," "meine Stadt," an acknowledgement that she, like Anna, one of the film's other protagonists, has chosen to create a new "Heimat," one in which she can live and explore her own identity. At the close of the film, Anna, who besides working as a psychotherapist for immigrant chil-dren in inner-city schools also works as a go-go dancer in various strip clubs, perhaps best summarizes the attraction that exile has for her and others like her: "I think somehow we all have a city or a landscape in us which is the image of that which we all carry within us. . . . In New York I immediately felt at home. The extremes, the contradictions, the brutality, the friendliness—that's all in me as well and I think that's why I fit in here so well. In Germany . . . I find that the people protect themselves too much and I don't want to retire or grow old there." The idea which Anna expresses of finding a reflection of one's inner self in the space or landscape of an exiled community is characteristic of many of these immigrants' experiences: the ahistorical desert landscape for Jasmin, the frozen tundra for Roswitha and the extremes of the metropolis for Vicki, Claudia and Anna. In the end, the decision to stay or return rests primarily on the indi-vidual's ability to achieve independence and self-actualization, elements which Jasmin, Vicki, Anna and Claudia are able to find but which remain questionable for Roswitha and Uli, the naive young woman in New York from rural Germany who expresses a desire to return to the peace of her

Heimat and escape the chaos of New York. The trauma of exile and the mourning or melancholia associated with it are overcome by the freedom and desire to find a new Heimat which either allows the freedom of self-expression or the ability to control the determinants of its creation.

Conclusion

While German films of the 1980s and early 1990s reflect many of the issues of the new "Heimat" discourses, the events and cultural transitions surrounding the fall of the Berlin Wall in 1990 have altered the German cinematic landscape to a degree, whereby the "German question" is now much more far-reaching. The conflict many on the left felt toward Germany as a nation, however, found expression in the cinematic representation of exiles in several West German films in the late 1980s. German unification in 1990s, on the other hand, led to even more traumatic confrontations not only with Germany's fascist legacy but also that of the former GDR. To that end, the mourning over the inability to reconcile these issues of identity and identification became manifested cinematically in a more pathological state characterized by melancholia. Other films at the time, though, viewed exile as a means of liberation not only from the constrictures of modern-day Germany but also the conflicts of the past. What is interesting at the end of the twentieth-century is that Germany, like its neighbors, has evolved into a modern, mobile, multicultural society in which the influx of immigrants has necessarily changed the face of the nation. Whereas the leftists of the first post-war generation struggled to come to terms with the "German question" and often sought alternative societies abroad which reflected their views or at least permitted them to forget their "Heimat," younger generations have a different attitude toward issues of Germanness and the concept of "Heimat." German identity today is constructed as much by the immigrants and minority groups within the country as by historical and/or mythical determinants. The desire of these individual groups to create a space and culture within Germany which allows them the potential to develop their own personalities and identities, both politically and personally, will continue to play a major role in shaping the identity of the nation in the coming century. Already young filmmakers have begun to explore the tensions and trauma that immigrants to Germany experience toward their homelands. Films like Tevfik Baser's *40 m² Germany* (*40 qm Deutschland*) and *Goodbye to a False Paradise* (*Abschied vom falschen Paradies*) as well as those of Fatih Akin and Yüksel Yavez explore many of the same issues of identity and nostalgia for the homeland but from the perspective of immigrants and exiles within Germany.[18] While the construction of "Heimat" is of course different—as are the reasons why many of these characters left their homeland—the feelings of trauma and melancholia are similar. Whether these individuals stay or return depends much on whether they, like their exiled German counterparts, are able to establish or find communities which support and foster their personal growth better than in their own "Heimat."

6. The Desire of the Other

Balkan Dystopia in Western European Cinema[1]

—Rodica Diaconescu-Blumenfeld

Reflecting on current debates on the nature of representation there necessarily come to mind those two key pronouncements against representation at the foundations of Western culture, the Hebraic and the Hellenic: the Hebrew scriptural injunction against graven images (*Ex.* 20:4, *Lev.* 26:1, *Deut.* 5:8), and Plato's attack in the *Republic* (X595A-602B) on artistic mimesis, though Plato swiftly passes from visual images to representation in poetry, his true concern.

We, as postmoderns, in a time and place that aspires to some sort of pluralism, again find a fierce problematization, through the notion of the Other and the awareness of dynamics of power that conjure, configure, or deny this other. How does desire of the other—as desire for the other, constitution of subject through consumption of the other—relate to the other's desire, the other as desiring subject? It is this question that underlies my essay, in which I set out some of my explorations of how this question motivates aesthetic/political strategies in certain trends of contemporary European cinema. Some artists seek to refuse or undercut a sovereign power of creation through a variety of means of hyper-representation and diffusion, and it is no accident that various techniques of deconstructing narrative so often confront the idea of history.[2]

This essay is prompted by issues that have emerged, mostly in postcolonial theory and heterology, around the question of an "ethics of representation." My broader argument is that what is at stake is any given text's cognitive position: that is, whether the artist is aware that to use the other as material is a matter of privilege, and whether he or she succeeds in integrating this awareness in the work itself. The essay will center on representation as both remembrance and occlusion, through the concept of diaspora of history. I will proceed by examining a narrative film, one quite explicitly focused on history, the history of the other, Gianni Amelio's film about Albania, *Lamerica* (1994), to then sketch out some points of interaction but also of contrast with films that seem to me significant texts for these issues: Pier Paolo Pasolini's *Notes for an African Orestes* (1970), Chantal Akerman's *D'est: Bordering on Fiction* (1993), and Jean-Luc Godard's *For Ever Mozart* (1996).

Using a play of historical and metaphorical dislocations, *Lamerica* performs two contradictory movements in relation to Albanians-as-other: one of recognition and affirmation (giving voice/image to silenced/invisible subjectivities), and one of erasure (these subjectivities become the raw material for a theorization of the Western self). Thus this essay will ask two questions: is History itself always in diaspora within a consolidated narrative? and, is *Lamerica* ultimately reinscribed in the discourse of cultural neocolonialism it attempts to demystify? or: is representation necessarily aphasic? Aphasia is a place of silence defined by the structure of language, a diaspora of signification. Along the axis of the syntagm, we may fail to tell the story. Along the axis of the paradigm, we may fail to recognize same and different. And like language, cinematic representation is at once exile and recuperation. Through the ellipses of memory, a narrative is constructed.

Lamerica is the story of a young, smug, but also naive, Italian entrepreneur, Gino, who finds himself caught in the political and social chaos of post-dictatorship Albania. Having come to Albania to set up a shoe factory (which turns out to be a money-making scam of his partner), Gino's life becomes entangled with that of an old, illiterate Albanian, Spiro, who turns out to be an Italian soldier, Michele, who had deserted during the war, and had spent most of his life in a Communist prison. The two travel together with the itinerant masses of Albanians, whose only desire is to embark and flee to Italy. As Spiro rediscovers speech in his native Sicilian dialect, and starts to generate crazy narratives, alternating with lapses and disorientation; and further, as Gino is increasingly waylaid by the countless Albanians' own narratives of misery and desire, the balance of the discourse changes, and Gino grows progressively quieter, and in the last 15 minutes of the film is completely silent. In the course of quasi-incomprehensible trajectories, Gino is gradually dispossessed of his capitalist goods—his jeep, his clothes— and his body is transformed from a consumer body into a vagrant, cast-out body. His very identity as a passport-carrying free man, based on the laws of another place, is dissolved. It's as if the unstable identities of the mad old man and of the muddled Albanians proliferate to the point of engulfing the one previously seemingly stable identity, that of the young Italian.

My initial interpretation of this film was "resistant": Amelio seemed involved in what has been termed "unthinking Eurocentrism" (Stam and Shohat)—an enterprise of straightforward "epistemic violence" (Spivak "Subaltern Studies" 18), whereby the Western European subject is able to gain self-knowledge at the expense of the colonized, subaltern, other. Thus the category of occlusion (of the subjectivity of the other) was a central one in that interpretation. It focused primarily on Amelio's declared project of allegory: "The prime mover of the film is memory, necessary for rediscovering in others—in the different—one's own origins, one's own past, oneself, and, if possible, a future" (Detassis 33).[3] Amelio's allegorical use of Albanian history as Italy's earlier history is a classic colonialist/evolutionist trope, and is related to Western conceptualizations of traveling and discovering, which are forms of the self's desire for a return to origins.[4] Postcolonial cultural critic Marianna Torgovnick writes,

If primitive societies resemble our prehistory and exist in contemporary spaces accessible to individuals, then origins remain accessible. Our need for the primitive to be eternally present accounts in part for the anxiety often expressed by anthropologists and adventurers about the speed with which primitive societies vanish. The primitive must be available or our "origins" may no longer be retrievable, re-creatable (187).

As corrective to the forgotten past of Italy, Amelio offers the present of Albania, an embodiment of it (indeed he lays claim to real Albanian bodies, the most acute occasion of which is the "landscaping of pain" in the final boat scene).[5] Albania is the shadow, the subconscious of Italy being raised to consciousness, mediating self-identity in an other. In this sense Amelio's artifact of retrieval, with its investment in the idea of origins, is not very different from Pier Paolo Pasolini's imagined others, as I shall presently argue.

Upon further reflection, I came to see that the film is more complicated than this. The other may still be raw material for the constitution of the protagonist as Subject, but not to the extent of an absolute silencing. Occlusion still occurs, but it is the kind in which representation itself finds its possibility. This is very much connected to Gayatryi Spivak's concept of the subaltern. Her question "can the Subaltern speak?" is of necessity answered with both yes and no. But also, as dramatized in Amelio's film, the question becomes, "whose speech is it?"

Amelio's film means to raise the question of two dilemmas in the Western/Italian sociolect. The first is the relation to history, the second capitalism. Contemporary Italians are portrayed as ignorant/forgetful of their own history of poverty and emigration, and thus are now arrogant and exploitative. Intersecting this is the issue of Amelio's intended audience: it is the Italians at home that he addresses, the forgetful, complacent, xenophobic Italians who, as consumers of his product, might be rendered more susceptible to acknowledging the (presently hated and feared) other of Italy: Albania. This is done very well in the formal choice of the split screen of the beginning, where the loud, bombastic fascist propaganda film of Italy's "civilizing mission" to Albania is set against the (as if) silent, austere, titles of Amelio's own film. Historical memory is invoked here in a double articulation. First, as signal of cinematic self-reflexivity, the status of the image in relation to its history is called into question. Second, as a false memory, a lie—since the real history of relations between Albania and Italy is that of occupation and colonization—it offers an analogy with present-day fraudulent Italian businessmen (and a contrast, implicitly, to

Amelio's own endeavor).[6] But Amelio isn't engaged here in a reconstruction of historical events, nor in an extensive analysis of the two cultures. What history signifies for him is remembering what it means to be hungry.[7]

Moreover, if Amelio criticizes the Italians' forgetfulness, he also criticizes the Albanians' desire to forget, desire that forgets. Amelio's Albanians are in a double-bind: they *speak* their desire to *not speak* their own language. In a very moving instance, in an extraordinary but desolate countryside, one of the many young Albanians, expressing his hope that in Italy there are no laws to prohibit his marrying an Italian girl, says in broken Italian: "Now I go to Italy, I find a girl in Bari. I want to marry that one, make many children. And I want to never speak the Albanian language with my sons, I want to speak always Italian. And so the sons forget that I'm Albanian."[8]

Amelio authorizes his characters to speak, but what they say denies them. Identity is denied by what should constitute it: speech. And on one side, we seem to understand, what they are and have is valueless. Who would not want to forget an identity, a past that's made up of isolation, exclusion, erasure of an earlier past?[9]

Alternatively, the Albanians watch on Italian television that country's version of "The Price is Right" in silent incomprehension. This, the Italian television, the true but insidious enemy, dealing out Pasolini's "cultural genocide" beyond its state-given borders, is a recurrent topos in *Lamerica*, and it is done well and with great economy by Amelio. His is a subtle but extremely pointed analysis, along neo-Marxist lines.[10] With no material context, no accessible referent, television is for the Albanians the place of desire and of denial of memory. Or, in fact, the place of the constitution of a different memory, as a possible (but totally illusory) future. The images project beyond themselves, not to obtainable objects, but to another life. But also, here, in the wasteland of nonsensical prices for never-to-be-seen, brand-name garden furniture, where there is no price that can be right, Gino is offered non-specific, universal food, and his money is not accepted.

Amelio strongly criticizes/demystifies capitalism, consumption and exploitation through consumption, and television as the specific medium of the episteme's "silent programming function" (Spivak, "Can the Subaltern Speak?" 282–83). This critique, though particularly poignant in a Western society, falls under the economy of postmodern, posthumanist deconstruction of the Subject, but, as in the case of women and emerging nations, is somewhat inappropriate here. In fact, when Gino tries to tell the Albanians that their Italy, as glimpsed through the myth-making capitalism of the media, is not the land of opportunity, that it has been already claimed by other groups and they are too late in history, exclaiming with contempt, "Go ahead, come, you'll be lucky if you get to be dishwashers,"—the response can only be: "better dishwasher in Italy than hunger in Albania," the undying dream of the emigrant.

Yet, even if the question "can the Subaltern speak?" is answered with "yes, but only in hegemonic language," even if the Albanians are incapable of speaking, of narrating a self in a critical manner, the film still offers them the possibility of speech, a self's expression nonetheless.

There still remain two points I would like to raise in a critique of Amelio's endeavor. Even reduced to silence, the deconstructed Italian remains central, because this silence is only fleeting, while the Albanian other remains the raw material of representation and self-knowledge. And, in like manner, Amelio's own product is reinscribed in the capitalist circuit.

On the other side, though, it could be said that any representation does all this. The question then becomes, to represent or not to represent? or more specifically, how to represent the other? There is real sophistication in Amelio's film, used to integrate conventions of perception in capitalist cinema with the possibility of seeing—he made a popular film which portrays the Albanians as sympathetic to his intended audience. What enables the capitalist Italian/Western consumers of this film to recognize the suffering of the Albanians is the process by which the Albanians are set into a paradigm that makes them the same as the Italians. A paradigmatic axis is to be set up: the Italians went to America, the Albanians go to Italy; the old man had been made into an Albanian; and while he re-becomes Italian, the young Italian (almost) becomes Albanian. But the point is that in setting up a taxonomy of sameness that enables you to recognize the existence of something, you are also occluding difference. In *Lamerica*, the Italian's suffering displaces the story of the real hunger of the dispossessed Albanians. And in the end, the process of film consumption requires the well-known, beautiful actor; his suffering does give access to the suffering of

Enrico Lo Verso as the destitute Italian at the end of Lamerica. *Courtesy of Photofest, New York.*

the other, but that suffering must needs be fascinating. One might say we can, indeed we yearn to consume the abject, but only if filtered through an acceptable aesthetic, through a symbol, not raw. What kind of film would this have been had the protagonist been ugly?

There are discrete moments of the narrative, what I would call "nodes of inscription," where the reality of representation coheres as writing/ rewriting. One relates to the one character that mediates the two cultures and the two historical times, Spiro/Michele, the old man. Early in the film, we see that while illiterate, he can still sign his name, yet that name is a false one (Spiro), designating the diaspora into which his Italian identity has been sent by his Albanian one. At the very center of the narrative, the two travelers stop by a derelict communist farm compound filmed in wide-lens against a mountain-side on which a huge inscription reads "Enver Hodxa"—an homage to the now-deposed dictator. Gino asks the old man what the inscription says, which the latter takes as evidence that Gino is illiterate as well. But illiterate as he is, Michele is still better equipped than the ignorant Gino to interpret the meaning of the inscription: he tells Gino, "It says: 'Duce! Mussolini!'"

One dictator is assimilated to another, producing a symmetrical move: one past (Albanian) sent into diaspora by another (Italian).[11]

The paradigm rendering possible such correspondences is in fact already dramatized by the spelling of the title as the aphasic form of *Lamerica* (without apostrophe)—another node of inscription. The misspelling of the name of a utopia renders it not a dystopia, but rather serves to emphasize the utopic as intrinsically dysfunctional, its nowhere-ness (the mapping of a nowhere place). Thus Spiro/Michele's *mad History* is continuous with a *mad Geography*, also echoed in the Albanians' own dysfunctional utopia. They ask constantly, is Sicily near Bari? Is Bari near Turin? The geography of utopia also goes into Diaspora, suddenly nothing is anywhere it should be.

Finally the titles of the film, in which the juxtaposition with the news-reel footage alludes to cinema's own historicity, is yet another interesting node of inscription: what we have here is, at once, old against new cinema, old against new capitalism, the unethical past, with its false representation displaced into a more valuable, more moral, more correct representation.

History is narrative, but it is also not the narrative. In a consolidated narrative (representation), history is always in diaspora. The past is dispersed, occluded, scattered, "sent out." In selecting its pieces and assimilating them to the trajectory of the story, narrative always enacts a silencing as well as the possibility of utterance. Something is always being silenced by something expressed. You can't say everything at once: that's the essence of narrative, indeed of language. Speech comes at the cost of turning somebody else's speech into a silence. Aware of his shooting of the film as "invasion," Amelio seems to say that representation, even as mechanism that operates on occlusion, must be undertaken.

The dilemma of representing something that ultimately remains beyond representability cannot be solved in a definitive way. We might say that today, in this age of self-reflexivity, we must look at every work and examine its ethics. The privileged can engage in political struggle; they can become subverters of the order that has (falsely) empowered them. Amelio attempted this mainly through the creation of an identification (the becoming-Albanian of character of Gino), and his ironic use of cinema-scope (a medium that, he said, was hardly innocent).[12]

At this point I would like to ask the original question in a more specific way: What do the Balkans or Eastern European countries seem to have come to symbolize for contemporary European filmmakers in relation to the issue of self and other?

In some quarters (mostly in the mass media) with renewed, revitalized lack of critical awareness, or with the kind of awareness that can never settle the matter of representation, we have a conflation: between the East and the South, in a dynamic of same and different. Anybody dealing in post-colonial discourse knows: we can't invent Africa any longer these days.[13]

But—without seeming to invent—we can still talk about Eastern Europe, perhaps with less need for remorse and doubt (after all it wasn't conquered through shameful genocidal wars! At Yalta, it was only a tactical settlement, presumably necessary for the good outcome of a just war). But at work here are the same mechanisms of occlusion as those of the colonial project: Eastern Europe is both Europe and Africa, and at the same time is neither. It is the East that now embodies difference, strangeness, a space of both (pure) origin and compromise, while at the same time it is neither absolute purity nor absolute compromise. Another topos of "unthinking Eurocentrism" is the notorious atavistic fratricidal violence that resists "civilization"—a danger at our door (so far, so other, yet so close, so like us); the phantasm of our past (that we would prefer forgotten, which we had considered already deciphered), that might besiege our present, with real or symbolic warfare. The Balkans are "the other of Europe" but also, as Slavoj Zizek writes in his project of uncovering the hidden dynamics of this process of othering, "Europe itself in its Otherness, the screen on to which Europe projected its own repressed reverse" (Zizek, 212).

In relation to art as well, the Balkans appear as a newly discovered, "unnarrated space." Thus, both in the West (from positions of power) and in the East (from positions of internalized colonization or self-marginalization), there has been a proliferation of texts, most of which reveal this inescapable dialectic. In Italy in particular this proliferation is strongest and the intensity of investment is of such proportion that it calls for an analysis of Italy's own function as site of the other of Europe, a site it has occupied for (at least) the last two centuries.[14]

As a relevant link to earlier historical forms of fascination with the other in Italy, a brief examination of Pier Paolo Pasolini's "erotic ethnography" might be undertaken here. Reality for Pasolini was mythical, belonging to a past—idealized, pre-historic, primordial—inscribed in the symbolic order of the sacred, yet made manifest in the jouissance of the life of violence in the slums of post-war Rome, the Italian South, the Third-world countries where he filmed ("Una visione del mondo epico-religiosa" 13–14). Consistent with his theory of reality as epic and religious and his vehement anti-naturalism (Stack 51–52), is Pasolini's highly self-aware concept and practice of "contaminazione stilistica" [stylistic contamination], a series of dissonant elements in his films, through which he sought to disrupt, to denaturalize narrative and perception itself.[15]

Pasolini's passionate interest in the other, in the so-called primitive cultures, functioned as a scornful blow to the ego of Italy's alienated middle class. I am referring mostly to his *Appunti per un'Orestiade africana* [*Notes for an African Orestes*], a 1970 montage of travel diary, footage material from different African liberation wars from the 1960s, conversations with African students in Rome, and a bizarre jazz version of the myth of Orestes. In what I would call his "pastiche of primitivism," Pasolini honors the people he uses. The use he makes of African people relates mostly to laying claim to their bodies as image, and sometimes to their customs, which are to be transposed in his reapplication of the Greek myth of the origins of democracy, and also, especially, to their suffering in fratricidal wars. But Pasolini's ultimate objective is to shock the Europeans, by suggesting to them that this (Africa) is their birthplace, that there's continuity between them, that somehow the Africans are their ancestors. He's trying to make something manifest by evoking a time of ancestral exaggeration, violence and opulent misery—the very roots of psyche and culture. But Pasolini understood in some measure that the only way to represent the integrity of a "pure primitive" is through the construction of a pure, utter pastiche.

Pasolini is also useful for my purpose since he recorded his film diaries, in a way that Amelio also does. In another diary, of the film *Medea* which he shot in Turkey, Pasolini acknowledges that he was "invading" with his entourage a particular site of "pure" origins, but he seems unaware that he found what he had set out to find, such as an ancient dignity in the poverty-stricken Turkish peasants ("Travestiti da poveri" 574). Just as, when in *Appunti* he comments on the vivacity and laughter of the African girls, he betrays no suspicion that the natives' eternal essence was in fact simply reaction to the camera. (Not to mention that in the case of Turkey he preferred to lay the blame for the disruption at the feet of Maria Callas, his Medea, a diva and a Greek as well!). Amelio, writing in a different socio-cultural context, is much more articulate: he knows that there's violence in the gaze itself. "We were, with our troupe, our technical means, like the bad guys that came to Albania after the collapse of communism" (Sesti 57).[16] He also writes: "no matter how I might have tried I could not become Albanian. I couldn't have become invisible." But then he adds, "nor could I ever have their purity of gaze"!

It is in fact a nostalgia for *purity* that underlies both Pasolini's and Amelio's endeavors: Pasolini sought what he thought the other, the African, the Turk or also the Arab, still had, and what he felt that he himself (and his bourgeois society) had lost, the purity of nature, of vitality. For Amelio it is the purity of hunger. Both exist in the domain of classic ethnography, of a modernist illusion of origins.

Another way of looking at the dilemma of representation in post-colonial times is through a deconstruction of the idea of honorability. We cannot tell what is honorable today (or for that matter whether absolute hedonism and asceticism are so far apart, whether they are not assimilated into one construct, a sort of "ecstasy of abnegation"). Honor belongs to the *polis*, a closed space, where good taste dwells. Once you open up the world, when good taste seems to be "in exile" and when hunger and the desire to consume things are not different from one another, all honor can mean is trying to understand pain. The construction of any kind of morality at present, I believe, can only be done through attention to pain, an enterprise that can have its triumphs but also its failures. How much access is given to pain, and how our political thought might change through such knowledge is really the only meaning of honor today. The self-reflexive mode, whose results are somewhat problematic in Pasolini and Amelio, comes to fruition in two other Western European films about the East: Chantal Akerman's 1993 *D'Est* and Jean-Luc Godard's 1996 *For Ever Mozart*.[17] Brief discussion of these films will analyze their cognitive positions.

Akerman's feature-length documentary was filmed in the East (Poland, Germany, Russia) after the fall of Communism. Already the film itself, with its composition of fixed frames, very long pan-shots, its procession of images, its live sound-track that contains almost no conversation, is constructed for the maximum of space for reflection. Subsequently, throughout the 1990s, the film was then was incorporated into a museum "installation," staged at different galleries and museums in the States and in France, Belgium, Spain and Germany. It is through the particular concept of the exhibit that Akerman succeeds in integrating all the awareness I was talking about, of the other, of the representation of the other, of the medium itself. The show, a critic writes, was a "deconstructive tour of the production process, working back from the completed feature film to the individual shot segments and . . . in the end, back to language itself" (Halbreich). The installation began with a room in which the film was continuously played, followed by a gallery with video monitors playing simultaneously sequences from the film, and ending in a final room with a single monitor on which images enlarged to the point of becoming quasi-abstract were played, accompanied by the sound of a cello piece and Akerman's reading of the biblical injunction against images. In her notes Akerman wrote: "While there's still time, I would like to make a grand journey across Eastern Europe . . . I'd like to film there, in my own style of documentary bordering on fiction . . . everything, everything that moves me . . . faces, streets, cars, train stations and plains . . . fields and factories and yet more faces . . . all these countries in the throes of great change" (Halbreich and Jenkins, 17–18). But Akerman, unlike Pasolini or Amelio, comes almost immediately to question her own investment: "I was saying: while there's still time. Time for what? Time before the Western 'invasion' becomes too blatant? as if there had been a before and after . . ., the time of a realized utopia and the time of a fallen utopia, or the time of yet another utopia? . . . of course, there's no pure 'before' that would now be perverted or contaminated" (22–23). Akerman understands that "she who seeks shall find, find all too well, and manipulate things a little too much in order to find them" (23). Thus Chantal Akerman does not deny her work, but places it in a decentered position, challenging all sorts of perceptual expectations. Against the pull of images that draw the spectator into stories, the film is deconstructed into its constitutive elements. Moreover the title of the installation became: *D'Est: Au bord de la fiction* [About/From the East: Bordering on Fiction], which both acknowledges representation and the struggle against it. Of course the precedents to *D'Est* must be sought in Duras/Resnais' *Hiroshima mon amour* (1959), and Lanzmann's *Shoah* (1985), both of which problematize the visual representability of historical cataclysms.

In like manner, Godard's fiction film *For Ever Mozart* tracks its own complex, excessive discourses, seeking to lay open its production, in this case through an operation of abstraction.[18] It follows, among other narratives, the doomed voyage of a small theater troupe traveling from France to Sarajevo during the siege in order to put on a play by de Musset ("One Must not Play at Love"). A critique of both the attempts at representing the horrors of history, and the Western humanitarian projects of "bringing culture" to war-torn lands, *For Ever Mozart* refuses to exploit the pain of real people. The "Bosnians" virtually do not exist; the "Serbians," who will kill the French actors, are a fantasmatic bunch of armed peasants, mobsters and drug-dealers, noir-like terrorist females. In fact, Godard went so far as to decline to film in Yugoslavia, his "Bosnia" was the barren landscape of his grandfather derelict estate (Rosenbaum 53), and his "Sarajevo" in only a graffito on a wall: "Sarajevo = Whore"—for sale to the West, where money can buy symbols for ineffectual intellectuals. Towards the start of the film, the fictional middle-aged daughter of Camus, explaining that it was under the politico-literary incitement of a Philippe Sollers article that the troupe takes up the scheme, exclaims: "As if that's what France needs!" France, not Sarajevo. It is France that must give up (the pretense of) war. What Godard defies is not the atrocities of the war against Bosnia, nor even the usefulness of Western solidarity, but the very use of Western privilege to "play" in Sarajevo. Capitalism, elitism, the compromise of leftist intellectuals with State apparatuses, power to create, are all brought together in the multiple threads of this film. *For Ever Mozart*, with its hyperbolic stagedness, constructedness, its freeze-frames, and its citational excess of overlapping texts, through its very pretentiousness, does not permit he audience to accept the story through emotional impact, thus giving it the possibility of reflection. Here, the disjunction between Life and Representation remains intact, the pretentiousness and hysteria of representation is

Godard's For Ever Mozart. *Vicky Messica as Vicky Vitalis, the director of* Fatal Bolero, *the film-within-the-film, in a mise-en-scène of double screens. Courtesy of Photofest, New York.*

made intrinsic to representation. By contrast, Amelio's film is one that while it requires deciphering (it is a text *a clef*), it does not block its spectator from entering into the story.

With all its problems, I believe that Pasolini's "stylistic contamination," his hatred for naturalism which was operative even in his "slum-films" and which issued later in utterly extravagant pastiche that in a way doesn't touch the other, is a more successful self-deconstruction than his more writerly acknowledgments, and as successful as Akerman's or Godard's deconstructions of their artifact. Compared to these, Amelio's cinemascope remains a more simple, less competent gesture. Amelio seems to think that by symbolizing the compromised nature of cinema, he distances himself from something that is truly compromised.

In closing, I need to return to the idea of the other's desire raised by the injunction against representation with which this study began. Very simply, the desire for the other is in fact desire for the other's desire. In obscurantist, colonial, patriarchal modes, the other is perceived as site for retrieval of a lost self. In recent feminism, as in postcolonial texts, however, we have a shift: the other is the site of an epistemic privilege (Narayan 258, 262–65),[19] the source of knowledge, not of ourselves, not of some sort of ultimate Reality, but simply of itself in its historicity. This is the other as subject, agent of its own desire. But this too is extremely attractive, and, if acted on unthinkingly, it too may taint, even such works as Akerman's and Lanzmann's: the other has access to the unthinkable itself. It is possible that the same old desire for the other—as overpowering fascination—work its way into an erasure of the specific contents of the other's desire (which in most cases is simply to survive or be free): they (the survivors of the Nazi death camps, of Hiroshima, of the Iron Curtain) have got something we don't have: they have the Thing, they have "it"—and there's nothing more "it" than the inscrutable (to us) historical cataclysms to which they were the subjected. They have had a glimpse into the abyss of meaning. They possess the real "post-something"-state, as opposed to our lost postness, and they may reflect it back to us. In fact they *know* what the end of the world looks like.

As a provisional conclusion—in favor of representation—I would invoke an insight from Deleuze and Guattari on creativity. Although not interested in actual pain, they understood its creative possibility (144–45).[20] Creating memory out of pain is the possibility of culture, or, in other words, creativity has its own contingent, historical circumstances, but it has to be able to happen despite the guilt that's laid on it.

7. Voices Unveiled

Mémoires d'immigrés. L'héritage maghrébin

—*Mark Ingram and Florence Martin*

Although issues involving immigration receive considerable attention in the French media, seldom are the "immigrants" themselves heard. The documentary film *Mémoires d'immigrés* breaks this silence by giving a voice to Maghrebi immigrants and their children. In French public discourse on immigration, the category *les immigrés* often includes many who have not in fact immigrated: the second generation, born and raised in France. In its tripartite organization ("Fathers", "Mothers," and "Children"), Yamina Benguigui's film highlights the distinctions between generations, while also tracing the continuity of a Maghrebi legacy in France from the end of the Algerian War to today.

In its emphasis on personal narratives, Benguigui's film provides a new perspective on immigration issues in France. Through interviews with representatives of the French state and with immigrants, the film reveals the personal impact of state policies on the daily lives of their intended subjects. One can also read this collection of vignettes as a feminist memoir composed in "*Beur écriture*," telling the tale of Yamina Benguigui, immigrants' daughter. The resulting transcultural and polyphonic film unsettles the stereotypes about Maghrebi immigration in French public culture.[1]

Mémoires d'immigrés as "transcultural cinema"

Like Yamina Benguigui, many cultural anthropologists have aimed to capture the experience of individuals as they move across the boundaries of conventional national, ethnic, and other categories of identity. Ethnographic filmmaker David MacDougall has focused on the unique qualities documentary films possess for representing cultural differences and similarities. MacDougall holds that films have a number of advantages over the written text in this regard. Chief among them is the ability of images to challenge a simplistic understanding of cultural difference.

> Ethnographic films have been widely understood as transcultural, in the familiar sense of crossing cultural boundaries . . . but they are also transcultural in another sense: that of defying such boundaries. They remind us that cultural difference is at best a fragile concept, often undone by perceptions that create sudden affinities between ourselves and others apparently so different from us. (245)

MacDougall's aim is not simply to argue for a more humanistic approach in documentary filmmaking: "the transculturality of cinema should not finally be taken as a new key to human universals, but rather as a *provocation* (279)." The transcultural qualities of film call for new attention to individuals as they negotiate across cultural boundaries. They emphasize an understanding of culture in which people confront cultural precepts, rather than submit to their dictates. This focus on negotiation also reflects a heightened self-consciousness about issues of identity in a world increasingly marked by flows of people, capital, and commodities across national and other borders.

In order to avoid the excesses of an overly "culturalist" approach, many anthropologists have chosen to place individual narratives, rather than "cultures", at the center of analysis. These narrative forms, MacDougall notes, "make possible a view of social actors responding creatively to a set of open-ended cultural possibilities, rather than being bound by a rigid framework of cultural restraints" (271).

Mémoires d'immigrés is composed of a series of individual narratives and inasmuch as it shares the goals of crossing and challenging cultural boundaries, may be considered as an example of "transcultural cinema." But its presentation of multiple narratives also raises a number of questions. Is this collection of stories to be read as a statement regarding "Maghrebi" identity? Benguigui's title is ambivalent in this regard. The singular Maghrebi heritage is located in the past, and the memories of immigrants are plural. To what extent do these interview subjects from various North African nations share a collective sense of belonging? If such a sense exists, will it continue in the future? In short, what can the narratives of these interview subjects tell us regarding cultural identity among those of North African descent in France today? Answering these questions requires attention to Benguigui's own narrative choices and aesthetics, and to what goes unsaid, as well as what is said, in the presentation of her subjects' stories.

Mémoires d'immigrés and French Discourse on Memory and Immigration

As the many positive reviews of the film in the French press note, Benguigui's discussion of immigrant memory is particularly important in France, where there has not traditionally existed the same kind of venues for the expression of immigrant identity, as, for example, in the United States. As Gérard Noiriel has noted, the concept of republican rights which eliminated any consideration of the citizen's ethnic or religious origin has made it impossible for 'foreigners' to have a place in the collective memory of the French nation:

While many American textbooks celebrate the contributions to the American republic of the various communities that settled in the United States over the years, in France immigration is always approached as a question extrinsic to the country's history. It is seen as a temporary phenomenon, something fleeting and marginal. Similarly, while Ellis Island, through which millions of European immigrants passed in order to enter the United States, has become a museum, comparable sites in France, such as the Toul selection center, which processed most Central European immigrants in the interwar period, have been torn down, as if something dictated that a history so starkly at odds with the myth of the soil, had to be magically erased. (151–52)

In depicting the transitional status of individuals caught between two worlds, Yamina Benguigui's film transcends the extremes characteristic of much debate on immigration in France. The film makes evident how much is left out of the simplistic dichotomy composed of a homogeneous Maghrebi or Beur identity on one side, and the assimiliationist Jacobin state on the other. Because there has been no place in French public culture for discussion of issues of immigrant memory, Benguigui's film marks an important development. As the *Libération* journalist Nidam Abdi noted in a 1998 review of the film,

> *Mémoires d'immigrés* is one of these productions which arrive at a propitious and awaited moment. . . . In the French audiovisual environment, we are told that there is an absence to be filled, a pressing need for images and knowledge about immigration. We could not continue to be in this imbalance between a constant presence of this question in the news and an absence of accounts from the fathers and mothers and these 'children' who, by virtue of the urban crises of this country, return to center stage regularly.

By providing access to voices previously unheard, Benguigui opens up a new area of discussion within French public culture. In spite of its depiction of immigrants and their descendants in an uneasy relationship with French society, the film is clearly situated within a national discourse on issues of memory and identity, and provides a new voice within that discourse.

Mémoires d'immigrés: State policy and Personal Narratives

The film's three sections (Fathers, Mothers, Children) are each fifty-two minutes long. Benguigui's tripartite division allows her to situate her subjects with respect to the history of state policy toward immigration. In interviews with "the fathers," she recounts the recruitment of men from

North Africa in the years between the Algerian War and the early 1970s. The accounts of "the mothers" are situated with respect to the change in state policies in the 1970s, which led to the unification of families in France. The third part focuses on the lives of "the children" in the 1980s and 1990s, and on the lives of the first generation as seen through their children.

The great advantage of this organization is that it allows Benguigui to trace the historical development of attitudes and feelings among these immigrants and their children. Through the course of the interviews, one can see all the pieces of a chain stretching from the state's policy toward immigrants in the 1960s to the perspectives of young Beurs today. Benguigui has included interviews with state officials who either crafted policies or put them into practice. Much of the film involves the juxtaposition of individual narratives with accounts from state officials and others responsible for shaping public policy toward immigrants. A central dynamic in the film is the contrast between the impersonal directives of the French state and the impact these policies had on the personal lives of their intended subjects.

The film begins with a focus on the difference between the first generation of immigrants from the Algerian War era and their children. The opening lines are from one of the "fathers" saying "Our children are here today. They should know why we are here, why we came, and how we came." Another adds that his children are not able to understand him because when they came into the world all was given to them: "They did not suffer." Much of this first section of the film is devoted to explaining the painful experiences of these men and the reasons why they felt so unwelcome and looked down upon in France.

For example, the section entitled "the Fathers" includes footage filmed in a classroom for Maghrebi workers in the greater Paris region in 1966. We see adult men sitting in what appears to be a high school classroom and repeating French vowels for a teacher in a white jacket. The men are interviewed by a man who remains invisible. While the disembodied voice sharply poses a number of questions to the men, the camera looks down on them as they respond. Some of the men answer quickly and look away, while one smiles and answers informally.

The following is a question and answer dialogue.

Sir, what do you learn here?	I learn to read and write.
Why do you come to study here?	Why?
	To speak with French people. To not waste time, to read the newspaper. To speak with my boss, at the factory. To speak French well.
Do you have the intention of returning to your home later?	Yes. To see my parents from time to time.
For vacations.	Yes.
But do you want to go back to Algeria later, definitively?	I haven't yet organized things. I am from Morocco.
Oh, you are from Morocco?	Yes, but it's the same.
Yes. It is the same.	One never knows. For the moment, I am here.

The film makes clear that the state was a central intermediary between immigrants and French society, and that the primary goal of the state was to fit these workers into the French workforce easily and productively. Often recruited from the most rural areas of North Africa, these men were intended to be malleable and adapt to the needs of French society. They lived in crowded conditions with other men and were expected to do what they were told.

That these workers were considered primarily as "labor" rather than as men is well expressed in the interview which concludes the "Fathers" section of the film. Philippe Moreau Des Farges is identified as the *Conseiller Technique du secrétaire d'état chargé des travailleurs immigrés de 1975 à 1977.* Describing the state's attitude toward North African workers during his tenure, he states that the notion of doing something "human" for them was discussed, but

Fundamentally, these men were perceived not completely as men. . . . for them we did not ask ourselves a lot of questions—they just had to deal with it—it's their problem, it's not our problem.

Yamina, one of the interviewed "mothers", concurs: "When the men were brought, it was forgotten that they were men. It was forgotten that they had wives. That they had children."

This consideration of men as units of labor is also evident in the language of other state representatives interviewed in the film. Joel Danoui recounts his experience as a state recruiter of labor in Morocco between 1963 and 1995. In praise of the high percentage of workers who were able to adapt and do well in France, he states (while apologizing for the term) that there was very little in the way of *"déchets"* (waste).

Benguigui suggests some of the harmful implications of this impersonal attitude by showing interview footage with a worker in the 1960s who has contracted severe lung problems from working in a bleach factory. In the film clip, the man is asked, "Did you learn a trade?" and the interviewer uses the familiar "tu" form to address him. "Yes", he replies. "But this trade made me sick."

Benguigui also shows the longterm impact on the personal and family lives of these men. Some of those she interviews still live alone. Today, a footnote in the film explains, of the 130,000 beds provided by the state for older men living alone, 60% are occupied by men of North African descent.

In addition, her presentation of the problems faced by the Maghrebi men in the 1960s and 1970s helps to explain the differences between this generation and the children interviewed in the third section of the film. Many of these young men and women express their frustration with their parents for their meekness with regard to state authorities. One man recounts that his own period of revolt and juvenile delinquency was a reaction to the exaggerated fear of drawing attention to oneself that he saw in his parents. Benguigui also shows the changes provoked by a younger generation. One young man tells of confronting his father's employer for routinely using the *"tu"* form of address with his father, noting that it led to a conflict between the two. Benguigui's film is valuable in providing an understanding of both the larger picture of state policies toward immigrants, and the acts of individuals as they negotiate the implications of a "Maghrebi heritage" in their daily lives.

By showing such details in personal narratives and linking them to the history of policies toward North African workers in France, Benguigui provides for a deeper understanding of the changing status of Maghrebi immigrants and their descendants in France. Ultimately, the contrast Benguigui emphasizes between the impersonal directives of the French state and the personal lives of these subjects is resolved to some extent in one of the final interviews with Soraya Guezlane who, as a lawyer, has become an agent of the French state. The contrast between this urbane young woman shown walking down the steps of the courthouse in her lawyer's robes and the men presented at the very beginning of the film could not be more complete. But even here, in what might be considered a model case of integration, Benguigui's interview draws out the singularity of Maghrebi experience in France. Soraya Guezlane says that she wishes she could stop being in a constant state of "*démonstration*", of having to prove that she is not illiterate, a failure, or a problem to society. She wishes that she could have lived for herself rather than in counterpoint to the negative images of "immigrants" found in the media. Even with the case of Soraya Guezlane, Benguigui shows the legacy of state immigration policies in the daily lives of those of North African descent in France today.

Mémoires d'immigrés as a Polyphonic Autobiographical Documentary

Although the voice of the film-maker is not heard, her presence is very much felt throughout the documentary.[2] Her status wavers between outsider and autobiography film-maker, and she succeeds in achieving an intimate look at strangers by not recording her own questions to her interviewed subjects. However, the fact that Benguigui is in a dialogic relationship with her interviewees is made very clear. For instance, in a scene taken from the first part ("Fathers"), Hamou tells her that she and her contemporaries find it difficult to believe in the actual hardships undergone by the fathers' generation because they have a much easier life (they live like "kings' children"). "You, the young ones, you do not know this, you do not believe this. You are young. You were just born yesterday." The openness of the dialogue is further illustrated by a frontal, medium shot of him. At the end of this scene, he asks Benguigui (who is located at the viewer's place so that it sounds like an invitation to us too): "*Bon . . . on boit un café?*" (OK. Shall we have a cup of coffee?). Although he is perfectly understandable (in spite of his heavy accent), everything he says is subtitled in French, except for his invitation for coffee in the end, as if this were offscreen, a little piece of intimacy left there unintentionally.

The systematic erasure of Benguigui's voice from the sound-track is a device to authenticate the documentary:

> I think that, this way, the person is with you: there is no one in the middle, no intermediary! Similarly, there is no commentary. When Canal + heard that the film was going to be three hours long with no commentary, they started to scream! I explained to them that I had a gaze of a cinematographer rather than of a reporter. (Barlet 38)

Benguigui's collective narrative of an uprooted people helps her sort out her relationship to her own roots. In an interview in *La Tribune*, Benguigui claimed that it was "a kind of group therapy for parents and children, as well as for French society" (Tinazzi). However, the film can also be seen, beyond a group therapy, as an attempt at "re-membering" in Toni Morrison's sense of the term, i.e. stitching together various individual memories to reconstitute a past identity which has been erased, denied, or misunderstood. In this sense, the collective memory essay becomes an attempt at defining one's own memory, past and identity—in this case Yamina Benguigui's—and runs contrary to the unwritten rules of silence of the immigrant group (the parents). Benguigui remembers her own silence while growing up: "They found me rather pale, but I would say nothing. It was this way: The more you shut your mouth, the less you might catch flies in it, as writer Azouz Begag says in the movie, quoting his father" (Mingalon). Disrupting silence is risky: opening one's mouth makes it vulnerable (unwanted elements from the outside world might invade it) and leaves it exposed to danger in the (ironically) termed "welcoming country" (*pays d'accueil*). In the eponymous book that accompanies the documentary, Yamina Benguigui spells out her project in a first person preamble: "This book is the narrative of my journey at the heart of the Maghrebi immigration in France. The history of fathers, mothers, children, the history of my father, of my mother. My history" (*Memoires* 11). The book is her rendition of the Maghrebi interviewees' testimonies, and, this time, her narrative voice appears clearly in her comments, and recorded impressions as she describes her subjects and their surroundings. In a startling passage, an interview even brings back a memory of hers. She interrupts her transcription of the interview to retell her own memory. "Naima's serene voice bring me back to my own childhood. I can see myself in this little northern town where my parents had immigrated." The memory is then reconstructed but not analyzed. Rather, Benguigui lets the reader draw her or his own conclusions.

Mémoires d'immigrés as a Project in *fémi-humanisme*

This is not the first woman's project of doubly breaking the silence (in a film and a book) which has shrouded her reality, stories, identity, or those of her people. For instance, the controversial documentary *Warrior Marks* (1993) by author Alice Walker and film-maker Pratibha Parmer, focused on the painful and taboo topic of women's genital mutilation, and was followed by their 1996 book on that subject.[3] In this film and book dyad, Walker and Parmer interview women throughout the world who were implicated in the process of genital mutilation. The film is hard to watch. The camera films little girls (the youngest is four) on their way back from two weeks of initiation, freezes on their gaze and records their silence. The latter is twofold: the silence of fear and physical excruciating pain, perhaps even incomprehension, and also the silence of the initiation secret—they are to tell no one what has just happened to them. Breaking that silence would be sacrilegious. Hence Alice Walker and Pratibha Parmer, as foreigners, take on the blame for the sacred offense.

Yamina Benguigui's breach of silence takes on a different value from Parmer and Walker's womanist one. Benguigui is not an outsider but a member of the Maghrebi group and broke its patriarchal rules personally by escaping from a traditional, arranged marriage, knowing she would never see her father again as a result. Her first documentaries are meant to share and continue to enlarge her private initial breach in silence and to understand, not to denounce. And as with Parmer and Walker, her first film *Femmes d'Islam*, was elaborated by a companion book.

Book and film form two complementary sides of a text which shed light on each other in a dialogic relationship, although they can be read or seen independently from each other. They let previously mute people tell their tales both orally and on the written page. In Benguigui's case, the question of audience is crucial: she wants everyone from Maghrebi descent and from French descent to witness and learn. She has therefore opted not for Arabic—the parents' mother-tongue, but not always spoken by their children (Benguigui herself does not speak it)—but for French, to be understood by all generations, and by all members of French society (whether "rooted"—*de souche*—or not). It is a movie, and as such can be seen by an illiterate audience. It is a book, and can also cater to members of a written, Western culture.

Benguigui's political feminist concerns seem to be those of Évelyne Accad's *fémi-humanisme*, a brand of humanist feminism which is adamantly non separatist, and takes upon itself the defense of all victims (women, children, men) of oppression, whether local or global (Accad 25–26). Hence, her initial recording of individual memories intended to cover her own history becomes a political gesture which exceeds her own individual narrative or even her group's. Her resulting narrative not only addresses the Maghrebi-French community and the larger French society, but also becomes relevant to a more universal discourse on exile and displaced populations. And yet, she conveys her message by using *Beur* aesthetics and rules of discourse.

Mémoires d'immigrés as an Essay in "*Beur écriture*"

Here we are using *Beur* as an opportune shorthand to mean: relating to the immigrants' children generation (and not necessarily the political, ambiguous term it has become). As oversimplifying and reductive as such a term may be which attempts to define a whole generation almost by default, we are keeping it, with the ironical distance of Azouz Begag's definition in mind.[4]

Crucial to this aesthetics and mode of discourse is the unsaid, what is concealed between the words, which Benguigui translates for the viewer/reader through her bicultural lens. Her role as an interpreter in the film appears in several instances. First, she provides French subtitles to late Dahmane Elharrachi's Arabic songs, as they frame the film. The first song provides a running commentary to the black and white images of the

1950s' and 1960s' footage on immigrants arriving in France (the Fathers settling in their makeshift lodgings):

> *Memories awaken in me, after I forgot everything;*
> *I left everything, my village, my friends;*
> *I ended up all alone, facing myself.*

Here, the focus is apparently on the past tearing away from home, and only refers to the present situation through a mention of intense solitude. The silence around the present is thunderous. Similarly, when the film shows women arriving, and simultaneously evokes the myth of the return to the motherland, the same singer's husky voice is heard lamenting in another subtitled song: "It is high time to leave, suitcase in hand,/If we live longer, we will come back to you." As the wives finally join their husbands, the song also announces the years of transit to come, the hope of a return slowly fading away, yet the suitcases never out of sight. This mode of representation which skirts the issue, is highly effective: the narrator uses detours and contours instead of addressing the thing itself. Elharrachi's deep, husky voice is a perfect choice to accompany these images. The singer migrated to France in 1949, and became extremely popular in the Maghrebi community in France and North Africa. After singing songs in the Shaâbi urban tradition (an originally religious folk-song tradition turned secular this century), he started to compose his own songs on homesickness and the daily problems of immigrants, thus turning into a Maghrebi immigrants' bluesman of sorts.

Speaking out is not the rule in the parents' generation. In fact, the whole documentary constitutes a major infraction of their unwritten law. Their children—the *Beur* generation—want to voice their needs and concerns, and negotiate a space for discourse between the loudness of the society they inhabit and the silence of the parents. Benguigui's first gesture is to "unsilence" the parents, give them their voices back, push them to express their past and their feelings, unfettered by modesty. Khémaïs cries as he remembers the cold welcome he received upon his arrival in Marseille: "The warmth of Maghreb, of the people there, I did not find it here." Yamina also cries as she tells how she "learned to keep quiet" on her wedding night.

At age 40, after she had raised her children, she finally broke out of the silence and entrapment of her marriage. She discovered herself as she discovered freedom. "I was finally free. I was finally myself," she declares, her eyes immense with joy and wonder.

There are several reasons for the silence. As Wahib, remembers, quoting his father: "Here, you must keep your eyes down, you must shut up, you are not at home, you see." Not attracting attention, blending into the bleak landscape of the 1950s' and 1960s' French slums, then the 1970s' and 1980s' projects and at the assembly lines, walking on egg shells in order to avoid being fired, sent back, deprived of a precious job, seemed to be the main reasons for not talking. Another one was language. Some of the workers had to take night classes in order to read and write French (although others, like Khémaïs, quote Victor Hugo and Pierre Loti as their inspiration to come to France). The mothers, who had been waiting for years in the *bled*, the village in North Africa, usually did not speak French and were illiterate. Their children—especially their daughters—became the interpreters of cultural codes, the deciphering messengers between the French culture and the Maghrebi one. Myriem remembers translating the words of a social worker for her mother; Warda volunteers to help Maghrebi parents fill in their social security papers in the projects. In her book, Yamina Benguigui herself, remembers an instance where she was the go-between between her mother and a French "rooted" neighbor:

> At the time of the Aïd celebration, in one of her famous generous moments, my mother asked me take to the neighbors a plate of cakes, to be given away in memory of a dead relative, according to the custom. "Go to the neighbor's, and do tell her that the these cakes are from Uncle Moussah.—Yes, Mother" I replied, an obedient thirteen-year-old. I can still see myself, ringing the bell, petrified, holding the plate as straight as possible, afraid I would drop the cakes. I can still hear the uninviting, sour voice: "Who is this?—It's me, Yamina, your neighbor's daughter. My mother told me to bring you cakes on behalf of Uncle Moussah!—You tell your mother I do not know that uncle of yours!" the neighbor's cold voice had answered.

According to Mireille Rosello's pointed analysis of this passage, the messenger, although bi-cultural and bilingual, fails doubly: her mother's cakes in memory of Uncle Moussah will not be delivered; and her neighbor will remain uneducated about the Muslim custom. As a result, the messenger is doubly isolated, while this whole episode could serve as "a warning against the temptation to transmit legacies completely unchanged" (Rosello). True, literal obedience to the mother (which here means repeating her words faithfully) does not strike us as an efficient strategy to communicate with the outsider. Hence, we would venture, at some point, the children need to disobey, change, translate *and* betray the parents' generation (*traduttore, tradittore*). Speaking out will therefore mean negotiating a third space in-between the parents' discourse at home, and French discourse behind closed doors.

The anxious pursuit of this third space has been at the crux of several books and films, and perhaps best expressed in the novel *Georgette!* by Farida Belghoul (who is also a film-maker).[5] In this fictitious narrative, the eponymous protagonist, haunted by two voices—her father's beautiful declamatory voice in Arabic and her school teacher's voice in French, writes in one note-book. One side is occupied by the French "homework" (from left to right) and the other by the Koranic verses in Arabic (from right to left). In the middle of the note-book, blank pages reflect the silence and failure to translate from one into the other. The protagonist remains muted, caught between both cultures, both genders (the school teacher is a woman), both languages. The disharmony and tension between both worlds are not resolved in the novel and end up precipitating a tragic dénouement. In *Mémoires d'immigrés*, on the other hand, the film-maker succeeds in filling the white pages and effectively translates the realities and aesthetics of transit. "Time went by. My father did not ask for the return subsidy, but my mother kept on steadily piling up the boxes. My brothers and sisters grew up, their hands on the suitcase handles. So did I." Not only were the Maghrebi immigrants lodged in *cités de transit* (temporary projects), their whole lives were suspended by the vague notion of a return to the motherland, which was reinforced by French authorities and by the initial attachment to the place of origin. It is further illustrated in the film by the notion of the fathers initially not belonging, afraid to be seen or heard, for fear of being disposed of, against a slow traveling shot in black-and-white of a French graffiti which spells: *La France aux Français* (France to the French). The graffiti is painted on a wall which, we are led to believe, is on the immigrants' way to work so that they have to pass it at least twice a day. This slow-moving shot introduces and closes the film, thus framing it. Its reappearance at the end, however, might bear different meanings. The *Beur* generation is French. In light of that reality, the xenophobic slogan seems outdated at best, and further denounces the absurdity of the statement. Furthermore, the first time the graffiti is shown, at the beginning of the movie, we hear Elharrachi's song and read its French subtitles. The second time, there is no subtitle. We, the Francophone viewers, are now in a position to understand and remember.

This shot also comes as a counterpoint to Warda's comment on the symbolic importance of wanting to be buried in France. This new phenomenon signals a desire to become part of French earth, part of France (even if the latter only has one Muslim cemetery and fifty *carrés musulmans*, i.e. Muslim sections of larger—probably catholic—cemeteries). The choice of a place of burial is a constant theme throughout the film, but perhaps more so in the women's interviews. Some subjects want to have their bodies shipped back to North Africa; others are starting to want to be buried in the *terre d'accueil*. "I already have my place in Saint-Pierre," Adjia declares, wishing to be buried next to her dead son in France.

Perhaps electing France as one's place of residence in death does signal the end of transit, of holding on to suitcases. However, such a choice or decisive move towards one culture over the other remains individual, and cannot be subsumed under the *Beur* label, so ill-fitting in its generalizing stance. Right now, the decision about one's final resting place (as opposed to one's work place) still points to the diversity of individuals, to the plural nature of the title of the film (*mémoires d'immigrés*) rather than to the unifying singular mode of its subtitle (*l'héritage maghrébin*). Perhaps the key to the third space in which a freer *Beur* discourse can resonate lies in the multiplicity of voices and possibilities of choice.

The immigrants' children seem to have carved such a space for themselves between both cultures. Speaking of Algeria, one girl says "I have the mentality but I couldn't live there." In this phrase, she expresses both a sense of difference with respect to French people, and a sense that she is much more at home in France than she would be in the home of her "mentality." She expresses the same paradox later: "I don't even feel like the daughter of an immigrant. At the same time, I don't consider myself the same as Magalie, as Aurore, as Stéphanie."

Ultimately, it is in showing this sense of holding both identities together, of using each one to look at the other, that the film provides a "transcultural" cinematic narrative. Benguigui's film shows cultural identity among Maghrebi immigrants in France today as composite to such a degree that it cannot be reduced to a mere choice between complete assimilation within the larger French society and the assertion of a distinct Maghrebi identity. Yamina Benguigui's polyphonic documentary shows the artificialness of the public distinction between Maghrebi "immigrants" and others in France. Her film introduces new images to French public culture with its moving representations of individuals claiming their own complex identities in their own voices.

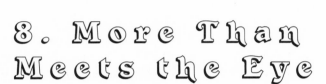

8. More Than Meets the Eye

Meandering Metaphor in Claire Denis's *Chocolat*

—*Carolyn Durham*

Perhaps travel inevitably involves some element of risk. Clearly it is always possible to lose your way in unfamiliar surroundings; and even if you make a return trip to someplace you have already been, nothing guarantees that it will look the same—the familiar, too, can be elusive. Regardless of the circumstances, moreover, your visit need not necessarily turn out to be welcome. Although I would not propose as a matter of course that the film spectator is in any meaningful way analogous to this hypothetical traveler, even if both experience a certain displacement in space and time, viewers of Claire Denis's *Chocolat* (1987) are in fact taken on a literal, as well as a metaphoric, journey. In what Thierry Jousse has characterized in *Cahiers du cinéma* as "a kind of African road movie" (132), the camera's meanders through Cameroon are explicitly filmed from the perspective of its audience.[1] Perhaps it is not surprising in that case that we should share in something like the vague disorientation of even the seasoned traveler to whom I refer above. Whether or not it is a quality they admire, reviewers consistently describe *Chocolat* in terms that stress the film's curious capacity to attract and escape us simultaneously; indeed, its appeal appears to lie in its very elusiveness. "One of the strengths of the film is precisely that it explains nothing," notes Jousse, for example, only to worry a bit later that Denis "seems to have lost track of her subject along the way" (132–33); for Desson Howe, *Chocolat* "seems to hold enigmatic truths"; Stanley Kauffmann finds the film able "to speak of what is not being said" (29); and Hal Hinson concludes that "in some peculiar, not entirely explicable way, the movie is a kind of mystery" (C9).

That *Chocolat* should provoke a sort of wonderment, not unlike that experienced by the first-time visitor to a foreign land, is no doubt consistent with the complexity and the ambiguity that characterize the film as a whole and underlie, in particular, its metaphoric structure. In *Unthinking Eurocentrism*, Ella Shohat and Robert Stam suggest that beliefs about nations "often crystallize in the form of stories," whose original expression in print media (see Anderson) has more recently taken shape on the screens of movie theaters: "The cinema, as the world's storyteller *par excellence*, was ideally suited to relay the projected narratives of nations and empires" (101). Such films, in which female protagonists often carry the primary symbolic weight of French identity, tend toward what Frederic Jameson identifies as "national allegories," in the sense of "texts which metaphorize the public sphere even when narrating apparently private stories" (Shohat and Stam 230; see also Kaplan 166).[2] In the case of a film whose female protagonist bears the very name of the nation that she represents, a connection gently mocked even as it is made ("What's your name? . . . France? Long live France!"), allegory and irony would seem to coexist. Shohat and Stam identify *Chocolat*, along with Brigitte Roüan's *Outremer* (1990) and Marie-France Pisier's *Bal du Gouverneur* (1990), as unusual examples of "critical" colonial nostalgia films (123). These contemporary women filmmakers appear to reenact within film history the same contradictory role that women originally played within colonialism (see Shohat and Stam 166, and McClintock 6), a duplication that is particularly appropriate in the case of Denis, whose autobiographical film not only draws upon her own life and that of her mother in colonialist Africa but also (re)figures this relationship within the text.

What is surprising, in that event, is that the name of the central character of *Chocolat*, once revealed, subsequently tends to disappear from
view. If critics and reviewers inevitably mention its presumed importance
in passing, they also invariably fail to see where further exploration might
lead them. To take a single, but highly significant, example, E. Ann
Kaplan, whose reading of *Chocolat* is both openly ideological and explicitly
symbolic, is nonetheless content with the following parenthetical—and,
arguably, tautological—comment: "her name is not only apt but surely
symbolic" (161). To the extent that Kaplan does discuss what the film has
to say about France as a nation, she focuses diagetically on characters other
than "France"; moreover, her primary interest, which lies in why the film
might have been produced in the late 1980s, is clearly extradiegetic in
nature. In addition, and perhaps more importantly, critics also tend to
ignore the larger function served by calling our attention early in the film
to the heroine's name: to alert us to the potential significance of names and
of the act of naming throughout *Chocolat*; to reveal a strategy of allusion
and metaphor that supports a reading of Denis's film as national allegory.
By pursuing this further, I will argue, we also come to appreciate more fully
the characteristically meandering structure of *Chocolat* that takes France
and the spectator on a similarly circuitous journey.

In general terms, Denis's first feature film tells the story of France
(Mireille Perrier), a young French woman who attempts to return as an
adult to the 1950s Cameroon she knew as a child (Cécile Ducasse).
Chocolat is framed by France's literal journey along the coast of Cameroon,
from the beach to the airport at Douala, which provokes an extended
flashback to her childhood in northern Cameroon, divided between
French and British rule, on the eve of independence. Denis illustrates the
daily routine that constitutes the life of Marc Dalens (François Cluzet),
military commander at Mindif, and his wife Aimée (Giulia Boschi) in
a place so isolated as to merit its designation as "the last house on earth."
Aimée gardens; Marc tours the colony; France rides her donkey; there are
occasional visits, made or received; most frequently of all, there are meals.
The dramatic interest of the film stems from Denis's particular focus on the
relationships between and among different characters, the most important
of which center on Protée (Isaach de Bankolé), the black servant who

The composition of interior shots in Chocolat *calls the importance of frames and of the act of framing to our attention. Protée (Isaach de Bankolé) serves Aimée (Giula Boschi) and France (Cécile Ducasse) under the watchful eye of Luc (Jean-Claude Adelin). Courtesy of Cinédoc, Paris.*

cares for France and to whom Aimée is sexually attracted. A plane crash midway through *Chocolat* temporarily expands the colonialist community and introduces overt racism into the daily lives of the family and its native servants. Prejudice comes in many forms: the weary cynicism of the pilot Védrine (Didier Flamand) and his navigator; the hypocrisy of the planter Delpich (Jacques Denis), a comic caricature of cruelty and stupidity, whose black mistress travels with him in the guise of his servant; the naiveté and fear of Machinard (Laurent Arnal), a young colonialist official, and his bride. Luc Segalen (Jean-Claude Adelin), the former seminarian who has set out to "walk across Africa," is a much more ambivalent figure, whose disturbing presence will upset the delicate balance of race and gender relations. After Protée throws Luc out of the house, Aimée dares to reach out and touch her "boy"; when Protée rejects her advance, Aimée engineers his exile from the house to the garage; the last time we see Protée, he knowingly allows France to burn her hand on a generator hot enough to scar her for life.

In keeping with the connotations of the word *meander*, which suggests a somewhat leisurely wandering over an irregular or winding course, I want to begin closer consideration of metaphor in *Chocolat* by doubling back on the story that encircles the film as a whole. Denis's determination to ignore advice that she cut the narrative of travel, which provides the framework for France's return to her childhood, already points to the fact, if not necessarily the nature, of its potential significance: "Everyone who read the screenplay for *Chocolat* told me to abandon the contemporary part, to keep only the autobiographical section about my childhood" (qtd. in Strauss 31).[3] Within the film, moreover, the importance of frames and the act of framing are constantly called to our attention. The camera periodically interrupts its characteristic tracking motion to hold on an image, whose careful composition provides an internal duplication of the visual strategy at its origin. Enclosed within the frame of the screen appear other representations of borders and boundaries. Frequently, for example, we view the Dalens's house from just beyond the verandah so that we look both *at* the doorway and *through* it to see its spatial configuration repeated, first by the walls of the room within and then again by the legs of the table that the room contains. Such self-reflective shots, which metaphorically remind us that the movie screen exists apart from the actual world of the spectator, help to destabilize the apparent realism of Denis's film. The formal function served by such images is further reinforced by the unconventional, and therefore unexpected, fact that they often show us empty, i.e., unoccupied, space. At the same time, of course, this framing of emptiness might also be seen in ideological terms as ironic, given that Cameroon's history is in reality one of long and multiple "occupation" by the principal colonialist nations of Europe (France, Britain, and Germany).

In the frame story of *Chocolat*, a man, whom we first see swimming with his young son in the opening sequence of the film, picks up France as she walks along the road ("I'm out for a walk") and insists that she accept a ride back to town ("This is Africa. It's too hot to stroll along like that"). Although he asks France her name almost immediately, he does not reveal his own until very near the end of the film; indeed, we, like France, are deliberately misled about whom he might be. In a film whose characters are generally more representative than realistic, the driver of the car is the only one whose name evokes a real person. Yet, despite the attention that has been paid, at least in passing, to certain names in *Chocolat*, only Luc Sante appears to have considered it significant that France's traveling companion in the contemporary portion of Denis's film finally introduces himself as one "William J. Park," now called "Mungo," in what is surely one of the more curious and intriguing examples of the wide-ranging influence of the original Mungo Park.[4] An eighteenth-century Scottish explorer (1771–1806), Park undertook expeditions along the Niger river in 1795 and 1806 as part of a plan for commercial expansion sponsored by the "Association for Promoting the Discovery of the Interior Parts of Africa" (see Pratt 69ff).

But if Park's reputation is such that the call for papers for the 1999 national convention of the Modern Language Association announced a special session on "Mungo Park's Travels, 1799–1999: A Bicentennial Review," this results not from Park's actual adventures as an explorer but from the written work that this experience subsequently inspired. One of the earliest examples of the best seller, the first edition of Park's *Travels in the Interior Districts of Africa* appeared in 1799 and sold out in a month. Since then, according to Mary Louise Pratt, "the book has been anthologized, excerpted, and re-edited constantly. . . . Its dramatic scenes and unassuming style became touchstones for European travel-writers for decades to follow" (74). More specifically, Pratt argues in *Imperial Eyes: Travel Writing and Transculturation*, which she introduces as both "a study in genre" and a critique of ideology (10), that Park's narrative of his journey to the interior of Africa established a model for "sentimental travel writing on the imperial frontier" (75). In keeping with Pratt's focus on the tropes or representational conventions of European travel writing in the interest of proposing ways of reading that may act as a stimulus for others thinking about similar materials (11), I want to suggest that Denis's reference to Mungo Park functions for the viewer as a kind of signpost that marks one point of entry into the film or opens up one path for its exploration. In this sense, the frame *story* of *Chocolat* appropriately provides a frame*work*, a *frame of reference*, in terms of which certain elements contained within the narrative of travel, which circumscribes the film as a whole, can be interpreted in particularly revealing ways.[5]

In the first place, the presence of Mungo Park acts as an important confirmation that *Chocolat* both permits and even encourages not simply an allegorical reading but one of a specific kind, whose significant attributes include irony and ambivalence above all else. Initially, the immediately evident fact that this Mungo Park is black might seem sufficient to destabilize the real Park's association with white European expansionism into Africa. Despite potential evidence to the contrary, until Mungo follows up the revelation of his name by that of his nationality, we no doubt share France's naive assumption, based on nothing more than the color of his skin, that Mungo is a native of Cameroon.[6] Thus, it is our ignorance, as much as hers, that merits Mungo's gentle sarcasm: "I'm an American black [*un nègre américain*]. Are you disappointed? Were you looking for a real native?" But if Mungo's words suffice to call into question France's own illusions about her place in postcolonialist Africa, in all probability they do not yet undermine a second assumption on the part of the viewer, one which follows, automatically and for the same reason, from the first, i.e., that Mungo, unlike France, does belong in Africa. Mungo will need to turn his irony toward himself for us to understand that his fictional journey to Africa not only reverses but also repeats that of his historical namesake.

Mungo Park, notes Pratt, "wrote himself" as a sentimental hero (75). Indeed, what he describes in *Travels in the Interior Districts of Africa* as a "passionate desire to explore into the productions of a country so little known" (2) includes, at least initially, a fundamental belief in the common humanity of black Africans and white Europeans: "I was fully convinced that whatever difference there is between the Negro and European in the conformation of the nose and the colour of the skin, there is none in the genuine sympathies and characteristic feelings of our common nature" (84). Once Park journeys into Africa, however, he experiences a series of encounters whose threat to his liberty and even his life challenge his optimistic assumptions about the native population; the adventurous hero must at times rewrite his character as that of a sympathetic victim. Although the original Park operates on premises that are dialectically opposed to those of Denis's contemporary Mungo, for whom racial identity now functions as the determinant of commonality rather than an insignificant mark of difference, he too draws upon the trope of the romantic hero to tell the story of his arrival in Africa. Contrary to their expectations, Park's cinematic counterpart, like his historical predecessor, will also find his illusions of a warm welcome quickly shattered:

> I remember the day I arrived in Africa. I was totally drunk. At customs, I wanted to kiss the officers, my brothers. I said to myself—that's it, you've come home. Of course I got screwed at the airport by the first taxi driver. He didn't give a damn that I was black. And, you know, he was right. My brothers over here, my brothers over there. I'm still an American. They don't give a damn here about guys like me. Here I'm nothing. I'm dreaming. If I died right now, I would entirely disappear.

In having Mungo tell the story of his own arrival in Cameroon as a false "homecoming," parallel to that of France herself, Denis confirms that her film functions explicitly as an allegory of *nation*. If an African-American—who might rightfully, if naively, claim Africa as at least an ancestral homeland, however distant and impersonal—does not belong in contemporary Cameroon, then clearly the possibility that the citizen of a former colonialist power might go home again is not merely incongruous or naive but arguably absurd. Indeed, France, unlike the historical Mungo Park, will never manage to travel back to the "Interior Districts" of northern Cameroon where she grew up. From the beginning, Mungo has identified her as a tourist ("Are you a tourist?"/"If you say so"), whose inappropriate insistence on traveling on foot he denounces as an inauthentic attempt to fit in ("It seems more typical, is that it?"); at the end, as he advises her to leave Africa, he evokes her metaphoric death as the price of any further attempt to move inland: "No, honey [*petite*], get out quickly—before you're eaten alive." The original Mungo Park, of course, undertook a second expedition to Africa only to die as a direct result of what had become a highly militarized endeavor to open up markets for European expansion.

Mungo himself, as his words suggest and the filming of the sequence confirms, enters Africa as a foreigner, who risks the loss of identity, if not of life. Not only does his disillusionment coincide with the literal passage of the frontier ("at customs," "the first taxi driver"), but he metaphorically evokes his own presence in Africa as an experience of absence, disappearance, and invisibility ("I'm nothing," "I would disappear"). Throughout this episode, moreover, Mungo speaks as a disembodied voice; we see neither him nor

France as the camera tracks forward to frame only the road ahead and the surrounding countryside through the windshield of the car. In general, Denis's stylistic preference for tracking shots, filmed from a distance and a perspective that imply our presence within the frame, just behind or next to France, construct the spectators of *Chocolat* as fellow travelers. Unlike other filmmakers for whom tracking is a signature shot, such as Alain Resnais and Agnès Varda, Denis's camera does not seek or explore; it simply visits, recording what it encounters as it passes by. In this instance, *le travelling*, more consistent with the word that names it in French, is simply traveling through, as Mungo Park once did.[7] Indeed, the capsule summary of contents that introduces each episode of Park's record of his adventures in Africa reproduces his voyage as one of perpetual motion, a repetitious cycle of arrivals and departures, conveyed by a series of synonymous verbs of movement—it reads, that is, not unlike a plot resume of *Chocolat*.[8]

The textual presence of Mungo Park, once evoked, can be seen to resonate as well throughout the double flashback—to France's childhood, on the one hand; to France's colonialist past, on the other—at the center of *Chocolat*. This superimposition of character and country serves as a constant reminder of the particular significance of names in decoding Denis's film as an allegory of nation. According to Pratt, as I noted earlier, what Park himself announces as "a plain, unvarnished tale" (vii), consistent with the predominantly scientific and informational travel writing of the eighteenth century, in fact "richly exemplifies the eruption of the sentimental mode into European narrative" (74–75). If Pratt's analysis depends, in particular, on evidence of Park's interest in a newly (re)discovered realm of the emotional, the private, and the individual, she also notes that the influence of "that great sentimental obsession, transracial erotics" is not entirely absent from his text either (82). Indeed, the conventions of representation that characterize Park's *Travels in the Interior Districts of Africa* clearly include a certain tendency to romanticize his encounters with native women, for whom he always expresses particular sympathy and affection. Moreover, his stories of their curiosity about the anatomy of a white male body might fairly be described as rather risqué (see, for example, Park 136–37).

Within a more recent category of what we might still call sentimental travel literature, constituted by the "colonial nostalgia films" that have appeared in the last 10–15 years (Shohat and Stam 123), the love story has become so fully developed and so prevalent a plot that it might well qualify, in Hayden White's terminology, as a "master trope" in its ability to shape our conception of history (58).[9] The questions that I and others have raised about the politics of using the narrative of romance as a metaphor for colonialism in such recent French films as Brigitte Roüan's *Outremer*, Jean-Jacques Annaud's *The Lover* (1992), and Régis Wargnier's *Indochine* (1992) clearly apply to *Chocolat* as well. Notably, to take one example, the confinement of France and her mother to the house, visually reinforced by tightly framed shots of its interior, suggests an analogy between the restrictive lives of (white) women and the oppressive regime of colonialism that could well obscure the complex interrelationship of race and gender in imperial discourse (see Durham). In addition, given the evident mutual attraction that characterizes the relationship between Aimée and Protée, visually reinforced in this case by the frequent use of point of view shots, the complicity of women in colonialist oppression may itself be similarly obscured. In concluding a general discussion of "transracial love plots" in imperial narrative, Pratt makes this very point much more absolutely and emphatically: "The allegory of romantic love mystifies exploitation out of the picture" (97, see also Kaplan 89).

No doubt *Chocolat* has been read in this way; more importantly, some significant number of people apparently wanted Denis to direct a film that could be so read. In another intriguing, if this time coincidental and extradiagetic, parallel between the frame story of *Chocolat* and the flashback it contains, Denis had to fight not only to retain the metaphoric presence of Mungo Park but also to prevent the disappearance of Protée into a world of convention. The difficulties that Denis encountered in financing her first feature film did not result from the story she wanted to tell—"I did not experience any problems in actually discussing colonialism"—but rather from the way in which she chose to tell that story:

> I was, however, strongly advised to construct an affair between Protée, the male black servant in the film, and the white woman. The producers saw this outcome as good box office. . . . I resisted the pressure to alter the script. When it came to doing the scene in which Protée resists the possibility of a sexual encounter with the woman, I shot it quickly in one take before anyone could

even attempt to suggest an alternative. I know this was a big disappointment for the production company, because they really wanted me to re-shoot the scene and to change it, but Protée's refusal was the purpose of the film. (Qtd. in Petrie 67, in English)

Significantly, if Denis does not wish to realize the trope that informs the relationship between Protée and Aimée, neither has she any desire to abandon it. Indeed, the possibility of a sexual liaison was introduced into Denis's original script only after she began to collaborate with Jean-Pol Fargeau in a deliberate effort to distance herself from her own childhood memories. Far from originating in reality, the suggestion of an affair comes pre-encoded in an explicitly literary form; Denis borrows it from a remembered reading of a Cameroonian novel, Ferdinand Oyono's *Une Vie de boy* (Reid 68). As a result, Denis reveals that there are ways, short of elimination, to undermine the romance narrative from within. In *Chocolat*, she makes its very absence at once significant and visible by deliberately arousing, the better to thwart, our expectations, themselves largely based on our knowledge of literary and cinematic conventions, that the erotic potential of the plot will be fulfilled. This refusal to comply with traditional codes of representation enables Denis to turn the allegory of love, denounced by Pratt and others as a sentimental mystification of imperialist exploitation, into its virtual opposite: a strategy for the subversion of colonialism as a form of romance.[10]

In the case of Protée, Denis's disruption of the discursive tropes of colonial cinema is deliberate: "His rejection of this white woman demystifies the prevalent screen image of the black stud and the exotic black, something imagined in Hollywood films like *Out of Africa*" (qtd. in Reid 68, in English). I have quoted at some length from two different interviews with Denis, not simply to confirm the extraordinary importance of Protée's gesture to her conception of her own film, but to reveal something rather curious about how she refers to the other character in this relationship. Three times, in two different statements, Denis refuses, or at least fails, to so much as name Aimée, whom she identifies successively only as "the white woman," "the woman," and "this white woman." This reluctance to individualize is no doubt consistent with an allegorical interpretation of Denis's film, particularly since official France literally represents itself as a white woman through the symbolic figure of Marianne. If the daughter's ultimate confinement to the *periphérie* in *Chocolat* is suggestive of the ambiguous status of postcolonialist France, the mother's role in the last days of imperialism is still structurally central, if equally ambivalent. Aimée's name clearly identifies her with the "beloved" nation. Her metaphoric significance is foregrounded early in the film by the unexpected and dramatically gratuitous visit that Jonathan Boothby (Kenneth Cranham) makes to Mindif in the absence of Marc. Boothby is visually juxtaposed to the huge framed photo of the queen, the British version of the adored empire, which he displays even in his guestroom. The scene in which Boothby and Aimée dance in tux and long gown, carefully framed and filmed from a distance as if we were watching a theatrical performance, reduces colonialism to a fantasy image, a nostalgic memory, whose representation is characterized by frivolity, sterility, and artifice.

Because Aimée is loved (or desired) by all of the men in the film and yet fundamentally passive in her own right, the most important function of her character lies in its ability, first, to unite male characters who otherwise appear to have little in common, and, second, to undermine this entire group—and therefore the gender and the ideology it represents—in the process. Anne McClintock argues that imperialism and nationalism must be understood as gendered discourse, whose central focus, as in *Chocolat*, on the domestic world of the house tells us as much about male identity as female and about the political sphere as the private (352–58). Shohat and Stam conclude even more forcefully that "the imperial narrative is ultimately masculinist" (166). That the male characters in *Chocolat* both bond and self-destruct specifically in the role of "sentimental hero" demonstrates once again the mobility of the metaphoric presence of Mungo Park in Denis's film.

Park's influence in the flashback sequence of *Chocolat* is most evidently reflected in the character of Marc Dalens. Like the historic Scotsman, Marc is both colonial explorer and writer; and the record he keeps—"just some notes I make when I'm out on inspection"—is strongly reminiscent of Park's own travel writing both in content and in appearance. It functions, moreover, as the transitional device that moves us from present to past; the camera follows Mungo's glance back at France, who is reading her father's travel journal, and then tracks directly from a close-up of the book, lying open on her lap, out the car window and into the countryside of France's memory. Marc too is driving through Cameroon in the opening scene of the flashback, and he is often on the move. Notably, in the first part of the film, the routine daliness of domestic life for France and Aimée is intercut with Marc's tour of the province, a sequence that foregrounds the reality behind the very written page we have seen earlier, as if to signify once again the importance of representation in *Chocolat*.

But Marc is not simply a fellow traveler of Mungo Park but an equally sentimental one; his idealism, sensitivity, and self-awareness also recall his historical predecessor. In particular, the only passage from Marc's notebook that we hear read aloud, in which questions of nature and culture, of difference and superiority, are addressed through the symbolic framework of skin color, directly echoes similar reflections that recur at several points in Park's *Travels*:[11]

Amidst the brownish-black faces of Africans, white skin definitely evokes something very like death. In 1891, when I first caught sight of Europeans again after months of seeing only people of color, even I found white skin unnatural compared to black. So how can one blame the savages native to the region for viewing the white man as a creature opposed to nature, as something supernatural or demonic?

Although most spectators will be inclined to find Marc sympathetic, he is gently denounced within the film as naive and ineffectual by both Aimée ("You always get taken in, Marc") and Jonathan ("Marc's a dreamer, you know. He loves the land, the people, insects, everything. Is he still keeping his bloody *bororo* diaries? Marc and his notebook"). Indeed, even in his role as military commander, Marc is essentially portrayed as either romantic hero or sentimental writer, roles that are at best incongruous with his position. During his tour of the colony, for example, when he is not shown simply meandering through the countryside, we see him up on a hill, writing in his diary, while his escort waits below; and we hear him sing "Ma Mie [My Beloved]," an old French song whose words ironically state a clear preference for love over empire: "If the king had given me/His great city of Paris,/But I had to leave/The Love of my life,/I would tell King

Henri/Take your Paris back./I prefer my beloved, *au gué.*"[12] In English, Marc's last name evokes the word *dalliance* whose double meaning appropriately, if no doubt purely by chance, identifies Marc as simultaneously a lover and a dawdler, a waster of time.

In contrast to Marc, Luc should be suspect from the moment he is introduced into the film, for we know him to have been the lover of one of Aimée's married friends, and his interest in Aimée herself quickly becomes evident. Still, this mysterious white man, of whom we know nothing, except that—like Mungo Park once again—"he's walking across Africa," initially seems to expose and to challenge the racism of the other colonialists by his insistence on living and working among the Black servants. But this pretense of "going native," an act of questionable merit in and of itself, is quickly exposed as a parody of Park's compassionate interest in the customs and peoples of Africa. Luc, whose motives are entirely personal and self-serving, is a hypocrite, a fake, a parasite, a presumptuous impersonator, whose forced entry into the community and "occupation" of the servant's quarters metaphorically repeats the invasion of Cameroon by colonialist France, performed once again in the guise of a seduction. If Marc tells Luc that "this isn't your place," it is Protée who throws him off the verandah and "out of the picture," literally as well as metaphorically.

Luc, then, would seem to be the last person for whom we would expect Marc to show friendship, especially since the latter acts the polite but distant host with the rest of his guests. Yet, it is Luc, to our surprise, whom Marc allows to read his journal; and the two become allies in the climactic sequence of *Chocolat*, whose meaning must be counted among the most elusive of the film.[13] One theoretical development within feminist film criticism has privileged a "symptomatic" method of interpretation that seeks to identify moments of apparent textual incoherence at which mainstream cinema reveals its ideological contradictions (see, for example, Cook and Johnston). I want to suggest that this scene in *Chocolat* works in a somewhat similar fashion, but that the "gap" or "rupture" opened up as a result of the plane crash works in this case to reveal the ideological consistency of Denis's film, read as national allegory. Curiously, although the scene includes what Denis identifies as the most important sentence in the film, it almost seems to elude her as well; she speaks of it as if *Chocolat* were a film she had once seen rather than one she has directed:

> One line from *Chocolat* has always stayed with me. François Cluzet and Jean-Claude Adelin are on the terrace, it's the typical colonial night, two men with their whiskey. A horrible scene has just taken place in which they've driven off the black doc and the only thing they find to say to each other is, "*So what, one of these days we'll be kicked out of here.*" Cluzet couldn't keep from laughing during the scene; he knew intuitively that it could only be acted that way. It's a useless line as far as the plot is concerned, but it's the most important one in the film. (Qtd. in Strauss 33)

The "black doc" has a name, of course, one which is carefully called to our attention within the film, and one which, once again, functions metaphorically.

When Machinard's wife falls ill, Marc goes in search of the native doc-tor, Prosper, whom he tracks down at a meeting at the school. Back at the house, Machinard's refusal to allow a black man to treat his wife provokes Luc to perform an exaggerated parody of the racism expressed by Machinard and supported by Védrine and his navigator (" 'Filthy nigger!' That's how you have to talk to them," etc.), but what begins as a strategy to expose the intolerance of the others evolves into a re-enactment that is indistinguishable from the original, and in which all of the colonialists, Marc included, are fully implicated. Refusing a ride home, Prosper walks away alone to the sound of Védrine singing "Prosper, Youp la Boum." Marc and Luc sit laughing on the verandah, and we hear Marc say, "One of these days, we'll be driven out of here."

The inevitable end of colonialism does indeed appear to surface in the moment that Luc's performance in some sense "slips" from an act of deri-sion to one of authentic imitation, opening up what Homi Bhabha has identified as "this area between mimicry and mockery where the civilizing mission is threatened" (86). Octave Mannoni has coined the expression "Prospero complex" to refer to "the inbred dependency of the colonized on the leadership of white Europeans" (Shohat and Stam 140).[14] But if, as the doctor's name and professional status within the colonialist community suggest, Prosper has "prospered" under colonialism by an act of mimicry of his own, on this night he is metaphorically freed not only by the mockery

of the white men but by an act of independence on the part of his own people. Marc is clearly disturbed to learn that Prosper is at a public meeting
organized by the school teacher ("What the hell are they doing at the
school?"/"They're talking, monsieur."), and when he calls to Prosper to
come out, he—and "France," who on this night accompanies him—are
confronted by the entire group of men, lit from behind so that the teacher
projects a huge, menacing, black shadow that suggests the threat of the
insurrection to come. That the imperial narrative is not only gendered but
may well be "ultimately masculinist" (Shohat and Stam 166) also becomes
clear in this scene. What essentially comes down to the denial of the body
of the white woman (Machinard's wife) to the black man (Prosper) will be
repeated in reverse on subsequent nights, in which the gift of the body of
the white woman (first Aimée, then France) to the black man (Protée) will
be rejected with increasing violence. The connection is already made during Prosper's departure by the ironic words we hear sung, which reduce the
man of science to the hustler of the streets: "Prosper, Youp la Boum, he's the
darling of the ladies/Prosper, Youp la Boum, he's the king of the streets."

In a discussion of the future of self-representation in European cinema,
Stuart Hall includes *Chocolat* among what he characterizes as "traveling
films": "They open with traveling shots, and end in airports. . . . We are in
the world of movement, of migration, of the dissolution of boundaries, of
national borderlines" (47). What makes Denis's film of particular interest
in this context is the degree to which the motion of her film leads not only
through the specific world that is visually represented on screen but simultaneously reveals the very conventions and codes of representation that
enable imperialism to write itself into reality and history as well as into fiction and film. Metaphor and allegory are also, of course, forms of displacement that mediate in indirect fashion between one place and another.
Shohat and Stam describe colonialist discourse as "*protean*, multiple,
adopting diverse and even contradictory rhetorics" (139, my emphasis).
Appropriately, then, Protées name, whose importance I have reserved for
the end, may well be the most significantly allusive of all, for it points to
the meandering and metaphoric nature of Denis's film as a whole.[15]

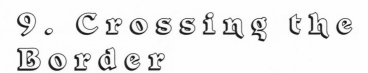

9. Crossing the Border

The Post-Colonial Carnival in Neil Jordan's *The Crying Game*

—*Catherine Wynne*

In 1806 a feud emerged in East Munster in the South of Ireland between two large factions calling themselves the Caravats (Carabhaití) and the Shanavests (Sean-Bheisteanna), or in translation, the Cravats and Old Waistcoats—the opposing groups derived their names from the costumes of their adherents.[1] The Caravats emerged from the poor and attempted to exercise control over local economic and agricultural interests. Indeed, such agrarian secret societies were a feature of the rural Irish landscape of the eighteenth- and nineteenth-century. Operating against changes in agriculture and the monopoly of land by landlords, their response often involved aggressive violence against the symbols of colonial rule, landlords, and their agents. The Shanavests were a middle-class movement who expounded an ideological belief in nationalism and saw the activities of the Caravats as destructive of any attempt to forge a political separatist alliance.

137

The opposing factions acquired their sartorial appellations in the Winter of 1805–1806 when a Nicholas Hanley, nicknamed after his elegant cravat or "caravat," was hanged in Clonmel before a violent and effusive crowd of supporters and enemies, the latter camp being led by a Patrick Connors, noted for his battered old waistcoat or "shanavest." According to tradition, Connors shouted out a pun on Hanley's nickname and its association with the hangman's rope. Despite his imminent garrotting, Hanley replied with a cutting comment on his adversary's waistcoat. Hanley's execution operated as a catalyst as the groups took their names and inspiration from their leaders' dress. "One can discern here," Paul Roberts argues, "the clash of two different moral and cultural worlds, and the rival leaders seem to have personified many of the different values and aspirations of each. This was reflected in their evocative nickname and dress, which is surely the reason why tradition places such emphasis on an exchange of insults about clothes at Hanley's execution, and why the factions automatically seized on cravats and old waistcoats as their rival emblems" (Roberts 72).

What has this got to do with *The Crying Game* (1992)—a late twentieth-century film, preoccupied with a radical re-visioning of gender and politics and the implications and complexities of the post-colonial condition? Of course, the film emerges out of an Irish social and political context that has its roots in nineteenth-century colonial politics, in fact it can be said to mobilize such politics as the Belfast carnival converges on the London "Metro." In line with this, the Munster story underscores the very composite nature of nineteenth-century Ireland, and moves away from a reductive interpretation of the colonial engagement. The tensions between the colonized classes, of economics versus nationalism re-frame the colonial landscape as it shatters the notion that colonial conflict exists in binary politics of landlord and tenant, colonizer and colonized. Equally, binary politics are contested in Jordan's film, as the protagonist is forced to see outside the conventional framework of colonizer versus colonized, of us versus them, embodied in Fergus's (Stephen Rea) early remark to the British soldier Jody (Forest Whitaker) that "you guys shouldn't be here."[2] Execution is the hallmark of both historical anecdote and contemporary film; Jody's inadvertent execution (in fact, carried out by a British Army Saracen,[3] just as Hanley's execution was conducted by the agents of colonial rule in Ireland) forms one of the film's crucial spectacles and fundamentally sets Fergus in opposition to his former colleagues. The execution is the cata-lyst that forces him to question the binary nature of his political engage-ment, just as Hanley's execution fragments the agents of colonial resistance into opposing factions.

The other feature that makes this historical moment interesting is, of course, the centrality of dress. It demarcates the economic preoccupations of the labouring class from middle-class nationalism in the anecdote, whilst in the film clothes designate the females' race and class as well as their political and ideological positioning. The gendered preoccupations of the film have their antecedents in the colonial manifestations of nineteenth-century Ireland. Indeed, the Caravats and the Shanavests emerge from a tradition in which agrarian secret societies dressed up in women's clothing to perform their nocturnal rampages. The Whiteboys wore linen frocks over their trousers, whilst the Molly Maguires went further both cognomenally and sartorially. Disguised as women they dedicated themselves, according to Kevin Kenny, to a "mythical woman who symbolized their struggle against injustice, whether sectarian, nationalist or economic" (Kenny 22). As such, they operated as agents of an informal system of law and punishment, a feature that their contemporary counterparts in Northern Ireland retain.[4] Kenny aligns them with the cultural practices of mummers, cross-dressed groups who infiltrated the Irish countryside on feast days, travelling from house to house demanding food, money and drink in exchange for a per-formance (Kenny 23). Mummers and agrarian secret societies demonstrate the convergence of cultural and socio-political practices.

Ultimately, the social and cultural roots of cross-dressed agrarian secret societies lie in the practices of carnival. In Ireland, such ritualized mani-festations outlasted their European counterparts, and their validity and potency re-emerge in Jordan's film where carnivalesque spaces function to legitimate the illegitimate, allowing for protest, excess and gender inver-sion. *The Crying Game* moves from the colonial to the post-colonial but in its crossing over, it bridges (like the bridge of the film's opening sequence) the complicated and transgressive colonial politics of nineteenth-century Ireland and the (post-) colonial milieu of late twentieth-century Northern Irish and British politics. Spectacle, display, sartorial preoccupations and the carnivalesque are significant points of reference within a film that insistently crosses gendered and political borders.

The post-colonial era is one of constant crossing over, of voluntary and forced migration, of mutating and hybridized identities. As Edward Said posits, identity accrues from constant crossing over, from exile and return (*After the Last Sky* 164). All of this is manifest in *The Crying Game*, a film that embodies what Richard Kearney calls the need for "new paradigms of political and cultural accommodation" in Ireland (*Postnationalist Ireland* 11). It is a film preoccupied with transitional states where the negotiation and re-negotiation of position and identity are discovered, but not fixed, at the point of crossover. The idea of traversing boundaries reverberates not only in the social and political arena; it has yet more implications in terms of gender and psychology. The analogy in *The Crying Game* between societal politics and body politics is crucial, most explicitly articulated in how its initial political focus becomes rapidly sexualized. Thus, a heated early interchange in which Jody calls the IRA "tough undeluded motherfuckers" moves from a political emphasis that physically (as can be seen in Fergus's posture) and psychologically alienates the IRA man, to draw him into body politics as Jody seductively beckons Fergus to come over to him to seek in his jacket pocket a wallet that reveals a picture of the soldier in cricket attire and even more pertinently a picture of a smiling woman's face, designated as the soldier's "special friend." The body becomes the locus for an interplay of disparate forces. As John Fiske notes: "the body is where the social is most convincingly represented as the individual and where politics can best disguise itself as human nature" (70). Such a point intersects with the film's obsession with and interrogation of what constitutes nature or the natural.[5]

Cross-over, advanced by the film, is not only a political and social manifestation; it is equally a matter of sexuality and gender. The various crossovers in *The Crying Game* operate in a space in which order is suspended. This suspension of order is noticeably reminiscent of Bakhtin's notion of carnivalesque space wherein boundaries can be transgressed, rank inverted, roles exchanged: "carnival celebrated temporary liberation from the prevailing truth and from the established order; it marked the suspension of all hierarchical rank, privileges, norms, and prohibitions. Carnival was the true feast of time, the feast of becoming, change and renewal. It was hostile to all that was immortalized and completed" (10). The carnivalesque spaces of *The Crying Game* facilitate this cross-over into sexual and political otherness.

I. Carnivals and the Dancehall

Robert Stam in his work on carnival and film sets out the tenets of the carnivalesque:

The carnivalesque principle abolishes hierarchies, levels social classes, and creates another life free from conventional rules and restrictions. In carnival, all that is marginalized and excluded—the mad, the scandalous, the aleatory—takes over the center in a liberating explosion of otherness. The principle of the material body—hunger, thirst, defecation, copulation—becomes a positively corrosive force, and festive laughter enjoys a symbolic victory over death, over all that is held sacred, over all that oppresses and restricts. (86)

At the same time, despite the carnival's threat to hegemonic order, its revolutionary appeal, its subversive anticipation of the overthrow of oppressive social and political structures, Stam cautions: "Carnivals can constitute a symbolic rebellion *by* the weak or a festive scapegoating *of* the weak, or both at the same time. We must ask who is carnivalizing whom, for what reasons, by which means and in what circumstances?" (95). For Stam, "carnivals must be seen as complex crisscrossings of ideological manipulation and utopian desire"; Bakhtin, he argues, "tends to overestimate the political efficacy of real life carnivals" (96).

Such a position intersects with another key thinker on the carnivalesque. Abner Cohen's work on the sociology of carnival (in particular on the Notting Hill carnival in London) raises the question whether the carnival operates as an adjunct to ruling class control—in other words as part of the dominant culture's political hegemony—or alternatively whether it serves as a counter-culture that constitutes "an ideology of resistance and opposition, or whether it is a contested ideological terrain" (134). Carnival may alleviate political tension within the society by simultaneously allowing for the articulation of conflict and protest. "Carnival's potentialities for fostering criticism, protest, resistance, subversion and violence are equally great," insists Cohen, "and at the best of times the celebration is poised between compliance and subversion" (130). Underneath the masquerade of such cultural display resides the political. Carnivalesque spaces and sites of festivity permeate Jordan's work and occupy at once the possibility of change and ossification, multiplicity and binary. They are nonetheless contested and contentious spaces that allow for processes of becoming, just as their temporary nature threatens a return to an existing order.

This is explicit in Jordan's earlier film that also deploys the thematics of the Northern conflict. In *Angel* (1982), which was released as *Danny Boy* in the States, the narrative centres around a showband and more specifically its saxophonist, Danny (Stephen Rea). After a performance at a rural ballroom, Danny leaves the hall and encounters a teenage girl, Annie, whom he had earlier danced with. After an implied sexual encounter the two find refuge by sitting inside a large pipe that is positioned so that the ballroom's red neon sign penetrates its interior. Its vaginal and womb-like connotations are rendered evident by Jordan, a technique that is mirrored in Dil's similarly lit flat in *The Crying Game* which is also framed in a womb-like manner.

Annie leaves the safety of this space when she sees a car pulling up to the dancehall and witnesses the band's manager being shot by a paramilitary group variously disguised in balaclavas and with women's stockings on their faces. When they see her watching them, she too is shot dead. Ironically, Annie is both deaf and mute—but such silencing does not prevent her annihilation. Her murder forces Danny to leave the security of the pipe—the metaphysical womb—to face the personal and political realities of the Northern conflict. He vows vengeance on Annie's killers and readily exchanges the saxophone for the gun in order to hunt them down. By conflating the musician with the vigilante, the film offers a critique of the aestheticization of violence (Kearney, *Transitions* 183).

Of even more pertinence here is *Angel's* exploration of dancehall and carnival. Ostensibly, the dancehall is the site of festivity, of relaxation and release. It marks a moment of celebration demonstrated in a new bride on her wedding day who comes in accompanied by her husband and some male friends. In a flirtation with Danny the bride initiates his request for her to dance, to which she then coyly responds with the words "I can't, I'm married." The site of liberation is also a site of confinement which is later substantiated in the woman's description of the brutal nature of her marriage when she accidentally meets Fergus in a café some time after the breakdown of her relationship. In addition, the male members of the bridal party are there to carry out the manager's assassination. Hence, the wedding festivity serves as a masquerade for political and criminal intrigue.

The dancehall is complicit with violence, but allusions to carnival initiate opportunities for its alleviation and the possibility for transformation. Danny finds temporary refuge in his Aunt Mae's house, which is demarcated from colonial politics, as demonstrated when Danny stands at the window and looks out at a British army soldier on the street corner. Pertinently, Mae is a fortune-teller, a reader of tarot cards. At one point she reads Danny's cards and he asks her if he will be "crossing water." However, Danny merely crosses over into political violence, while Fergus's physical and psychological crossing in *The Crying Game* is a more radical attempt to move away, if not altogether successfully, from the politics of the Northern conflict. A second carnival allusion occurs at the end of *Angel*. Danny revisits the site of the burnt-out ballroom, adjacent to which is a silver trailer. A carnival barker is peddling healing sessions with a boy, Francie, who as the seventh son of a seventh son is ascribed with spiritual powers.[6] When Danny enters the caravan and encounters Francie, surrounded by religious iconography, he collapses.

Dancehall and carnival finally converge in the film's closing scenes when a police official, Bonner, leads Danny from the caravan into the burnt-out shell of the dancehall, where the policeman is revealed as the final member of the paramilitary group responsible for the double murder of the band manager and Annie. When Danny is on the verge of being shot, Francie enters from the left to stand to one side of him. The boy's intervention is timely. Bonner fatally pauses to comment on the boy's mystical powers: "Here's a boy believes in miracles," "Do you?" he asks Danny. At the moment that Danny replies "I do"—a phrase that recalls how the dancehall became a site of marital celebration and ruthless murder—Bonner is shot from behind by a police colleague. The revenge is completed on the site of the murders. Appropriately, the presence of the boy with his carnivalesque associations ensures Danny's salvation and completion, and the film's final moments witness Danny leaving the dancehall followed by Francie.

Brian McHale argues that in the absence of a real carnival, fiction incorporates or constructs its own versions of carnival (174). *The Crying Game* certainly *constructs* carnival spaces. The first of these is represented directly in the carnival outside Belfast, where the soldier, Jody, is captured. The second, referred to only obliquely in the film but emphasized in the screenplay, is the carnival outside Monaghan run by Fergus's uncle. Furthermore, London, and more specifically the "Metro" bar, operates as the third carnival space. The Belfast carnival initiates a process, operating on sexual and political levels. McHale notes that "traveling shows frequently function in postmodernist fantastic texts as agents of disruption" (174). The sexual disruption is represented in the seduction by Jude (Miranda Richardson), the IRA woman, of Jody, the British soldier. At first, this seems an ordinary heterosexual relationship, a one-night stand practised and allowed in the daytime by the sexual license of the carnival. Jody, however, is homosexual. Intriguingly, when he later recalls the scene, he is baffled by his attraction to Jude. The carnivalesque atmosphere is implied as the agent behind the disturbance of Jody's sexual behaviour as he crosses into bisexuality.

The carnival also allows an illegitimate army, the IRA, to prevail, as the legitimate army, represented by Jody, is disempowered. Literally and metaphorically, Jude draws him into the carnival. This is the terrain in which Jude, as illegitimate IRA agent, is legitimated. The overtly heterosexual and seductive Jude, with her denim mini-skirt, black tights and white heels, represents a slightly outdated working-class girl on the pull. Her class position and feminine masquerade (though biologically female she has a male name) mark her as an inheritor of the tradition of cross-dressed Irish secret societies, who often targeted landlord's agents rather than the landlords themselves, just as Jude targets the agent, not the centre of British rule.

Jude knows her landscape and this is demonstrated when she catches the eye of her IRA colleague, Fergus. Initially, her seeking out Fergus's response to her connection with Jody would seem to be simply sexual—her coy glance could embody the hallmarks of an erotic game. Though the sexual does exist in her relationship with Fergus, the ensuing scenes will unveil the seduction's primary political imperative. With its milling crowds, activity

and noise, the carnival is the place where the capture of the British soldier is successfully carried out. Operating as a site of festivity, enjoyment
and relaxation, it ensures that Jody's defences are lowered. The locus of
relaxation is also the site of the undisciplined. Jody has succumbed to the
heterosexual masquerade to the extent that when he is violently captured
by the IRA he cries out Jude's name and shouts "are you alright, Jude?" The
scene ends with a shot of Jude fleeing over a field, like her nineteenth-
century counterparts, an image that variously and ambiguously positions
her as agent in the abduction or as innocent party.

The Monaghan carnival is problematic. Even though it is broached as a
carnivalesque space in the screenplay, its liberating potential is muted in
the film. For Fergus, the Monaghan carnival of the screenplay, intimately
connected with his youth, is a signifier of childhood freedom. When Jody's
fear of his imminent execution results in an emotional breakdown, his
tears and his desire for comfort remind Fergus of the security offered by the
Monaghan carnival. This operates as the antithesis of the insecurity of the
Belfast carnival, an opposition conveyed by way of an anecdote to the dis-
traught Jody:

Fergus: When I was a child. . . .
Jody: Yeah?
Fergus: I thought as a child. But when I became a man I put away childish
things. . . .
Jody: What do you mean?
Fergus: Nothing.
Jody: Tell me something, anything.
Fergus: When I was a kid my uncle had a carnival in Monaghan. I used to get
free rides on the swings.
Jody: And?
Fergus: Only when the day was finished and the place near empty. So I'd swing
as the sun went down.
Jody: And?
Fergus: Nothing. That's it. That was my little bit of bliss.
Jody: And that's the story.
Fergus: Yes. (Jordan 20–21)

Later Fergus returns to the Monaghan carnival, seeking the comfort he
earlier sought to extend to Jody. Implicit in this is an attempt to achieve a

psychological equilibrium which will prepare him for his escape to London. The Monaghan Carnival represents the innocence, purity and freedom of childhood. Childhood is the untainted state. The Monaghan Carnival is significantly situated in the Republic. It thus embodies the concept of the "Free State" that politically came into being after the Anglo-Irish Treaty of 1921 and, of course, established the border with Northern Ireland. The convergence of political and psychological resonance in the term "Free State" in an Irish context hardly needs to be further underlined. Politically, union with this free state embodies Fergus's ideological aspirations. Psychologically, the return to childhood represents freedom. But the "free state" of the Monaghan carnival offers an alternative interpretation. The representation of this site as a carnivalesque space in the filmic image is significant. The scene opens with an old man pushing a bicycle, as the door of a car (revealed as scrap) opens and Fergus emerges. The clapped-out car underscores the carnival wasteland; this is a carnival in decay. It is no longer functioning.

Fergus's uncle can be therefore interpreted in two ways. On one level he represents innocence. He asks no questions and desires no answers. He refuses to become complicit with, or tainted by guilt and thus rejects entrapment in post-colonial politics. Secondly, Tommy's refusal to engage and the failure of the carnival to work in this "free state" signify both atrophy and completion. If nationalist politics is the acme of Fergus's political ambitions, then the Republic should embody his political philosophy, but the "Free State" embodied in the Monaghan Carnival is in decline. At best it can offer only temporary refuge, and a passage to England aboard a cattle ship. Agricultural economics outweigh political and social transformation. The potential of the Monaghan carnival is undermined in the film as it presents a sealed political system that is cut off from the potentiality of change, just as it allows Fergus to hide. Contrary to this, the Belfast carnival is where Fergus first encounters Jody who will ultimately disrupt Fergus's closed political vision. Fergus initially employs a simplistic pattern of binary thought. His position is simply encapsulated in an interchange with Jody:

Jody: What do you believe in?
Fergus: That you guys shouldn't be here.
Jody: It's as simple as that?
Fergus: Yes. (Jordan 17)

Fergus is still operating within a colonial binary paradigm. Questions need to be asked about the extent to which Northern Ireland is still trapped within the political and psychological dynamics of colonialism. For Frantz Fanon, the second stage in the process of decolonization is that of nationalism. But nationalism is an essentially conservative political aspiration which mimics the ideology of the mother country (121–63). For Kearney, "Irish and British nationalism are Siamese twins. Britain has always been obsessed by Ireland, and oblivious of it at one and the same time. Ireland, and in particular Irish nationalism, its alter ego, its ally and enemy, familiar and foreign. The other which defines, and undermines its very identity. The double which haunts and fascinates. Its phantom limb" (*Postnationalist* 9–10). The Irishman, embodied in Fergus, must remain "other" in Britain. Hence, Fergus's imitation of the batsman's motion with his sledgehammer is interrogated by Deveroux (his Anglo-Norman name is apposite) who tries to reinscribe Fergus's racial identity and by implication his inferiority through naming:

Deveroux: So Pat's a cricket fan, eh?
Fergus: It's not Pat, it's Jim.
Deveroux: Jim Pat, Mick, what the fuck. Long as you remember you're not at Lords. (Jordan 30)

If the scene serves as an indictment of the exclusivity of British national identity, Fergus, as if in limbo, is equally trapped within Fanon's second order of nationalistic dynamics. Contrary to Fergus's statement to Jody the post-colonial framework reveals that nothing is "simple"—a knowledge that Jody as immigrant West Indian has already attained. At the same time, Jody opts to join the British army—a move that interrogates not only colonial but class politics. For Jody, the British army is a job. It is only in the Belfast bar where Jude picks him up that Jody reaches a realization of his position. In what amounts to an interrogation with Fergus, he explains: "I'm saying to myself what the fuck am I doing here anyway." To which Fergus replies: "What the fuck were you doing here?" The unnamed Belfast bar is in direct opposition to the Metro. It is the place where Jody's colonial choices return to haunt him. It is at once the site of sexual deceit (his fling is adulterous) and colonial betrayal (Jody, the colonized other, is replicating imperial norms). Jody, who crosses over into the domain of the colonizer, primarily embodies the post-colonial's internalization of the pattern of the oppressor group. As former colonial subject, he returns to fight the colonizer's battle against another colonized grouping, on the last patch of Empire, Northern Ireland.

At this point it is necessary to enter a caveat: *The Crying Game* does not allow for an alternative (Unionist) viewpoint and as such is itself trapped within binary frameworks. At the same time, Jordan is careful to indict and conflate all groups who resort to armed violence. In *Angel* the paramilitary organization is perceived as Loyalist (one of its members is a Protestant), but police officer Bloom (a deliberate allusion to James Joyce's *Ulysses*) remarks that evil "is everywhere." Bloom is anxious to display his difference by attesting his Jewishness. That sectarianism is immanent is embodied in Fergus's reply: "Are you a Catholic Jew or a Protestant Jew?" Binaries replicate, but Jordan works to interrogate them. In *The Crying Game*, both colonized groupings are guilty of employing and replicating the stereotypes and the insults of the oppressor. Jody—in a Belfast accent—mimics the slur on his racial identity as he explains to Fergus how he is called a "nigger" and told to "go back to [his] banana-tree." Fergus, with a smile, attempts to dismiss the racist insult: "shouldn't take it personally." Significantly, Jody is never in uniform—or at least the only uniform that we see him in is that of his cricket gear, framed in pictures of him in his wallet, in Dil's apartment and in Fergus's dreams. If on one level, Jody usurps the Englishman's game and interrogates what constitutes Britishness, on another level, cricket remains a "toff's game" and Jody, despite his sartorial display, remains part of a disempowered underclass that joins the British army to avoid unemployment.

Ultimately, *The Crying Game* vacillates between the political paradigm of Otherness as subversion and the psychological condition of Otherness as regression. As a paradigm, carnivalesque is criticized as vigorously as it is endorsed. This is the essence of Jordan's cross-over: a radical discontent with the politics of identity, crossing over must be perpetual. A politics of subversion identifies with "subversion" as a category in a manner ultimately as arid as the original politics of colonialism which fostered the tragic response. *The Crying Game* takes Fanon's thesis and worries it to an unbearable extreme. If Otherness is not constantly finding its own others, what right has it to the claims made under its fierce sign? As such, the film constantly seeks to be its own other, galvanizing strategies for the ceaseless fracturing of its own identification with any definable position. It is a draining requirement.

The strategy is directly embodied in the carnivalesque space of the London Metro. This operates as the boundary site which draws in a diffuse and diverse range of Otherness. The marginalized converge on the centre, subverting the operatics of power. Or do they? Order is suspended in a confused and liberated carnival and otherness is celebrated. The Belfast and Monaghan carnivals are to varying degrees hermetic. The carnivalesque space of the Metro refuses binary frameworks and abjures definition and categorization. Or does it? All the deviant—sexually (Dil, Dave), racially (Dil, Jody, Fergus), politically (Fergus) converge in the Metro. That the Metro is a space of becoming, unveiling and transforming is evident. This is the place in which Dil can enact her femininity. This bar becomes the site of Otherness. It is Jody who initiates Fergus into the "Metro" carnival; in bequeathing him the wallet with Dil's photo he leaves him a passport and the possibility to change his identity. The picaro's quest is initiated which leads him to the boundaries of the world and beyond. It is here that Fergus is accepted as "Jimmy." If the crossing-over of names thwarts any hegemonic discourse, for the IRA his disappearance renders him a nobody, identity-less. The unnamed exists outside the discourse. For instance, in Catholic orthodoxy, the unbaptised or unnamed exists in a state of limbo or nothingness. Unnamed, the human is unidentifiable and entirely Other, but as "nobody" Fergus is also of use to the IRA operation in London and the discourse of law and order, embodied by the judge, is in danger of destruction by this nobody. Namelessness positions Fergus in a vacuum, as space waiting to be occupied. The exchange of names and the play on gendered names is more subversive. Col, Dil, Jody and even Jude interrogate the binaries. Yet the paradox remains: leaving behind a binarist politics of identity, carnivalesque subversion may secretly reinstall an identification with subversion. Poison is not just cure; cure may also be poison.

II. Needed a Tougher Look: Performing Gender

An obvious thematic preoccupation of *The Crying Game* is the crossing over of gender and sexuality. The fixity of the feminine is negated as the film has femininity shifting across the bodies of two female characters Jude and Dil (Jaye Davidson). Simone de Beauvoir's dictum that one becomes a woman is the crucial point that opens a gap between sexed body and gendered identity. This space allows for the redeployment of gender, as the link between gender and biological sex is loosened. Judith Butler develops this concept by claiming that "sex" is a gendered category already enmeshed within the cultural apparatus but, she argues, there is nothing that guarantees that the "'one' who becomes a woman is necessarily female" (8). Dil can be theorized in relation to the discrepancy between gender and sex. She seems to break down the binary dictating the feminine-woman/man-masculine distinction. Gender becomes an exchange mechanism as female gender identity becomes increasingly dislodged from its culturally determined counterpart—female biological sex. This is the point at which the film is most radical. Or is it?

Jude, as visual object and as passive/active political agent, is complicated. Her feminine display is not only established in the opening scenes of the film where she uses her femininity as a sexual decoy to entrap Jody, but is replayed in the love scene with Fergus outside the IRA hideout. She coquettishly flatters his vanity in claiming that she thought of him while she was seducing the soldier which replays the film's opening sequences, where she similarly seeks out Fergus's gaze at the carnival. She parallels, both physically and performatively, the bride in *Angel* whose wedding celebration at the dancehall is used as a decoy for an assassination. Later, Danny sleeps with her to ascertain information on her husband, reducing her to a mere pawn in a criminal and political conflict.

Even though Jude successfully uses her femininity and appears to have control of the image, she is reduced to a passive role by her male comrades. In the scene in the hideout she is told to make tea. She is ascribed to a position of complete powerlessness within the operation and is brutally silenced when she voices her opinion and pleads with Peter (Adrian Dunbar) not to allow Fergus to stay with Jody on the night preceding the latter's execution. Jude thus moves from tart to tea-maker. Her use within IRA masculine nationalism is limited as go-between, as mediator. The IRA colonial framework presented in this film fails to endorse any form of advanced or alternative feminism. Jude's racial and political identity is

inscribed and contained in her Aran jumper. Her desire for power is problematic and her violent display when she strikes Jody with the gun and
brings forth blood shows that she is out of control. She is the kind of
woman who is designated by Jody as "trouble," but at the same time Fergus
excuses her because "she can't help it." Her meaningless violence invokes
her nineteenth-century predecessors and parallels a colonial society where
"the word 'woman' often signified," as Kenny argues, "the passionate, the
disorderly, the violent and chaotic side of human nature, [where the] temporary assumption of women's identity by men was fraught with significance" (24). Misogyny is implicit in the practices of nineteenth-century
secret societies,[7] just as the misogynistic representation of Jude is endorsed
by the film.[8] At this point, *The Crying Game* is immersed in colonial ideology. The disused farmhouse that functions as the IRA hideout is located,
as the signpost demonstrates, near Newry, an IRA hinterland. The decaying
house is an implied symbol of a colonial past. The large conservatory in which
Jody is kept prisoner indicates this.[9] It is here that Jody and Fergus bond
as soldiers and as sportsmen, a bond inscribed in the re-enactment of a
hurling game—a game that was central to the Gaelic Athletic Association's
desire to politicize the Irish rural landscape in the late nineteenth-
century "giving it," as John Hutchinson notes, "a defiantly separatist democratic culture, and provided a reservoir of *manpower* [my emphasis] for
militant nationalists to subsequently tap" (161). The implications of the
statement reverberate in the late twentieth-century representation of the
politicized female. In such a masculinist environment, Jude is increasingly
alienated.

Thus, it provides a marked contrast to the Jude who appears in Fergus's
London lodgings. Her black business suit, black leather gloves and revolver
signify the assumption of a masculine-gender identification and coincides
with the cross over into London. Moreover, the film's historical moment is
apposite: It emerges after Thatcherism, and Jude seems to embody a bourgeois feminism that works within, rather than deconstructs the social and
political organization.[10] She has, by this stage, gained access to a position
of authority in the IRA hierarchy. This is indicated by her alleged presence
at a tribunal where she had pleaded clemency for Fergus. Significantly, she
makes an overt and aggressive pass at Fergus: "Fuck me, Fergus" (Jordan 49).

Her masculine gender identification empowers her political position. Jude's assumption of masculinity gives her greater managerial credibility in the mimic army's organization. London provides the backdrop for the unleashing of this masculinity. It is she who controls Fergus's London activities and coaches him in his rehearsal of the assassination attempt on the judge. On the contrary, Peter is more removed. She is calmer as he becomes increasingly hysterical. This is a direct contrast to Peter's earlier calm in the hut when Jude becomes hysterical after Jody's assault on her. Peter seems to increasingly lose control in London. This is made explicit in the car scene with Fergus and Jude. Jude is calmly driving while Peter turns and burns Fergus's hand with a cigarette while claiming that he is becoming emotional. However, the marking, representative of the stigmata, will take on an interesting association and forge a bond between both men's subsequent political actions. In a striking reversal of her earlier silencing by Peter in the hut, Jude is now in a position of equality with him. She gives him a direct order on the morning of the assassination: "Can't stay here, Peter— drive me around once more" (64). Her use of the imperative denotes parity—an equality that is newly acquired.

Jude's increasing empowerment in the film coincides with her developing access to the gun. In the early scenes in the film, Jude's body is fetishized. She represents the phallic symbol but cannot possess the power it implies, except through seduction. The males possess the guns, a dynamic encapsulated in the early scene in which the men point guns at the couple lying on the grass. If Jude entraps Jody with her body, power, however, must rest in her body. On the contrary, Jude has complete control of the gun in Fergus's London lodgings, a fact which corresponds with her development of a masculine gender identity. Markedly contrasted to this, Fergus is rendered increasingly powerless. It is noticeable that he does not respond to Jude's sexual advance, something perhaps not unrelated to her acquired masculine gender identification. In the climatic scene between the two females in Dil's flat, Fergus occupies an ultimate position of disempowerment: he is tied to the bed. Dil and Jude possess the guns in the final showdown, as they do battle for the sexual possession of his body. Fergus reclaims the gun after Dil shoots Jude. This is as much an attempt to reclaim his masculinity as it is a desire to protect Dil. The sacrificial nature of the act directly parallels Peter's blood sacrifice as he seizes the gun to kill the judge, bringing about his own annihilation. Similarly, Fergus takes the gun from Dil, takes responsibility for Jude's murder and serves time. Hence, the film replays the dynamics of masculinist nationalism, both British and Irish.[11] Otherness, whereby femininity crosses over into efficient masculinity, is also a swerve into gendered violence as much as politicized violence. The colonial paradigm of the feminine as weak is intensified rather than subverted in this film. Again, however, we are presented with a latent critique of Otherness as a paradigm. Masculinity as the Other of femininity emerges as *efficient*, an antidote to "feminine" hysteria. Yet this reliance serves only to replicate the patriarchal matrix of aboriginal colonial mentality. Tactical cure is once again ultimate poison.

Butler's theory that the compulsion to become a woman does not emanate from a female biological sex is directly *embodied* in Dil. As a transvestite, Dil represents the ultimate cross-over and negates the consolidation of any binary framework. Or does she? Jude psychologically crosses-over the gender divide in her psychic internalization of masculinity, but remains socially definable as a (heterosexual) woman. Dil, however, refuses conventional social definition. She is psychologically and culturally female. She crosses the gender divide, but also the sexual one by her transgression into homosexuality. But, Dil's femininity is culturally credible. Therefore, she underlines both the performativity and the construction of gender. Her credibility is endorsed by Fergus who reacts positively to this feminine display as he had similarly reacted to Jude's earlier femininity. On ascertaining Dil's biological sex, Fergus is still more attracted to her femininity than Jude's aggressive masculinity. In addition to her female clothing she internalizes feminine values, and a stereotypically female cultural value system— a system that is inscribed within a patriarchal ideology. She does not want to be perceived as a whore, when she affirms that she is "loud, but never cheap" (Jordan 34). She suffers from ennui, a condition which was attributed to Victorian females, and claims to be "tired and emotional" (Jordan 45). The mould of gender is reassembled and shattered at one and the same moment.

Dil and Jude both mimic an identity. Jude mimics a masculine norm of behaviour while Dil mimics a female identity. This mimicry exposes an excess; a performance which is so overdetermined as to be a vicious parody of the ideological prejudices of the onlooker. This relates particularly to the scene where she strips to reveal a male body. The exposition of the penis disrupts the pleasure of Fergus's gaze. His attempt to appropriate the female body is denied him. The deformed body displaces and subverts the looking process, and as Homi Bhabha comments, it throws the "gaze of the dis-criminated back upon the eye of power" ("Signs Taken for Wonders" 112). Again, it is appropriate to redeploy Bhabha's terms in a feminist context. Dil is "not quite/not [woman]" ("Of Mimicry and Men" 132). The fact that she is so close an equivalent threatens the ideological construction of gender. If gender identity can be so easily usurped, then it is so obviously constructed. Femininity, therefore, does not indicate a female essence, if an almost perfect imitation is so easily created. But *The Crying Game* daringly asks whether a subversive politics necessarily follows from this recognition.

The gender cross-over is consolidated through the process of making over. The makeover of the woman in this film serves further to underline the exchangeability of gender identities. Both females undergo a process of phys-ical makeover. Jude controls her own image as she dyes her hair brown. This is an attempt to defeminize herself. In an interchange with Fergus she explains her reasons thus: "I was sick of being blond. Needed a tougher look, if you know what I mean" (Jordan 49). Fergus cuts Dil's hair in an attempt to make her more masculine looking, and in order to protect her from Jude. Fergus similarly seeks to change Dil's gender-identity when he dresses her in the cricket clothing of her dead boyfriend. She subsequently externalizes a masculine gender identity. This is witnessed in the shot of a drunken Dil staggering across the courtyard with a whisky bottle. Dil, in keeping with her new image, becomes more aggressive and ties Fergus to the bed. She forces a declaration of love from him at gunpoint. Clothes are a crucial part of Dil's creation of a female gender identity, so it is hardly surprising that she demands to know what Jude wore to seduce Jody. It is also significant that she shoots Jude while dressed in cricket clothing. The awakening of a latent masculinity makes the acquirement of the gun and the killing credible. It is this masculinity that brings about the revenge and signals a return to order.[12]

The consequences of the shooting result in the annihilation of Jude and the reinscription of Fergus into patriarchal and nationalist discourse. British and Irish nationalism become, in Kearney's sense, each other's other. Peter's murder of the judge threatens British national identity just as his annihilation validates IRA separatism. Similarly, Fergus's imprisonment denotes that at last he is a good Irish nationalist, serving time for his political principles, just as this imprisonment, demonstrated in the glass wall separating him from Dil, allows him to return to binary political frameworks. The hermetic nature of the glass partition saves him from otherness, both sexual and political.

But Dil's crossover also offers the potential for a demobilization of order—a cultural indefinability. This comes to the fore in an interchange between Fergus and his employer, as Dil dressed in a mini-skirt, boots and sunglasses—crosses the cricket pitch to visit Fergus's building site. She is suitably framed in the glass window that Fergus is putting in place. It is apposite then that when he sees her approaching he lets go his grip of the frame and it crashes to the ground, smashing its glass. Dil is thereby appropriately framed in an opened casement, a position that invites and undermines Deveroux's sexist commentary:

Deveroux: It that his tart? Does Pat have a tart?
Fergus: She's not a tart.
Deveroux: No, of course not, she's a lady.
Fergus: She's not that either. (Jordan 44)

The interchange demonstrates that there are only two valid class and sexual positions for the female; tart or lady. Dil's non identity, her cultural indefinability defies the binaries—a point that is further exposed in an exchange between her and Fergus:

Dil: Can't help it, Jimmy. A girl has her feelings.
Fergus: Thing is, Dil, you're not a girl.
Dil: Details, baby, details. (Jordan 47)

In the London carnivalesque space, culture is open to multiple identities. It allows the prevalence of disorder and thwarts any form of a hegemonic discourse by its very plurality. Disorder is inscribed unquestionably, as Dil's gender or sexual behaviour fails to merit discussion. Col, the Lord of Misrule, presiding over the "Metro" carnival, is not disturbed by Dil's cultural abnormality.

Dil: When a girl runs out, like that, she generally wants to be followed.
Fergus: She's not a girl, Col.
Col: Whatever you say. (Jordan 52)

Alternatively, Janice Raymond argues that transgenderism has "encouraged a *style* rather than a *politics* of resistance, in which an expressive individualism has taken the place of collective political challenges to power. And in the process it has de-politicized gender by de-politicizing feminism. The new gender outlaw is the old gender conformist, only this time we have men conforming to femininity and women conforming to masculinity" (222). The operatics of sexual and gender disorder become the norm of behaviour. The Bakhtinian inflection of a temporary disorder bruises the paradigm of ubiquitous difference. Difference becomes a form of sameness when it is just as prevalent as the norms which bracket the carnivalesque space of the Metro. It is more a matter of respite, perhaps, than response.

Individual subjectivity is destablized throughout *The Crying Game* by Dil and Jody, in their crossing over or invasion of the Other's boundaries. Carnival licenses the grotesque body: "To Bakhtin, the grotesque is the expression in literature of the carnival spirit. It incorporates what are for him primary values: incompleteness, becoming, ambiguity, indefinability, non-canonicalism—indeed all that jolts us out of our normal expectations and epistemological complacency" (Clark and Holquist 312). Dil represents the grotesque body in all its ambivalence. She is in the process of becoming, existing on the boundary and shifting between two polarities. She renders the possibility of defining impotent. The urinating Jody similarly represents the grotesque body as he freely displays his bodily functions. Carnival celebrates this display of excess, licensing that which is normally controlled. The effect of Jody's micturition is to draw Fergus into a psychologically homosexual relationship.

Equally, carnivalesque laughter attains a deep resonance; as Stam observes, laughter becomes "a form of free and critical consciousness that mocks dogmatism and fanaticism" (87). It releases Fergus from socially imposed gender and political roles, enters him into the possibility of an alternative political and sexual visioning. Crucially, then it is Peter who cuts off this political possibility as he re-imposes order on Fergus and draws him back into the nationalist matrix. It is also shortly after this point, and by implication after a discussion with Peter, that Jude intervenes with her violent display, a premonition of her later attempt to eradicate Dil's aberrant sexuality. Ultimately, glass is again crucial. It is within the greenhouse space that political binaries can be re-enacted and destabilized while Jody, enthroned on his garden chair, presides over the potential misrule. It is significant then, that the greenhouse becomes the focus for destruction by the British army.

The Crying Game clearly embodies the idea of the cross-over in a many layered manner. It does not reflexively celebrate otherness. In political terms, while Fergus crosses over from the closed political system of colonialism into the polyvalent postcolonial society it is a fraught passage. Even though the film's closing sequence would seem to deny its ultimate achievement, nonetheless, this serves as an opening to the possibility of multiple voices and discourses. Northern Ireland is not the priority in this London Carnival. It is mediated as distant and removed. This is expressed in Dil's vague knowledge of Ireland. Even though her boyfriend is killed there, it never occurs to her that Jimmy could be Irish—she erroneously assumes that he is Scottish. Northern Ireland functions as one discourse in a multiple of political discourses which converge on the London Carnival. No political advance necessarily follows. Indeed, Dil's lack of any political conscience is troubling. Clothing in the film does not allow for a removal from established gendered or political roles. At best it interrogates them, at worst it merely leads back into a replication of gendered and socio-political categories.

In the historical anecdote that framed this paper, clothes decorate and obscure the larger cultural and political tensions. Jude's shifting gender identification does not allow her to achieve real political validity, just as the sartorial displays and violent disorders of her nineteenth-century counterparts did not achieve tangible political or social progress in the colonial framework. Dil's body becomes the focus where the political and the sexual converge. She becomes the postcolonial metaphor for the fusion of polarities, the convergence of divergences. The ultimate problems are, however, unresolved, indeed they are reinscribed in the confusion of an ongoing site of the carnivalesque. There is no getting away from the question of whether a flight into carnivalesque otherness is subversive or regressive, sustainable response or temporary respite, iconoclastic or conformist, a transformation or a replication of colonial ideologies. Jordan plays with all these categories and allows for the re-working and attempted destabilization of binaries. The carnivalesque otherness of the film is provocative, it occasions disquiet and allows for possibility. The film's achievement is that it denies any resolution of the dichotomies and contestations of the colonial, the political and the sexual, leaving *The Crying Game* sited on the tensest possible border.

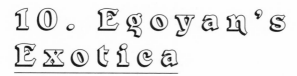

10. Egoyan's Exotica

The Uneasy Borders of Desire

—*Adam Knee*

As an Egyptian-born Canadian filmmaker of Armenian descent, Atom Egoyan has understandably shown a keen interest in issues of cultural and national identity—and the interplay among conflicting allegiances and identities—in much of his work. His most fully realized interrogation of the nature and potential flexibility of personal and national borders in an era of globalization is arguably the 1994 film *Exotica*, which quite appropriately opens at a border of sorts—an airport customs checkpoint. *Exotica*'s focus on "border matters" is particularly resonant and reflexive for a number of reasons—important among them the fact that firstly, it is a Canadian production, and secondly, it is the work of a director whose own national identity is quite complexly defined, who is himself living at a remove from a number of earlier homelands. Issues of national and cultural identity and self-determination have naturally often been a focus for Canadian mediamakers, not only because of the country's history of cultural heterogeneity, but also because of the overwhelming United States

159

influence in Canadian political and cultural realms generally and Canadian media production in particular. *Exotica*'s themes and imagery indeed bear comparison to those of other Canadian films (see Harcourt), but the work may also be understood as an exilic film, characteristic of what Hamid Naficy has identified as a transnational, "interstitial mode of production": Like many exilic films, it has come into being outside of the dominant industrial machinery of funding and production, and it is the work of people who are themselves astride or between existing national and social categories. Exilic cinema (of which Naficy cites Egoyan's work as a significant example) inevitably shows the traces of such distinct conditions of production in one form or another, and thus tends to take on a reflexive dimension, becoming "an allegory of exilic conditions, locations, and visions" ("Between Rocks" 132).

Exotica's concern with—and relation to—exilic and, perhaps more precisely, transnational and transcultural conditions and perspectives articulates itself most strongly through its offbeat drama about personal loss and desire and interpersonal exploitation; this drama, concerning a grieving widower's attachment to an "exotic" dancer and his chance acquaintance with a smuggler of exotic birds, is utilized in the service of a sophisticated allegory both about Canada's particular position in the current global context and about the nature of transnational relations more generally. *Exotica* thus extends Egoyan's ongoing project of refiguring notions of intercultural identity, and it does so, I would suggest, in a particularly provocative, complex, and nuanced fashion. Egoyan undermines simple binarisms of exploiter/exploited and dominator/dominated, offering instead the image of a world in which both interpersonal and international relations are often complex and contradictory, dictated by multiple, intertwined, often mutual desires. Yet while the film avoids positioning itself as a simple condemnation of cultural hegemony, it also takes pains to avoid the pitfalls of an uncritical celebration of transnationalism and hybridity—a celebration which can neglect "the powerfully oppressive socioeconomic forces underlying the changes" connected with globalization (Mitchell 220). In *Exotica*, the impulse to reach beyond borders of various kinds does indeed arise in part from a transnational capitalist logic with exploitative potential, but it also arises from very immediate, personal human needs—for love, for example, or for security. Egoyan's narrative, it shall be seen, in such ways manages to refigure and problematize the global in the most personal of terms.

The placement of the first postcredit sequence at an airport customs office immediately telegraphs the thematic importance of national borders (the edge of the country marks the edge of the narrative), and the scene itself engages many of the conceptual resonances of the border which will operate throughout the film. We see first of all a concern with the potential porosity of borders, as a young customs officer in training (hidden behind a two-way mirror, itself a semi-porous border) is taught what to look for when watching for smugglers. It is later revealed that the traveler (Thomas, played by Don McKellar) being observed in the scene is indeed involved in smuggling; unbeknownst to customs, he is bringing exotic birds' eggs into Canada.

This is the first of many of the film's quiet incursions of the "exotic," the foreign, the unusual into the local—witnessed on a larger scale, for example, in Thomas's overt business of running an exotic pet shop, or in the exotic fauna visible in the credit sequence which we later learn graces the film's eponymous strip club, as does an exotic stuffed bird. The highlighted heterogeneous national and racial make-up of the film's dramatis personae likewise suggests a thorough mixing of "local" (if a local can even be clearly defined in present-day Toronto) and foreign, of landed Anglo-Canadian, Jamaican, Armenian. As bell hooks describes it, "The culture we watch on Egoyan's screen, where difference is tolerated and border crossing more a norm than a contrived spectacle, has been created by immigration, mingling, and integration" ("*Exotica*"28–29). Sexual orientations prove as mixed as ethnicities, the film featuring much interaction between gay, straight, and bisexual characters. This sense of heterogeneity is suggested from that opening scene, where the young customs officer is black, while the older inspector coaching and observing him is white. The white main protagonist Francis's wife is black and his brother lives with an exotic bird over a Jamaican restaurant where the strains of rap and reggae music can always be heard. The proprietress of the club Exotica (Zoe, played by Egoyan's wife Arsinée Khanjian) is Armenian and the music selected by her floor manager and disc jockey Eric (Elias Koteas) is an eclectic international mix with a decidedly Middle-Eastern emphasis; when the music is not playing, exotic bird songs can be heard. As Francis (Bruce Greenwood) at one point observes apropos of their city, "It is, after all, a jungle out there."

The opening scene, like the film as a whole, alludes both to the foreign connotations of the exotic and to its associations with desire and the erotic as well. The black customs officer stares at the white traveler with intense interest—not only as the first object of his state-sanctioned investigatory gaze in training but also, we retroactively discover, as the object of the officer's sexual and emotional desire. And Thomas's own sexual preference, we learn over the course of the film, is evidently for men of color. The exotic/erotic connection is of course made manifest through the device of the exotic club Exotica, with its "exotic" dancers, as is a further association (also played out in the opening scene) between desire and voyeurism, sexuality and surveillance. Indeed, the club, like the customs station, is fitted out with two-way mirrors, which allow Zoe to keep a protective watch over her establishment and its dancers but which have also in the past allowed a rich customer to peek at the dancers and now afford Eric the opportunity to spy on the object of his desire, the dancer Christina (Mia Kirshner).[1] The gogo bar would at first appear the formal antithesis of the customs station, the one a brightly-lit and highly regulated national border, the other a dimly lit private establishment of questionable legitimacy—Canada's public face and its heart of darkness, as it were, the visible edge and the hidden center; yet what operates in both Canadian sites is an erotically charged and ambiguous fascination with the exotic. The exotic is intensely scrutinized on the one hand as a means of regulation (of border-crossings, of commerce, of behavior) and protection (of the nation, of the client/consumer—and also of the exotic itself), but it is also investigated as a function of voyeuristic desire. This fascination with the exotic—the desire to explore it—is ultimately revealed to have repercussions in many realms.

The rather unconventional narrative structure of *Exotica* highlights the pervasive theme of the investigation of the exotic or foreign or simply unfamiliar; a number of concurrent (though not, on the surface, causally connected) plot lines feature characters involved in the exploration of mysteries (and in particular the scrutiny of individuals) while, at an extra-diegetic level, spectators simultaneously try to solve the puzzle of the relationship between plot strands. As a tax auditor (another state-sanctioned spy), Francis pores over Thomas's questionable financial records; towards the end of the film he coerces Thomas to spy on Christina on his behalf (wearing a wire) because he has been ejected from the club. A jealous Eric spies on both Christina and Francis during their interactions at the club, in an effort to discern the nature of their intense relationship (and also to hinder it), while Zoe too spies on the young dancer and also keeps a watchful eye on Eric because of his increasingly erratic behavior. The customs officer goes out of his way to pursue what he finds so intriguing about Thomas. On a broader scale, the customers at the Exotica are lured with the promise that for five dollars a young dancer will "show you the mysteries of her world." And in a more conventional investigatory plot line (which, rather perversely, is relayed to us only retrospectively through obscure flashbacks and quick bits of dialogue), police investigate Francis in their unsuccessful search for the murderer of his daughter. While characters pursue their investigations, spectators, too, must work to piece clues together, to understand how and if the characters have significant plot relationships to one another. One of the first crossings of narrative lines is rather coyly presented as a literal crossing of ostensibly unrelated characters' paths, so that viewers are initially invited to suspect that the plot interconnections will be random: Thomas's taxi from the airport stops to drop off a passenger in downtown Toronto, and the camera waits as the taxi leaves, then follows a woman (whom we later learn is Christina) walking down the street and continues with her as she enters Exotica for her shift.

It is in fact eventually revealed that all of the characters are related in complex and sometimes profound and intimate ways, but these revelations only arrive gradually and often run counter to initial appearances. When we see Francis, whom we know to be a patron of Exotica (where he watches Christina dance in a schoolgirl's uniform), offering a teenage girl money in the front seat of his car and asking if she will be "available next Thursday," we are invited to assume (wrongly) that he is frequenting an underage prostitute. We are similarly coaxed into making misassumptions about the relationships of most of the main characters and are given minimal clues as to the narrative placement of a series of vignettes that punctuate the film and that feature Christina and Eric walking through a field. Characters

Eric (Elias Koteas) and Christina (Mia Kirshner) converse in one of Exotica's *idyllic field sequences. Courtesy of Jerry Ohlinger's Movie Materials Store.*

likewise misread the clues they are given in their various investigations. In that opening scene again, customs officers fail to "read" Thomas as a smuggler. Moments later Thomas himself (and we as well) begins to misread a man who has offered to share a cab ride to the city as someone who may be interested in more than a cab ride, especially when he asks Thomas if he is interested in ballet, but again Egoyan reveals his mischievousness: When the man hands Thomas some ballet tickets and Thomas says, "Oh, you mean, for the ride," the man curtly responds, "What did you think I meant?" These and similar false cues and clues keep reminding characters and spectators alike of the inadequacy of surface appearances to reveal truths. The truths about characters' identities and relationships which are ultimately so central to *Exotica* are only laid bare through lengthier contemplation and deeper intimacy with the characters—a fact which has led a number of commentators, as well as Egoyan himself, to note parallels between the film's formal structure and that of a striptease (see, for example, Coates 22, Romney, Klawans).

These identities and relationships are so hard to initially read, we come to realize, not only because they are bound up with a highly complex and by nature invisible past, but also because they are themselves convoluted and ambiguous. Francis's true relationship with the girl in the car, Tracey (Sarah Polley), will serve as an illustrative example. We learn that Tracey is not a prostitute, but is getting paid to stay at Francis's house and practice her flute while he is out. His need for this odd, if evidently benign, service, we discover, is related to his need to come to terms with the murder of his daughter (for whom he used to hire a babysitter) and the loss of his wife. Tracey's wheelchair-bound father (Harold, played by Victor Garber) seems to allow this arrangement in part out of a sense of guilt or obligation. This impression is eventually confirmed when it is revealed that he is in fact Francis's brother and had been having a secret affair with his wife, and that moreover his own crippling and his sister-in-law's death came as a result of an automobile accident when the two were driving together. This complex web of shared, intertwined histories extends laterally to other characters as well. We learn, for example, that Francis formerly knew Christina as his daughter's babysitter, and that Christina and Eric met not at Exotica, but during the search for Francis's daughter when she was reported missing—a search gradually revealed through the aforementioned field sequences.

As Byzantine as these various plot complications may sound (and the above account is only a sampling), *Exotica* is structured to highlight very distinct and significant parallels among its various character relationships. One such noticeable parallel among the relationships is that they tend to be at once emotional and contractual, familial and pecuniary—and often have a sexual valence as well. For example, the relationship between Francis and Tracey is, as noted, literally familial, but the comportment between the two is quite ambiguous and can possibly be read as that between intimate friends or lovers; at the same time their relationship is based in part on an economic arrangement, the hiring of Tracey to deliver her unusual services. In the case of Francis and Christina as well, while the relationship at first appears to be sexual and financial (she table-dances for him for pay), the film gradually reveals the connection between them to be more profoundly emotional and indeed familial in nature, its lurid context notwithstanding: Christina (as schoolgirl-cum-lap-dancer) very explicitly

Christina (Mia Kirshner) and Francis (Bruce Greenwood) play out their psychodrama in the Exotica nightclub. Courtesy of Jerry Ohlinger's Movie Materials Store.

serves as a substitute for Francis's lost daughter, while Francis just as explicitly serves as a father figure for the (as it turns out) emotionally needy young woman, giving her psychic support and protection. And while Francis's relationship to Thomas is initially only that of tax auditor, whom Thomas helps out under duress (he spies for him in exchange for having his illegal operations not reported), it eventually becomes an intimate friendship as well (Thomas ultimately helps out of personal loyalty).

A similar blurring of the borders between different kinds of relationships is evident among the people working at the club Exotica. Zoe's relationship with her employees, like that of Francis with Christina, is one that confusingly mixes exploitation and protection, as she has young women display themselves for money, but also looks after them. With Christina, the situation is more complex still, as Zoe is not only her employer but evidently her lover as well, and bears an at times motherly and protective comportment towards the young dancer. Eric's relationship to the two women is likewise multivalent. He is Zoe's employee and friend—and also the father of the child she is carrying, though the pregnancy is the result of a formal contractual arrangement between the two of them rather than a marriage; at the same time, however, it is also evident that Zoe and Eric have strong emotional and sexual feelings for one another, which threaten the supposed dispassionateness of their business agreement. In a similar vein, as a hands-on supervisor at the club Eric is technically Christina's boss and paid protector, but as the young woman's former lover and intimate friend he watches over her jealously and longingly, with anything but a professional disposition. As the foregoing should suggest, the blurring between kinds of relationships also extends here to the blurring between sexualities: Christina is initially linked with heterosexuality through her metier and retroactively through her revealed relationship with Eric, but she also appears to develop a sexual relationship with Zoe. Zoe, on the other hand, shows a strong erotic interest in Christina in a number of scenes—but in one scene also behaves as though sexually interested in Eric. And Thomas, though plainly presented as gay throughout the film, ends the film by touching Christina's thigh (at the behest of Francis) as she dances for him.

The ambiguity and multivalence of all the film's relationships appear largely a function of the complex and contradictory nature of the characters' desires—profound, multiple drives which are presented as evidently constitutive of human nature; as bell hooks notes, desire is here "the thread that connects, the common experience" for all ("*Exotica*" 29). There are, for example, the strong sexual drives—heterosexual and/or homosexual—exhibited by most characters, drives which in turn are linked, as noted earlier, with a fascination with the exotic. Characters likewise exhibit strong desires to create or retain familial connections—as witnessed in Francis and Christina's evidently therapeutic father/daughter substitutions, in Zoe's machinations to be certain she has a child of her own, and in Zoe's and Thomas's similar desires to continue businesses left to them by their families. Even Thomas's smuggling activity becomes associated with a procreative urge, as we witness him caringly remove the exotic bird eggs he has smuggled in around his waist (read womb) and later hear the customs officer inquire, "Shouldn't you be sitting on them or something?" Eric and Christina readily accept when, on separate occasions, Zoe offers each of them the opportunity to touch her pregnancy-swollen belly; and Francis

Christina (Mia Kirshner) performs for patrons of the Exotica nightclub. Courtesy of Jerry Ohlinger's Movie Materials Store.

Christina (Mia Kirshner) shares an intimate moment with her Exotica employer Zoe (Arsinée Khanjian). Courtesy of Jerry Ohlinger's Movie Materials Store.

too seems drawn to the womb, in that it is interestingly Christina's mid-section he chooses to reach for—rather than a more conventionally ero-ticized part of her body—when he breaks the club's no-touching rule. Another set of ubiquitous impulses in the film are material drives, as the dramatis personae are all observed attending to financial needs, to the eco-nomic requirements for their well-being, which call for varying degrees of willingness to have oneself exploited—as dancer or bouncer, house-sitter or baby-sitter, sperm donor or egg smuggler, state official or spy. These var-ious desires themselves have their overlaps, are not completely separable from one another: In *Exotica*, we see sexual urges and fascination with the exotic merging with procreative, familial, and emotional drives and also helping to fulfill characters' financial needs.

Indeed, financial exchange and other kinds of exchange are an ongoing part of human existence as presented in the film—a fact concretized in the numerous shots of characters (usually men) handing money to other char-acters. And such exchange, the film reminds us, is a two-way affair: rela-tionships here fulfill a range of varying and shifting needs for all parties involved and are therefore subject to on-going negotiation, to a process of give and take which is often manifested in quite literal ways. For example, in two paralleled gestures, we see Christina hesitate when being offered money for her services, in one instance by Thomas and in another by Francis, because of an uncertainty at the given moment over whether to understand the man as a client, friend, or "relative." When Thomas seeks out young men at ballet concerts with the offer of a supposedly spare ticket, there is likewise a negotiation predicated upon the ambiguity of roles: Typically, Thomas sells the potential "pick-up" the ticket, then later insists upon returning the money, saying he doesn't feel right about it, in response to which the new acquaintance relents, but asks if Thomas will accept a drink in return. One young man's response to the ploy nicely sums up the film's take on human relationships: "No one gives anything away." Thus, when Thomas later picks up and brings home a young man who is, unbe-knownst to him, the customs officer who monitored his entry into Canada, he finds he has had to give something up for the man's company: the exotic bird eggs, which the officer sneaks out with in the morning. Further nego-tiations ensue, however, as the officer offers their return in exchange for more time with Thomas, who in turn must negotiate for a new delivery date with his customer. Thomas is likewise heard in the process of renegotiations with a contractor who has botched a wallpaper removal job and with Francis, who is willing to set aside the findings of his audit in return for the favor of spying on Christina, the auditor explaining, "You do this for me, I'll do this for you." It is little wonder that Thomas later extolls the utility of negotiating skills when chatting with the dancer.

While relationships are here depicted as involving a two-way process of negotiation and exchange, the film also makes clear that power tends to be unevenly distributed in these relationships, that one party tends to be more vulnerable and less privileged than the other: As Christina points out to Zoe, "Not all of us have the luxury of deciding what to do with our lives." Or, in the terms of one of the film's motifs, those on the see-through side of the two-way mirror have the advantage over those on the reflecting side. We are all situated differently by circumstance, by individual history, by culture, and this affects who we are, how we enter into relationships, and how much power we have in these relationships. Francis highlights a similar notion when explaining Harold's evident tenseness around him to Tracey: "As you get older, you become aware that the people you meet, and the person you are, are carrying around a certain amount of baggage."[2] Harold's "baggage," the permanent mark of the past in his identity, is given concrete manifestation in the wheelchair he is bound to as a repercussion of the car accident: He is formed and disabled by his history.

This persistence of the past is also suggested through the narrative structure of the film, which not only interweaves various present-day plot lines, as noted, but also brings numerous flashbacks, often not clearly marked as such, into its fabric; the film is thus able to highlight not only the complex interrelations among different lives, but also the direct relation between history and the present. That various segments of one particular chronologically earlier plot sequence—that involving the search for the daughter's body—are repeatedly returned to throughout the film suggests its distinct resonance for all of the characters in the film; it is a highly charged narrative nexus point which yields the key relationships and trajectories of the film—the site which brings together Christina, Eric, and Francis with the loss of Francis's daughter. Significant as well is the fact that the event relayed in that set of flashbacks is in large measure a family trauma, a loss of family bonds: family as an historical entity—indeed as that which articulates and enforces one's relationship to history—is something strongly suggested throughout the film. People become who they are in large measure because of past familial experiences, as well as because of familial inheritances, the latter emphasized in Zoe's and Thomas's discussions about their inherited businesses, as well as in Thomas's separate comments that he has inherited his hair patterns from his mother, his gun from his father. Even the customs officer is presented as having "inherited" his profession from a parental figure—the inspector who watches over him carefully and coaches him in the art of surveillance, passing his technique down to a new generation

The fact that the flashbacks of the search in the field occur repeatedly and steadily is also significant, further implying an entrapment in the past if not a compulsion to reenact it, and this is suggested as well in the repetition of a video image, taped by Francis, of his wife and daughter at a piano in their home. The repetition of both of these narrative moments (and the repeated pauses within the video playback) moreover suggests not only a dwelling upon the past but, as can be seen in their subject matter, a sense of familial loss or exile, a desire to retrieve that which has been permanently lost—in this instance through traumatic deaths. This sense of loss is also evoked through the distinctly dreamlike, idyllic feel of the field sequences, generally introduced by soft, flowing music and characterized by simple, uncluttered compositions of human figures within the natural landscape; the field becomes a primal Eden, in which Eric and Christina's intercourse may be untroubled only up until the Fall—the discovery of the child's corpse, articulating the Original Sin of the violation of the exotic and forever changing the protagonists' lives.[3] The wife's final gesture in the video sequence, one of the very few images we have of her, concordantly projects a sense of the unattainable, as she playfully puts her hand up to the camera to keep it at arm's distance; the gesture becomes more resonant with retrospective knowledge of the wife's infidelity and death.

The relatively brief use of video here continues a function more explicitly and extensively served by the technology in some of Egoyan's earlier work, most notably *Family Viewing* (1987). In that film a young man tries to reclaim his past—in particular his ties to his maternal forebears and his ethnic (non-Canadian) heritage—by taking possession of family videos from his childhood, while his father attempts to escape this past by recording over the videos. In *Exotica*, the physical act of playing the tape is itself not clearly situated in narrative terms, but its repeated (and repeatedly paused) imagery takes on significance as part of the film's larger flashback structure, its compulsive infusion of the present with the past; and again, the past being sought is in particular a familial history, one with connections to a presently lost or displaced ethnic identity. The sense of compulsive repetition as a response to loss is also invoked by the almost ritualistic manner in which various characters repeat certain narrative actions: We see Francis following a regular ritual of having Tracey watch after his empty house, then driving back and chatting with her before giving her money (a ritual which repeats actions we later learn have been performed at an earlier point in his life, when he drove Christina home after her babysitting), and we also watch him in a compulsive pattern of visiting the Exotica. Christina also repeats her actions—always performing the same choreography on stage (presented with the same Leonard Cohen song and in paralleled craning and tracking shots), before shifting her attentions to repeating a father/daughter psychodrama of sorts—in the guise of a lap dance—with Francis. Thomas too develops a ritual (one paralleled with Francis's Exotica visits through a cross-cut), of arriving at a ballet performance with an extra ticket and using it as a means of meeting a young, usually non-white man.[4] Thomas and Zoe, in continuing the enterprises of their respective forebears, are involved in another kind of reenactment—one which again reclaims connections to a familial history; Zoe even wears her mother's dresses and wigs while on the job, working from an office adorned with photographs from the time of her mother's reign. And Harold's choice of lodging in a Jamaican quarter, his outfitting in a Bob Marley t-shirt, suggests his own need to return to the lost object of his perversely quasi-familial desire, his brother's deceased dark-skinned wife.

While *Exotica* focuses heavily on the losses and sufferings of its white male characters (particularly Francis), on how their "baggage" affects their present lives, the film also allows us to remember that those who tend to suffer most profoundly and consistently as a function of the past are in fact not white males. The most severe repercussions of history, resulting in a lesser status in present-day relationships, are clearly suffered by those in the categories of the "exotic," the non-white, the non-Canadian, the displaced, the feminine, the young, the financially needy, contrasted in *Exotica* with the financially more secure Anglo-Canadian adult male. Those in these groups are clearly those more likely to lack what Christina describes as the luxury of choice, more likely to be the vulnerable parties in relationships of power, by virtue of shared or paralleled historical circumstance. The past defines us all, but the shared historical specificity of certain groups involves more profound trauma than that of others—the trauma of forced exile and enslavement for example, or that of sexual exploitation, or of displacement from family and home for whatever reason. That said, Egoyan does in fact portray specific instances where white males are vulnerable or exploited, but these remain exceptions (albeit significant ones): For example, as a contracted birth father, Eric does in effect sell his body, but so do the numerous female dancers at the Exotica. And it is no coincidence that the film's most notably dark-skinned woman and her daughter are the two characters who have not managed to survive, always kept at arm's length from both the film's other characters and its spectators, for the most part absent except in videos and photographs and memories, distanced and exoticized by history, always already exiled to the past, as we from them.

The way more vulnerable parties are protected in their interactions with others in *Exotica* is through the quasi-contractual agreements which exist within these relationships—Francis and Christina's understanding that their relationship is about mutual emotional support (rather than sexual gratification) for example or, more overtly, the Exotica patrons' understanding that they may watch the table dancers but not touch them. It is when such understandings are violated that the earlier-noted protection-exploitation balance may get pushed over into exploitation. The most explicitly played out instance of this violation is when Francis on one occasion breaks the "rules" of his understanding with Christina. This happens when a jealous Eric, in effect breaking his own contract to keep order in the club, coaxes Francis into touching Christina in violation of both club rules and the couple's personal agreements; as Christina later explains to Thomas, what upsets her so much about the incident is that Francis violates "his role," that is, "what he's supposed to do for me"—to serve as father-figure and protector. The violation of such mutual understandings is evident elsewhere in the film as well—for example, in the customs officer's theft of Thomas's eggs while partaking of his hospitality, in Francis's betrayal by his wife and brother, in Eric's betrayal of Christina by fathering Zoe's child, or, at the greatest extreme, in the disregard of social contract that permits the murder of Francis's unprotected daughter.

Family relationships once again loom significantly here, as not only a source of personal gratification and identity for many of the characters, but a source of protection; however, family also appears a double-edged sword, as it can be a source of severe exploitation when familial understandings or arrangements are violated—as in Harold's coveting of his brother's wife or the incestuality implied in Francis's various father/daughter relationships or the lack of love and appreciation we learn, at the film's very close, that Christina has suffered from at home. In the closing scene Francis has just driven a young Christina to her house after a babysitting session and he chats with her before seeing her off (the scenario later to be repeated with Tracey substituting for a lost younger Christina, as Christina substitutes for a lost daughter). Christina alludes to the lack of love she feels at home (expressing envy over how Francis speaks of his daughter), and the camera stays at the car's vantage point as we watch her slowly walk away toward her house and then, in the distance, disappear inside. The shot takes longer than would be ordinarily expected for the modicum of narrative information given, and the camera remains for a long moment on the tidy lawn and housefront in an austere, formally composed, symmetrical image. We are thus given to note the ominousness of the shot, to dwell on the significance of this housefront we haven't seen before—and, more importantly, to ponder the lack of love we've just learned this housefront hides, indeed to wonder if, given Christina's later "choice" of profession, she isn't the victim of incestual abuse which will shape her future life and inform all her future relationships. Incest is indeed a central trope in *Exotica*—a figure through which is articulated themes of the blurring of borders between kinds of relationships/desires, themes of exploitation, and the theme of continuing fallout from traumatic past events.

Christina's all-too-perfect housefront, the film's final image, recalls similar images of the protagonist's home—and of advertisements for homes—in Egoyan's *The Adjuster* (1991). In that film the austerity of the dwelling—quite literally a "model home," for an aborted housing development—can be plainly seen as a correlative of the protagonist's emotional shortcomings: The house is an empty shell without the warmth of genuine family ties, of personal and community history.[5] The house takes on still darker tones in *Exotica*. Family and, in a very literal sense, home are posited as potential hazards here, as structures which may provide protection but may also foster and hide abuse. After opening on a porous barrier, the film closes on a barrier which hides everything behind it, a structure which calls out for protective surveillance. The closing image bespeaks the dangers of insularity, the need for interconnections with the outside. The qualified national border of the film's opening would now appear quite positive in comparison, a place allowing movement, interchange, potential cross-fertilization. Family, home, and, by implication, nation, this would imply, can become arduous, oppressive, dangerous as ossified entities; they must be fluid and open to outside influences, subject to the kinds of negotiation and exchange which (as the film dramatizes throughout) are the very stuff of human nature, the product of human desire. Indeed the perspective that certain family arrangements (even those rooted in biological and/or ethnic ties) may require restructuring if they are oppressive or inappropriate to individuals' needs is one which Egoyan has articulated repeatedly in interviews (Naficy, "Accented Style" 193–94; Pevere 25–26).

Once again, given the border concerns of the film, its discourses about the duality of protection and exploitation and the dangers of insularity in family and other relationships readily invite application to wider issues of nation in an era of globalization, and, given the geographical specificity of the film, to Canada in particular. Clearly, the concern over the dangers of exploiting the weaker party in a complex relationship can be directly applied to the profoundly intertwined security, trade, cultural, and diplomatic relationships between Canada and its notoriously persuasive neighbor to the south—but at the same time the film's nuanced view of cross-border relationships would appear to reject the unqualified dominator/dominated, oppressor/oppressed binarism which emerges within many critiques of globalized culture and economy. As articulated here, global relationships involve more complex, multi-directional interactions rather than a unidirectional flow of influence; it is the kind of perspective that suggests economic and cultural forces operate within "a decentred network, in which the patterns of distribution of power are shifting and, indeed, in which power is in some ways diffused rather than concentrated" (Tomlinson 185).

Egoyan begins to imply such a shift in historical relations of power through a range of images/instances which appear to reverse former schemes, former structural positionings (in gendered/racial/ethnic terms). For example, at the Exotica, the boss for whom young women strip and who takes sexual advantage of two of her employees is a woman and an Armenian immigrant, while the two employees mentioned are white Canadians. In the affair between Harold and his sister-in-law, it is the black woman who appears to be financially more well off. In the romantic liaison between Thomas and the customs officer, it is the black man who works for the law, the white man who is the criminal. The black man even describes Thomas in terms which recall negative stereotypes applied to blacks: He says that touching Thomas's hairy chest is "like petting a gorilla." (Still another sort of reversal is suggested when Thomas indicates that this hair is inherited not from his father, but from his mother.)

How relational shifts or inversions might start to come about, the film suggests, is through the kinds of two-way negotiations dramatized throughout, negotiations which, if they achieve the right kind of quasi-contractual understanding, may help redress historical injustices, may foster the healing or bracketing of past traumas and reconfigure exploitative power relationships. (And once more, while these negotiations are here dramatized on an interpersonal level, the film's allusions to a transborder context suggest their applicability to international relationships as well: In Egoyan's heterogeneous world, the personal is global.) Such a negotiation process occurs quite clearly in the case of Tracey's rejection of her use as a tool in Francis's emotional therapy—a rejection which, significantly, yields a revision of her family relationships. Tracey explicitly voices her impatience in being involved with the heavy emotional baggage and past psychic wounds of her father and uncle, asking, "What has any of this got to do with me?" and by the end of the film she manages to secure a willing, respectful agreement from the men to end their practice of hiring her to "housesit" for Francis. In a different context, Thomas, too, enters into a new agreement/relationship with Francis so that he can "wipe the slate clean," as the auditor describes it, and continue without the difficulties imposed by his history.

A need for healing or moving beyond past injury or difficulty in order to foster future growth is articulated a number of times in the film—in Francis's therapeutic sessions with Christina, for example, or in Christina's criticism of Zoe for putting her future in her mother's past business: "So you feel better about adopting her options rather than creating your own?" the dancer pointedly asks her boss. Eric too speaks of the need for imposing a new order in his life in order to make something of himself, to improve his future, explaining to Christina on their first meeting that "I just need to find a structure. . . . My days just slip by." The final scenes at the Exotica also suggest the importance of healing the past and taking control of the present in order to secure the future: When Thomas touches Christina's thigh (as part of an elaborate scheme to lure Eric outside of the club so a vengeful Francis can shoot him), she picks up the man's hand, holds it and makes eye contact with him for a moment, returns the hand and smiles, then continues dancing; it is she who determines the acceptable parameters of their relationship, managing both to avoid a hostile confrontation (by remaining in communication with Thomas) and to avoid inappropriate body contact. Outside the club, meanwhile, Eric has decided to approach an armed Francis, telling him it was he who found his little girl, revealing his own profound connection to Francis's historical trauma, and the two men spontaneously embrace—a healing embrace intercut with moments from the original trauma, the discovery of the daughter's body in a schoolgirl's uniform, at which Eric likewise embraced Christina.

The skillful editing of this emotionally charged sequence clearly suggests the subterranean bond among all the main characters, a bond with its roots in a single directly or indirectly shared past moment, a trauma which here is partially healed through human touch, through communication rather than violence and through an acknowledgment rather than a disavowal of a common painful history; as bell hooks describes it, the embrace constitutes a "moment of redemption and reconciliation" ("*Exotica*" 31).[6] There is indeed a striking sense of catharsis here—for the characters as well as the spectators—but it is also clear that the catharsis cannot be total, as the original tragedy cannot be reversed: The death of the schoolgirl—the violation of the young, the female, the "exotic," the issue and emblem of interracial love—cannot be erased. The white protagonists remain for now exiled from that interracial connection, linked by their guilt over exotica unprotected, their sense of culpability in the film's Original Sin. Egoyan refuses to close with the scene of white male embrace, to allow resolution to arise unproblematically across the interpolated image of the mixed-race child's body in the field. Rather, the film moves to a final sequence which emphasizes an ongoing sense of loss, pain, and vulnerability. The scene of reconciliation is followed by a flashback to the only scene where we see Francis's wife and daughter "live," as it were—the scene of Francis video-taping them at the piano just before babysitter Christina's arrival—followed in turn by the aforementioned closing scene of him seeing Christina to her ominous home.

While the film thus appears to end on a downbeat note, with its intimations of insularity and abuse, hope nevertheless does seem to lie in the profound desire evidenced throughout the film for what has been lost, in the drive to overcome that particular exile, to retrieve that transborder, transracial connection. The exile articulated here is not from an ethnic past—as indeed such a past is something Egoyan's films have consistently worked to problematize. In *Next of Kin* (1984), for example, a WASP gains a new sense of belonging by adopting a fictive ethnic past, by joining a family (not biologically his) with spurious claims he is their missing son. In *Family Viewing*, where the protagonist surprisingly manages to retrieve connections to his Armenian mother and grandmother in contemporary Toronto, the reclaimed heritage may not technically be quite as spurious—but it is just as clearly part of a mediated, reconfigured past, reconstructed from videos and memories and repositioned in a new time and space. In *Exotica*, however, the protagonist's sense of loss and exile remains at the film's close (appropriately a flashback), and it is an exile not from a lost heritage or homeland, not from a biological or cultural lineage, but from the possibility of a new social formation, from the beginnings of new transcultural, transracial family configurations; what has been lost here is not what once was so much as what might have been, not an idealized past so much as a possible future. Egoyan's narrative of loss may be structured around the vulnerability of the exotic in an inhospitable climate—but it paradoxically still offers hope in the generative (and regenerative) potential of transborder desire. As Thomas says of the exotics in his shop, "They're a lot hardier than you think."

11. Mediating Worlds/ Migrating Identities

Representing Home, Diaspora and Identity in Recent Asian American and Asian Canadian Women's Films

—Eva Rueschmann

In her ground-breaking 1990 book *Between Worlds: Women Writers of Chinese Ancestry*, Asian American literary scholar Amy Ling opened up the discussion of the ambivalent relationship between home, belonging and identity for the Asian diasporic subject in literature. Using spatial metaphors for Chinese American bicultural identity, Ling attempted to capture Asian emigrants' complex mediation between different cultures, their condition of existing between two worlds. She writes:

The very condition [of the between-world] carries both negative and positive charges. On the one hand, being between worlds can be interpreted to mean occupying the space or gulf between two banks; one is thus in a

180

space of suspension, accepted by neither side and therefore truly belonging nowhere . . . On the other hand, viewed from a different perspective, being between worlds may be considered as having footholds on both banks and therefore belonging to two worlds at once. One does not have less; one has more . . . the person between worlds is in the indispensable position of being a bridge. (177)

During the 1990s the critical and theoretical examination of diaspora, immigration and transnationalism has grown exponentially in the wake of postmodernist and postcolonial critiques of universalized Eurocentric regimes of truth, history and power. Cultural theorists and postcolonial critics such as Edward Said, Homi Bhabha, Salman Rushdie, Arjun Appadurai, Gloria Anzaldúa, Avtar Brah and Chandra Talpade Mohanty, to name but a few, have articulated a more multifaceted and complex conception of culture and identity as not bounded and fixed, but instead, as Salman Rushdie has succinctly stated, as "always plural and partial" (15). More specifically, Rushdie has written of a migrant sensibility at work in contemporary world literature and cinema whose development he believes to be "one of the central themes of this century of displaced persons" (124). The effect of mass migrations in the twentieth century has been for Rushdie the creation of people "who root themselves in ideas rather than places, in memories as much as material things . . . people in whose deepest selves strange fusions occur, unprecedented unions between what they were and where they find themselves" (124–25).

Just as Salman Rushdie and other post-colonial writers, artists and film-makers have sought to represent a migrant sensibility through new, hybrid forms of representation that combine fact and fiction, history and fabulation, cultural studies scholars today define global cultures by contradiction, syncretism and movement even though, to be sure, exile and migration reach far back into human history and have for centuries created culturally hybrid spaces.[1] This concern with a more globalized, intercultural account of migration history, characterized in cinema studies by Ella Shohat's and Robert Stam's call for studying "ethnicities-in-relation," has also in recent years been taken up by Asian American cultural theorists such as Lisa Lowe and film scholars such as Jun Xing.[2] Peter Feng has commented on the challenges of defining an Asian American cinema as a single hyphenated identity in light of diverse cultures, languages and ethnicities among Asian immigrants and their different historical and political relationships with each other and Western cultures (32–35). These critics each in their own way argue for a more complex, global conception of Asian American identities and history beyond the familiar fixed bipolar dichotomies of "native" and "other." According to Jun Xing, "Migration of Asians as cheap labor, the displacement of refugees, and the forced exile of large groups have developed the different Asian diasporas around the world. New cultural spaces, borderlands, or crossing began to emerge and to challenge any essentialized notion of identity and subjectivity. Asianness is increasingly viewed as a historical and cultural formation shaped in complex, related, and multiple ways through its interaction with numerous and diverse communities" (24).

While this view of ethnicity and diaspora presents identities as complex, in flux and performed rather than rooted in essential conceptions of culture, I contend that contemporary Asian diasporan films are valuably discussed as a group of works that re-imagine and recreate the particular history of Asian migration and experience of discrimination and exclusion in the twentieth century. Asian diasporan women directors specifically address in their films orientalist stereotypes of Asian women, the vicissitudes of patriarchal family structures, their invisibility in both domestic and public spheres, and the long-lasting effects of truncated families through immigration laws. In this essay I focus in detail on three films made in the mid-1990s by Asian American and Asian Canadian women directors that articulate different strategies of representing this diasporic condition and also provide a gendered perspective on the search for home and identity on screen: Hawaiian Kayo Hatta's historically inspired fiction film, *Picture Bride* (1995), Ruth Ozeki Lounsbury's auto-ethnography, *Halving the Bones* (1995), about her Japanese family history on her mother's side, and Chinese Canadian filmmaker Mina Shum's feature debut, *Double Happiness* (1995). These recent films join a growing and significant corpus of films made by Asian American and Asian Canadian women directors, including feature films, documentaries, experimental shorts and auto-ethnographies such as Lise Yasui's *The Family Gathering* (1988), Janice Tanaka's *Memories from the Department of Amnesia* (1991), Helen Lee's *Sally's Beauty Spot*, Shu Lea Cheang's *Color Schemes* (1989), Trinh T. Minh-ha's *Surname Viet Given Name*

Nam (1989), Rea Tajiri's *History and Memory: For Akiko and Takashige* (1991), and more recently Renee Tajima-Peña's *My America, or Honk if You Love Buddha* (1997), among others.[3]

Because of a long history in the United States and Canada of exclusionary laws barring Asian immigrants from citizenship and land ownership, the dislocation and incarceration of Japanese Americans in internment camps during World War II, and the invisibility or stereotyping of Asian Americans as either unassimilable aliens or model minorities, the question of home and belonging has historically been a particularly vexed one for Asian Americans and is doubly so for immigrant women who have had to negotiate their relationship to different cultural definitions of female roles and the gendered meanings of home. The three films I examine here focus on the different ways in which Asian American women directors have reimagined and reinterpreted the sedimented history of Asian migration through a narrative intertwining of history and memory, autobiography and fiction, focusing on the intergenerational relationships between women and the merging and contestation between different cultural landscapes in a single frame.

Hawaiian director Kaya Hatto's 1995 *Picture Bride* is the first feature film to explore early twentieth-century Hawaiian plantation culture with its multi-ethnic immigrant labor force. The director based her film on extensive historical research and interviews she conducted with actual picture brides, by then in their 90s. However, the film itself strikes a balance between historical documentation and a dramatic fictional structure to explore through individual characters the effect of picture bride marriages and migration on gender relations and cultural traditions. Through its focus on a central female Japanese sojourner, *Picture Bride* is concerned with the development or recovery of an effective relationship between self and place in the face of dislocation and xenophobia. In response to anti-Japanese agitation in California, the 1907 Gentlemen's Agreement between Japan and the U.S. so severely restricted Japanese immigration to the United States and its territories that only parents, wives and children of established U.S. residents were allowed to enter the country. While this measure did curb the flow of male labor immigration, "the Agreement also proved to be the benchmark for the greatest influx of Japanese brides to the United States" (Nakano 30). With the development of photography matches were often arranged by go-betweens through photographs of the bride and groom, and thus Japanese women embarked on their journey to meet husbands they had never met, to live in a country they had never seen.

Picture Bride is particularly interesting to me in the way it simultaneously encourages identification with, and invites a critique of its central female sojourner, Riyo. A 17-year old "city girl" from Yokohama, she is forced to relocate to the primitive conditions of the plantation and the grim prospect of an arranged marriage to a much older man who is clearly of lower class origins. The film traces her adjustment to hard labor in the sugar cane fields, her longing to return to Japan, and her conflicted relationship with her husband, Matsuji, who, suspicious of her middle-class attitudes, takes a long time to understand his new bride's resistance to him and her feelings of alienation. The film also alludes to the complex social and racial stratifications in plantation society, where Japanese, Filipinos and Portuguese workers are pitted against each other by white Anglo planters but nevertheless create and inhabit a new "creolized" cultural space drawing on mixed cultural and linguistic codes. There are numerous examples in the film that suggest the complex cultural hybridization of the migrant community. In one scene, Japanese plantation workers watch a silent samurai movie projected onto a white sheet in the open canefields, as the traveling performer played by legendary Japanese actor Toshiro Mifune narrates the story. This projection of traditional Japanese culture is followed by a conversation in which Riyo's friend Kana advises Matsuji to romance Riyo "like Rudolph Valentino"—a subtle reference to the remaking of Japanese culture and courting rituals through hybrid, even mass cultural influences.

Yet, the most significant aspect of this film is the connections drawn between the central character, Riyo, and the other women of the *issei* immigrant generation working on the sugar cane plantation, who take care of each other and create their own spaces of survival amidst a gender-segregated culture. Among them is Riyo's closest female friend Kana. Although she first appears to have made a more fortunate marriage, her husband feels threatened by her strength and endurance, seeing it as a challenge to his authority. Playing a central role in Riyo's development, Kana is tough and pragmatic, and her sympathetic friendship makes possible Riyo's survival in the new land.

   What is an otherwise realist film narrative of an immigrant's adjustment to the new world is complicated by a "haunting" substructure that links the Japanese spiritual world with the Hawaiian landscape and immigrant community. One magical realist scene in particular visually breaks with the realist linear narrative, signaling a certain ambiguity of meaning and, in the context of transnational cinema, the intrusion of alternate visions of cultural reality. After Kana has died in the canefields trying to rescue her small child, Riyo runs to the beach filled with grief for her dead friend and encounters the ghost of Kana. The beach is a liminal space of the imagination, a symbolic meeting place of death and rebirth, leavetaking and homecoming, dream and reality, and ultimately the space that connects Hawaii and Japan. An overhead shot of Riyo lying asleep on the multi-colored sandy rocks of the coast announces a dreamscape sequence. The color scheme changes noticeably from saturated, lush primary colors to eerie blues, blacks and whites, evoking an aura of the supernatural in a scene which makes specific cultural reference to Japanese tales of ghosts and the dead. Riyo hears Kana's voice and sees her friend moving between the black rocks on the beach. Dressed in a white kimono with long flowing hair, Kana evokes typical Japanese paintings of restless female ghosts who return to contact the living, bearing striking resemblance, for example, to Maruyama Ōkyo's woodcut "The Ghost of Oyuki" (Addiss 26). When Riyo confides to the apparition that she longs to return to Japan, Kana advises her to stay in Hawaii and make it her new home. What have you got waiting for you in Japan after all? she asks Riyo. Kana takes the plantation worker identification tag around her neck, which she had received earlier from one of the older Japanese women who moved to town, and passes it on to Riyo, asking her to "take care of the girls," meaning the next generation of female sojourners. Here Kana plays the complex role of a mediator between Japanese and Hawaiian culture, a haunting presence through which Riyo may negotiate a new cultural identity in Hawaii while remaining connected to her Japanese heritage. Kana's representation as a "supernatural" figure is even foreshadowed earlier in the film: As their friendship develops, Riyo's significant encounters with her always take place in the dark, in liminal spaces such as the edge of cane fields or water. Kana's voice becomes part of the mysterious disembodied voices heard by Riyo upon her very first arrival on the island, voices singing unseen in the dark, elusive amidst the rustling murmur in the cane fields of the Pacific's wind from the east. At the end of the film, Riyo, as an old woman, has affirmed her new identity in her new home and invokes in voice-over the ocean that separates Hawaii and Japan as a central image for passage and continuity: "Sometimes even now when the wind's blowing real hard, I think I hear Kana singing. But the singing is not Kana. It's the voice of my daughter, singing her daughter to sleep. But sometimes when I close my eyes, I can still see the moon lighting up the cane fields, like the ocean that carried me home, to Hawaii." Kana's voice becomes the aural link in Riyo's mind between the two cultural and psychological spaces she has been negotiating throughout the film, and Kana's ghostly presence embodies the memory of both loss and continuity that has allowed Riyo to make her home in a new and alien place.

As a structural and stylistic contrast to *Picture Bride*, Ruth Ozeki Lounsbury's autobiographical documentary *Halving the Bones* presents a very different, much more elliptical reconstruction of the history of Japanese picture brides though the memories of three generations of women who have, to varying degrees, all been separated—geographically and spiritually—from their Japanese culture and have sometimes felt alienated from each other. In this piece, half-Japanese, half-Caucasian filmmaker Lounsbury makes a journey in both time and space to trace her Japanese heritage through her mother and grandmother, a journey that is marked by discontinuities and absences—repeated arrivals, departures and returns. Traveling to Japan to retrieve the bones of her grandmother, who went to Hawaii as a picture bride in 1909 but later returned to Japan to give birth to her daughter, Lounsbury reconstructs the painful and fragmented history of her Japanese "half." Lounsbury traces in images and through material objects her own incomplete history and challenges conventional constructions of documentary truth by mixing a wide range of narrative devices: different film stocks and videotape, video interviews with her mother, fragments of untranslated letters, stark internment camp poems, immigration documents, newsreel footage of anti-Japanese propaganda during World War II, fake home movie footage and visual poetry. To use Stuart Hall's formulation in "Cultural Identity and Diaspora," *Halving the Bones* is not so much about the "archeological" excavation of the past as it is about the *production* of cultural identity and the *re-telling* of the past (224).

Salman Rushdie has written of the migrants' "broken mirror" of memories, whose pieces become the raw material for diasporic artists' creative construction of hybrid identities: "It was precisely the partial nature of these memories, their fragmentation, that made them so evocative for me. The shards of memory acquired greater status, greater resonance, because they were *remains*; fragmentation made trivial things seem like symbols, and the mundane acquired numinous qualities" (12). Similarly, Lounsbury focuses on those fragments and quotidian objects that seem to encode forgotten collective and family memories. Thus, the objects that Lounsbury's mother calls the grandmother's "junky things" during her videotaped conversations with her daughter—a cardboard box of old tattered clothes and scrolls, scraps of paper, passports and books of poetry—acquire heightened significance for the filmmaker herself who is trying to imaginatively reconstruct her family's history. Her grandmother Matsuye's *reversible* silk jacket, for example, becomes a poignant symbol of sojourner life, of traveling back and forth between Hawaii and Japan, of having to adapt to and balance two different cultures.

An interesting and provocative meditation on the role of the material object in transnational and intercultural cinema can be found in Laura Marks's recent book, *The Skin of the Film: Intercultural Cinema, Embodiment, and the Senses*. In her chapter, "The memory of things," Marks claims that movements through space and time and among cultures can be read through material objects in film, which she calls "recollection-objects" or "transnational objects." According to Marks, these objects, whether an heirloom, a souvenir, or a mass-manufactured article, are often presented in intercultural cinema in all their fossil-like strangeness and suggestive power.

Objects that travel along paths of human diaspora and international trade encode cultural displacement. Even commodities, though they are subject to the deracinating flow of the transnational economy and the censoring process of official history, retain the power to tell the stories of where they have been. Intercultural cinema moves through space, gathering up histories and memories that are lost or covered over in the movement of displacement, and producing new knowledges out of the condition of being between cultures. To coin another term, by adapting D. W. Winnicott's theory of the transitional object, they can be considered transnational objects. The transitional object is any external object that a person partially incorporates in the process of reorganizing its subjectivity. So it seems useful to suggest that "transnational object" might describe the objects that are created in cultural translation and transcultural movement. (78)

I quote at length from Marks's study because her concept of the transnational object holds special significance for Lounsbury's auto-ethnography and its depiction of Japanese diaspora identity. Much of the film is concerned with objects—both found and created—which are accented through repeated close-ups. As Lounsbury re-tells, even speculates about the story of her mother, grandmother and grandfather in voice-over—at times adopting a mock Japanese accent for her grandmother's voice—the camera pans in extreme close-ups across old geography books, Japanese paintings, stamp collections, and a wooden curio box filled with Japanese doll heads, family photographs, plants, and minerals, which retain their aura of strangeness and disconnection even as the filmmaker scans them for clues to her elusive family history and attempts to create a satisfying narrative. Identifying with her Japanese immigrant grandfather who was an amateur botanist, photographer, haiku poet and avid collector, Lounsbury herself becomes a gatherer of images and a "fetishist" of objects that have traveled the world and accrued layers of meaning through their contact with different people and cultures.

The two central "transnational objects" that circulate in this auto-documentary are the grandmother's bones themselves and various photographs and films that Lounsbury incorporates into her piece. Since Lounsbury's mother did not attend her own mother's funeral in Japan, Ruth Lounsbury went in her stead, taking the opportunity to pay her respects to her grandparents' grave—a traditional ritual she captures on film—and bringing both the film and three of her grandmother's bones back to the United States. After keeping the bones in her New York City apartment for five years, Lounsbury finally decides to bring them to her mother in Connecticut to initiate a long-delayed conversation about their Japanese heritage and identity, and to re-establish connections between herself and her mother through the grandparents. She and her mother together look through the grandmother's remaining possessions, translate a Japanese poem in a book written about the internment camp during the war, view the film that Lounsbury made of the cemetery in Japan, and finally the filmmaker presents the grandmother's bones to her mother. These actions become healing rituals, even though the pragmatic, present-oriented mother is at times reluctant to follow Lounsbury down the path of revisiting the past. The black-and-white film Lounsbury shot of the cemetery is particularly evocative and deeply moves the mother. Images of birds flying over the walls and of barbed wire in the cemetery film remarkably echo the metaphors used in the interment camp poem about the incarceration of Japanese during the war and the contrasting freedom of birds that mother and daughter had translated earlier. Here, in one of the subtly evocative points of the film, disparate elements come together as object-images, shards of memory separated by space and time connect, if only for a fleeting moment.

Both the bones and film footage become potent symbolic, even fetishistic objects of connection and rootedness, but also of transience and loss. Early in the documentary, Lounsbury cuts to some home movies that her grandfather supposedly made of his young, recently arrived picture bride in Hawaii. Introduced by intertitles hand-painted on rice paper, the impressionistic black-and-white film captures a solitary women walking in the unfamiliar landscape. Intercut are close-up images of strange roots and plants as Lounsbury intones in the voice-over that bones are tissue that grows and withers. The grandfather's haiku poems on the soundtrack pick up the theme of the ephemerality of nature. Later Lounsbury reveals that she herself invented these home movies, imagining the alienation and isolation her grandmother might have felt upon her first arrival to Hawaii. Her grandfather did make films, she claims, but the camera and films were confiscated when he was sent to the Japanese internment camp in Arizona. Lounsbury's film asks: How do we recreate an immigrant or sojourner past whose tangible evidence has been lost and whose representation has been distorted or neglected by American culture?

Fundamentally, *Halving the Bones* poses questions about the veracity of memory and representation, and about the possibility of capturing a truncated, interrupted diaspora history on film. Lounsbury employs her grandmother's occupation of hand-tinting black-and-white photographs to assist her photographer husband, as a powerful visual metaphor for the ways in which Ruth (and perhaps all of us) color the past—embroider and stitch together the tattered tapestry of family memory and history, filling in the gaps and silences left by parents and ancestors. As Lounsbury struggles to recover the history that shaped her mother and grandmother, their various journeys back and forth between Japan and the United States, she is actually forced to reconstruct and reshape it. Lounsbury imagines her grandmother's and mother's lives, and we, the spectators, are drawn in by the beguiling presence of images—the grandfather's poetic "home movies" of his picture bride in the strange Hawaiian landscape, images of birds caught in cages, of a baby feeding on a mother's breast, and close observation of domestic rituals that are later revealed to be Lounsbury's own cinematic constructions. In a truly Winnicottian moment, the filmmaker incorporates fabricated images and found objects, documents of cultural and political history not necessarily her own to "reorganize her subjectivity" and reestablish a connection with her ethnic heritage and family. Here memory intertwines with fantasy and wish, to recreate the lost ties and intimacy between grandmother, mother and granddaughter through the creative medium of film. Hence, the film openly acknowledges the subjective, even unreliable nature of memory. In the absence of a linear family narrative Lounsbury plays with her own desire to complete her family history with imaginary tales and hallucinatory images even as she emphasizes the necessarily incomplete and fragmentary nature of the project.

It is significant that at the very end of her journey, which includes an imagined trip to scatter the ashes of her grandmother *and* mother into the Pacific Ocean, Lounsbury stops at Pearl Harbor and makes a final discovery there. Touring the watery grave of an American submarine sunk by the Japanese during World War II, she discovers to her surprise among the names of the drowned men a T. W. Lounsbury, perhaps a relative of her white father. The filmmaker is forcefully reminded that she has, in her single-minded pursuit to recreate her mother's and grandmother's story, neglected her father's tale, yet another complication that suggests that the puzzle of the family album project has some pieces missing. As Lounsbury and her mother state: "So much gets discarded and forgotten in a lifetime. . . . I think family relationships are like family stories: You have to practice them to keep them alive."

The third Asian diaspora film under discussion here, Mina Shum's *Double Happiness*, approaches the theme of dislocation and biculturality through the mode of sharp-eyed social comedy. Focusing on a 22-year-old Chinese Canadian woman, Jade Li, *Double Happiness* dramatizes how she negotiates the generational disjunctures within her Chinese immigrant family, particularly in relation to her stern, tradition-bound father, and confronts the cultural disparities she feels as a young Chinese Canadian woman in the wider urban milieu of modern-day Vancouver. Finding herself caught between modern Western values of independence and ambition and traditional Chinese Confucian ideals of filial duty, piety and submission, Jade walks a fine line between her dual heritage, her desire to become an actress in a predominantly white profession and to please her family by finding a "good Chinese husband" and stable career. The film is less concerned with the recovery or reconstruction of familial and cultural history than either *Picture Bride* or *Halving the Bones*; rather it exposes, in a lively, self-reflexively essayistic style, the familial and social conundrums that beset Jade as she tries to navigate the pressures both inside and outside the Asian Canadian community. Jade's coming-of-age and eventual moving out of her family home can be seen as a miniaturized version of the immigrant journey, a variation on her parents' own migration out of a traditional Chinese cultural context via Hong Kong into an Anglo-Canadian space. However, director Mina Shum resists the lure of assimilationist myths. *Double Happiness* is highly critical of the racism toward Asians in Canada and their marginalization and silencing by, for instance, the media; yet neither does the film advocate an unproblematic, nostalgic return to ethnic traditions and heritage. Shum, in fact, explores in Jade's story the paradoxes and ironies of a hyphenated identity, the interstitial meaning of being both Chinese and Canadian.

The central metaphor in the film for the negotiation of these cultural spaces is acting. *Double Happiness* is both theatrically and cinematically self-reflexive. Jade's experience as an aspiring actress emphasizes the performance of Chinese Canadian identity inside and outside her household, and Shum's strategic use of non-realist cinematic techniques—Jade's direct address to the camera, slow motion sequences, insertion of fantastic backdrops to Jade's private rehearsals—and other witty expressionistic point-of-view shots highlight the connections between a constructed dramatic reality and the assemblage of cultural identity. *Double Happiness* is supremely self-conscious in the way it makes visible the gap between what Jade herself sees and feels and the different images of her identity imposed by both her traditional Chinese parents and Anglo-Canadian society. An example of Shum's method occurs at the very beginning of the film, when Jade breaks the illusion of filmic realism by addressing the camera in a frontal medium shot: "I want to tell you about my family; they're very Chinese if you know what I mean." What does "very Chinese" mean?, the film asks us. Rhetorically posing the question: why can't my Hong Kong immigrant family be The Brady Bunch?, Jade offers her own humorous punchline: the Bradys never needed subtitles, she winks, hinting at her essentially hybrid Chinese Canadian identity and double consciousness as an insider and outsider to Canadian culture—itself in constant dialogue with U.S. popular culture.

Jade effectively leads a "double life" as a respectful, selfless and nearly invisible Chinese daughter and a bold, playful and ambitious Canadian "twenty-something." However, Jade is not merely masking some true self. It is one of the central ironies of the film that all its characters must act out roles assigned to them by traditional cultural values or to conform to stereotyped notions of "Chineseness." Mr. Li stubbornly performs the role of the respected patriarch in the family even though his actions alienate his more independent-minded daughter. Meanwhile, when Jade's uncle Ah Hung visits from China, Mrs. Li asks her daughters to play the parts of traditionally submissive and academically successful model children in front of him to show how their father has managed to preserve Chinese customs in Canada, while pretending that their disinherited brother Winston is a prominent businessman. When the Li family picks up Uncle Hung at the airport, Jade and Pearl perform their carefully rehearsed traditional Chinese greeting. Ah Hung is suitably impressed by Mr. Li's having raised his daughters in Canada "with a firm hand," but Mina Shum then makes a serious point with characteristic humor: as Ah Hung proceeds to lightheartedly greet Mrs. Li in English, romantically taking her hand and kissing it in European fashion in imitation of the in-flight movie, the comic scene underscores the film's larger insight that cultural customs and identities are not essentialist and fixed but are conventions that can be adopted, changed, discarded or played with. Significantly, Jade later discovers that Ah Hung, like herself, leads a double life, when he reveals that he is secretly involved with his former maid and has had a child with her. Empathizing with Jade's dilemma of living between worlds, he advises her to choose her part carefully in life, to avoid becoming a "white ghost."

Jade's various auditions and encounters with casting agents—both white and Chinese—also underscore the prejudices and preconceptions that seek to "fix" her ethnic identity. A white director can only see Jade as Chinese, demanding that she read her English lines with a "Chinese accent," while a Hong Kong agent dismisses Jade for a part in an Asian production because she cannot read Cantonese, asserting that she is not "Chinese" enough. When Jade's mother and sister watch Jade's acting debut on television, her performance as a Chinese waitress in a soap opera becomes humiliating: Not only is Jade reduced to a stereotypical, marginalized role, she is literally pushed to the edge of the frame so that only her accented voice marks her presence. Tellingly, in the scenes of Jade's confrontation with her father, Mina Shum employs a similar mise-en-scène, relegating Jade to the very edge of the screen. After disobeying her father by staying out all night for a romantic encounter with Mark, a white Canadian student, Jade plays the role of the obedient daughter by bringing her father his favorite red bean buns and tea in an act of appeasement. Patiently waiting for her father's response as she holds out her offering, the camera focuses squarely on his figure and leaves her at the margin of the frame—a deliberate visual echo of her marginalized presence in the Canadian media industry.

In *Double Happiness* Jade's problematic role-playing as a female in a traditional Chinese family converges with the problem of being Asian American in the workaday Anglo-Canadian world, revealing the complexities facing the second generation with its more fluid alliances to multiple homes. When Jade realizes at the end of the film that her father will never break free of his rigid definition of gender roles within the Chinese family, she leaves home to live on her own. Her first gesture in her new apartment is to set up a photograph of herself, her brother and her sister, a visual affirmation of the importance of her sibling ties, which reflect the break between traditional immigrant parents and culturally more ambivalent second-generation children.[4] Jade also puts up curtains in her own apartment with images of Marilyn Monroe—a symbol here of an actress who was stereotyped in her own time by the media and underestimated for her considerable comedic skills as a female performer. Monroe's presence is clearly a semiotic sign both for Jade's independence from her Chinese heritage and her determination to break the mold of Asian female stereotypes.

I close with an observation by cultural critic Lisa Lowe in her book, *Immigrant Acts*, who critiques "orientalism" as it developed in the western imagination. "Although orientalism seeks to consolidate the coherence of the West as subject precisely through the representation of 'oriental' objects as homogenous, fixed and stable," writes Lowe, the limits of this fiction are ultimately expressed in what she terms "the non-correspondence between the orientalist object and the Asian American subject" (67). The three films discussed here take different cinematic approaches to the construction of Asian American and Asian Canadian female immigrant identities, yet all accentuate the fictitiousness of a "homogenous, fixed and stable oriental object." *Picture Bride*'s employment of magical realist elements signals a hybridized sojourner culture; *Halving the Bones* self-reflexively constructs immigrant history and memory and emphasizes the fragmented "transnational object"; and *Double Happiness*, with its focus on the "performance of ethnicity," suggests a more complex conception of mediating cultural identities. These films grapple with the diasporic struggle to negotiate a home, incorporating different geographical, cultural, linguistic, national codes and identities.

12. Feigning Marriage/ Befriending Nations

The Case of *Flying Down to Rio*

—Norman S. Holland

In the following pages, I argue that *Flying Down to Rio* (RKO 1933) is Hollywood's first attempt at articulating FDR's Good Neighbor policy. This attempt can be read nowadays as a larger project to imbue the Latin American geocultural space and its inhabitants with a set of character-istics, images, and values. Following analogously from Said's *orientalism*, Frances R. Aparicio and Susana Chávez-Silverman name this discursive practice *tropicalism*.[1] In its broadest possible terms, this study involves trac-ing the conceptualizations of cultural identity with respect to their visual inscriptions. Any formulation of identity points toward the local institu-tional and political necessities that frame this act of cultural recognition and (mis)identification. The "Americanization of Latin America" involves the "Latinization of the United States." This process reifies the binary "American" versus "ethnic." In the case of *Flying Down to Rio*, Latinization becomes complicit with the construction of a hegemonic U.S. (fe)male sexuality. Precisely because it conflates various genres of American popular entertainment, the film fails to resolve sexuality into a satisfactory—that is, coherent—reading. In the concluding remarks, I will address how the film's celebratory cross-border marriage becomes the collective historical memory that the subaltern subject has mined in such recent films as *La Bamba* (1987), *The Perez Family* (1995), and *Lone Star* (1996).

The overarching plot of *Flying Down to Rio* belongs to the genteel-comedy romance. The formula usually employs a bored, headstrong, rich girl looking for adventure and an imaginative, aspiring, poor man. He is entranced by her will, she by his imagination, and before they have reached their destination, they have fallen in love. What makes this version exceptional is its cross-cultural dimension. The American male played by Gene Raymond has fallen for a rich Brazilian girl played by Dolores del Río, the couple's destination, Rio de Janeiro. This film is thus part of a historically emergent project of restructuration not only of the Americas, but also of the United States imaginary due to changing economic, political and technological configurations. While mainstream criticism has ignored this film (*Flying Down to Rio* is a minor note in the Fred Astaire/Ginger Rogers critical corpus), my reading of this film traces primarily how Hollywood maps this project onto Latin America and in the process "interpellates" the Latin American spectator into its apparatus. To anticipate: *Flying Down to Rio* suggests that the price for the Latin American audience to enter Hollywood's reformulation of the Americas' political unconscious is to lose its "dignity." Hollywood invites Latin America to be part of modernity, not as Habermas's or Taylor's autonomous and dignified modern subject, but as pure spectacle.[2] In order to enter the modern—made possible by advances in transportation and promulgated by an incipient global popular media—the denizens of Latin America have to give up their dignity.

The essay concentrates on four aspects of the film: the "Orchid in the Moonlight" episode, the emergence of Honey Hale played by Ginger Rogers as the ideal, Belinha's regression from modern female to traditional woman, and the male-bonding sequence, culminating in Julio Rubeiro, played by

Raul Roulien, feigning marriage and thereafter parachuting into modernity. I will conclude by arguing that the film creates the ground for one of Hollywood's most enduring articulations of Latin American identity: "Carmen Miranda," who first appears in another traveling film, *Down Argentina Way* (1940).

Flying Down to Rio opens in Miami. Belinha Rezende, a wealthy Brazilian tourist who travels chaperoned by her aunt, has received a telegram at her hotel asking her to come home immediately. She cannot honor this request for the Rio de Janeiro flight has already departed. Roger Bond, the Yankee Clipper band leader, offers the services of an aviator-friend who is no other than himself. The narrative configuration of the traveler and the voyage is further underscored by the location's fluidity. Of Miami, we only see a nightclub and an airfield, spaces that lack any geographical or historical specificity. These sites are more or less self-contained and are clearly separated from a homeland or national community that might be implied, but instead is always absent. As an eccentric territorial location, Miami is inhabited by outsiders who have just arrived or about to depart. The film focuses on and unfolds at these junctions or nodal points.

On their flight from Miami to Rio de Janeiro, our protagonists make an emergency landing on what appears to be a deserted island. Immediately after their safe landing, Roger debates with his double, in a technically innovative split screen sequence, whether he should seduce Belinha. While Roger decides, Belinha questions her double as to whether she should overthrow convention and let desire run its course. After a passionate embrace, the next shot of them sleeping separately creates the impression that they have decided to remain friends, "good neighbors."

The next morning when Roger pretends to be going to look for help to fix the airplane, naked black torsos surround Belinha. At the same moment that she exclaims "Cannibals!" Roger is knocked down by a strange object, which turns out to be a golf ball that has gone astray. Whatever fears emerge are put to rest by a black golfer searching for his errant shot who informs them, with a proper English accent, that Belinha's cannibals are the caddies of the Port au Prince Country Club going for an early morning dip. Roger, it turns out, landed his plane on the beach next to a golf course somewhere close to the Haitian capital.

All too often these types of sequences are readily dismissed as proving the old adage that Hollywood (and the media) is far better equipped to produce caricature and sensation than deal with the process of culture and history. Seldom are they read as points of entry into studying Hollywood's cultural practices. Precisely because it appears as a kind of innocuous, extra-territorial space, the site of countless love affairs, the perfect spot where Roger can woo Belinha with his composition "Orchids in the Moonlight," this sequence offers up a fascinating zone within which to examine Hollywood's (ethnographic) power. Through its capacity to construct and promulgate *Latinidad*, Hollywood becomes an ethnographer. This allows, in the words of Ana M. López, for "the analysis of the historical-political construction of self-other relation as an inscription among other factors, of Hollywood's power as translator of otherness" (405–06).[3]

Although romance motivates the narrative, their landing on Haiti is not a mere accident. The sequence begs to be read as Hollywood's earliest attempt to implement the Good Neighbor policy that FDR had articulated during his inaugural speech nine months earlier.[4] The film dates from the end of 1933, the year when Theodore Roosevelt's policy of "speak softly and carry a big stick" was rearticulated by his nephew as the Good Neighbor policy whose ideal was "the neighbor who resolutely respects himself and because he does so, respects the rights of others."[5] In 1915, disorder was so constant and violent in Haiti that the United States government applied the Teddy Roosevelt corollary to that nation. Eighteen years later, Roger and Belinha's respective soliloquies voice the new policy's ideal.

In an effort to expiate past excesses of United States imperialism, Hollywood has Roger and Belinha voice the emergent discourse on the Americas by recombining elements of a residual discourse on Haiti. Roger's view of Haiti reiterates how Americans have tended to view the island, that is, as a void onto which they could project their own ideas and desires.[6] This view depends on the widespread belief in the absence of civilization, thematized as cannibalism. Belinha's exclamation—"Wild men! Cannibals!"— activates the missing element of the discursive pattern. As long as the island and its people represent degeneracy and racial inferiority, Haiti can be perceived as a void. As an imagined space, Haiti is made visible in terms of antithetical extremes: a utopia, the possible horizon of romance, and a dystopia, the land of savagery. This Manichean notion marks its inhabitants as well. The head caddie is shot half-naked or half-dressed, depending on our biases. His image repeats the opposition, now in terms of noble savage/cannibal. Drawing on nineteenth century Afro-American stereotypes, the film further denies the caddie the possibility of seriousness by concentrating on his peculiarities of speech. The peculiarities are accentuated by a geographical confusion. He speaks all too perfect English in a former French colony. What we get is not only a hollow and hackneyed stereotype of Haiti as an interchangeable island with Bermuda or Jamaica, but more importantly a glimpse of the future.

While this conversation is taking place, airplane sounds are heard in the distance. Informed that it is the Rio plane that makes a scheduled overnight stop in Port au Prince, Belinha orders the head caddie to take her there. Her voice takes on a racial superiority, even though she is from Brazil, deflecting and glossing over continental hierarchies. "Yes Ma'am," retorts the caddie. His reply reinscribes him as a gregarious hospitality worker, to employ a current euphemism. Their exchange not only reveals the interplay between an emergent and a residual discourse but also discloses what will become the dominant discourse on Haiti and the Caribbean: a tourist destination made possible by commercial aviation. This future is once again predicated on Haiti as void insofar as tourism will promote the same images the film's audiences see—golf, deserted beaches, and romance. In this new world order, the cultural identity of the subaltern is not constructed through a system of identity and difference, but identification and belonging.

As I noted, the sequence begins with the assumption of savagery, of the existence of "wild men." As the plot unfolds, this impression is reversed. The "native" relates to the new modes of experiencing the world. He plays golf; he knows about modern means of transportation. Rather than being exclusionary like the colonial system always seeking to reproduce its differences, epitomized by the Caddies' Englishness, Hollywood's presentation of Americanization is absorptive. Although inclusionary, the new colonialism is still centered on the technologies and images of the West. Once absorbed, the other's potential for contestation, for resistance, is neutralized. This Haitian interlude comprises a perfect cinematic example of what

Homi Bhabha has described as "the discriminatory effects of cultural colonialism" in "Signs Taken for Wonder." A disavowed cultural differentiation grounds the existence of colonial-imperialist authority. Bhabha underscores this disavowal by noting that "what is disavowed is not repressed but repeated as something *different*—a mutation, a hybrid" (111). What follows is an exploration of this mutation or hybrid.[7] I will begin by returning to Belinha and decipher how Hollywood translates her otherness.

As ethnographer of the Americas, Hollywood undertakes a double imperative around the figure of Belinha: on the one hand to translate the ethnic and sexual thread of Latin American otherness into peaceful good neighborliness, and on the other, to elaborate an assimilation model more easily negotiable for a sector of the United States audience in the aftermath of the massive immigration from Europe in the late nineteenth and early twentieth centuries as well as for a sector of the Brazilian populace.[8] As we have seen in the Haiti interlude, Belinha brilliantly speaks to and collaborates with the Good Neighbor ideal so well in fact that her aura of modernity begins to slip.

At the beginning of the film, Belinha appears as utterly glamorous, that is, modern. Citing historian Peter Bailey, the cultural historian Linda Mizejewski writes, "Glamour is a modern concept involving public visibility of a desirable object" (11). As male fantasy, the danger is interpreting desire as exclusively masculinist in its origin. While the film portrays Belinha as the cool seducer, sure of her sexuality, exemplifying Mulvey's category of "to-be-looked-at-ness," her recognition as glamorous depends on her female audience. Her appearance prompts the (in)famous inquiry: "What do South American girls have below the Equator that we don't?" By erasing national differences, the question foregrounds the female body as a site among many cultural practices in which glamour is being re-defined. For her American (girl)friends who ask the above question, Belinha's body enacts the ideal female body. By 1933, this ideal was totally familiar. Its antecedents were European—the opera and ballet girl. Belinha articulates a code of behavior that is readily identifiable as glamorous though presumably other, and yet in its otherness, attractive because it resonates with the modern. Because of her liminal status in relation to bourgeois respectability and ethnic and national categories she becomes the object of male desire.

On first seeing her, Roger falls in love with her. As his opening move, he presents her with an orchid. She exclaims that in her country orchids grow like weeds. It appears that for the first time Hollywood is not going to discount the overlapping experiences of North and South Americans, the interdependence of cultural terrains. The upshot of this interdependence is far more complicated than the plot ever admits. Class, race, nationality and sexuality constantly intervene and disrupt their romance.

If we return to the triangulation of desire encapsulated in the sight lines of a panicky Belinha first trying to revive Roger who has been hit by a golf ball and then both staring at the "naked" head caddie observing them through the bushes, the scene evidences the fears and anxieties centered on cultural taboos in the area of sexuality. The scene's sight lines position the head caddie as a father figure who has caught the two youngsters in the act. Before the audience sees them being observed, Belinha calls him "darling," thus revealing her "true" feelings for Roger. What is striking in the close-up is their physical coloration. Gene Raymond is an extremely—and unusually by Hollywood standards—Aryan leading-man. Contrasted with his whiteness, del Rio's famous aristocratic exoticism takes on ethnic overtones. For a fleeting moment, she takes on the looks of a *mulatta*. By postulating that Belinha's character is neither incidentally or obviously white, I am underscoring how the privileging of one race and ethnicity over another occurs in an organized way within and outside the film.

As a creature whose life appears not to be cramped by a strict moral code, by the confining values of Puritanism, the film positions Belinha in the role occupied by Afro-Americans in the twenties. She recalls post-war America's fascination with "the Negro" and Harlem, specifically. From this angle, "Haiti" (the island sequence) becomes a more authentic Harlem. The head caddie diffuses this potentially heavy-handed treatment of race and ethnicity when he scolds Roger for moving his golf ball. The film's negotiation of inter-ethnic relationships anticipates the Hays Code that will prohibit black-white sexual relations to be represented on the screen. In passing, the Hays Office did not implement the Production Code until 1934, after *Flying Down to Rio* was released.

Belinha and the caddie's foreignness mark them as valuable sites in Hollywood's attempt to liberate America's sexual, racial and ethnic unconscious.

Upon them can be projected the tensions in the daily life of a large sector of the United States audience as they negotiated their passage into the desirable American lifestyle, momentarily threatened by the Great Depression. As a favored activity among courting couples, cinema, Hollywood—that is, cinema—was ideally positioned to instruct audiences about the changing social mores.

Film critics, such as Robert Sklar, have remarked that romance is one of the cultural constructs that Hollywood uses to model social behavior. As such, romance is related to the changing social conceptions of marriage. In terms of this film's cross-border romance, courting and marriage are defined as the right to follow the dictates of the heart. Belinha lacks these cultural rights when we discover that she travels with a chaperone and has agreed to an arranged marriage. Like the head caddie, Belinha is constructed out of a single Manichean discursive opposition that is repeated *ad nauseam*. What term of the opposition liberated/repressed, modern/traditional, same/other is highlighted shifts as the film negotiates the path between a domestic comedy with a foreign twist and a fallen-woman film. The markers invite different readings. For her American friends, Belinha at the beginning pertains to the first genre and to her chaperone, to the latter.

The film's actual opening shots are of the newly appointed Swiss hotel manager inspecting his work force of waiters and chambermaids. Before he dismisses them, he announces that he has been hired to impose discipline. When he attempts to impose his militaristic standards on the band, the band's singer Honey Hale played by Ginger Rogers deflates him by addressing him as "Pop Eye." Her remark attests to the popularity of the snappy, comic chorus girl. His reminder that if Roger is not on time they will all be fired squelches the momentary outburst of laughter and insolence. Roger is still airborne seconds before their live radio show is to begin. Exactly on the hour like a Swiss watch, Roger arrives. Honey begins her rendition of "Music Makes Me," whose lyrics are variations on the refrain "Music makes me do things I should never do" including, I would add, saying "Pop Eye."

When heard in relation to other films of its era, Honey Hale's wise-guy remark—"Pop Eye"—invites an intertextual reading. It echoes Mae West's devastating one liners. As Andrew Bergman reminds us in *We're in the Money: Depression America and its Films*, Mae West was the sensation of 1933.

More than any other actor, she destabilized the moralism of the "fallen woman" films. In an intertextual reading, the downward movement of our title—flying down—alludes to the downward path that the heroines of such films would undergo once a fatal misstep occurred. This allusion suggests that Honey, to avoid the breadlines, has gone "south" no longer as a "chorus girl" but as a "lead" singer. Furthermore, the opening sequence appears to be a continuation of the *Gold Diggers of 1933* in which Ginger Rogers plays the most forward gold digger of them all. One of her cohorts comments in the *Gold Diggers* that the show producer would not know her "with clothes on."

While the film pretends to speak Belinha's modernity, in fact, the film sets out to teach Belinha and her American friends how to become Honey. It is Honey who is totally modern: she embodies the accumulated meanings of the chorus girl body as a new image of womanhood. Both in musicals and films, chorus girls circulated as independent, often sassy, resourceful modern women.[9] In this instance, Honey's crack punctures stuffed shirts. Her remark overthrows the decorum and values of the Swiss manager.

I will have more to say later about Belinha and Honey, but I want to underline right now the confrontation between the Swiss hotel manager and the American band leader, Roger. Before that, I want to stress that *Flying Down to Rio* foresees in startling ways the profound transformations in the organization and spaces of the economy. Despite the shakiness of the United States economy, this film, unlike other films of the period, never doubts America's institutions or its institutional myths about work, fair competition and success. Instead it evokes the economic crisis as an opportunity to challenge traditional European values. It explicitly ties the transformation of American culture to the changing technology. Not only this sequence but the entire narrative pivots on the notion of precision and technical proficiency, supposedly neutral attributes of an advanced economy. While both the Swiss and the American are representatives of Fordism, one is characterized as reactionary, the other as progressive. The film casts the various attributes of power as well as the pursuits of profits as European, as part of an earlier imperial economy, as archaic. The Swiss's job to regimentalize leisure dooms him as an object of derision. Although the film depicts Roger following generic conventions, as a working person, all the cinematic indications of his class origin operate to make his working class background seem more a matter of whim than of necessity. Roger is so torn between his love of flying and composing music that he solves the dilemma by installing a special piano in his airplane. His easygoing affability gives him an air of detachment. He appears furthermore to be a person who feels comfortable, literally, at any level of society. He is the perfect invoicer of leisure as work. As I noted earlier, the band strikes up the music on time.

Images of mobility that are predicated on new technologies permeate the film. All the various sequences begin with an assumption of cultural backwardness. Belinha has her chaperone. The Haitians run around semi-naked. Julio, Belinha's future spouse, is depicted as an old-fashioned guy. Even the Brazilian musicians are filmed stereotypically as lazy. In terms of Hollywood's preexisting grid of stereotypes, they recall Mexicans. As these fragments or plot segments unfold, first impressions are reversed. Unlike many earlier films that had irked Latin American moviegoers and their governments, no negative stereotypes circulate for long. The few villains that appear are of European origin. In this film, either you relate to the modern means of communication or you are excluded. No space or time is available for those located outside the modern network of telegrams, radio, airplanes, and tourism. This network constructs a map of the possible and proper trajectory for the individual and the social group to accumulate cultural rather than economic capital. Inasmuch as they can relate to the new modes of experiencing the world, the Latin Americans are shown to have the potential to be modern. For both Julio and Belinha their passport into modernity is predicated on a radical rejection of their own national cultural allegiances. These allegiances, constantly interconnected to issues of sexuality, race and gender, are set in motion once again in Rio.

While both Julio and Belinha call Rio de Janeiro home, the film presents the city as a series of postcards as if it were extra-territorial. Like Miami, it is conceived as marginal to the mainland. Rio's marginality grants legitimacy to relationships that are taboo in a number of ways in the "home country." As I have pointed out, flying, the impulse to undertake journeys, to cross borders, marks the film. Belinha's journey to Miami opened new possibilities for her. It created a space in which Belinha's sexuality and pleasures are legitimated. These are romanticized and defined in relationship to a male partner. Furthermore these are re-inflected as the possibility to escape her class structure of control and discipline (the chaperone, the arranged marriage) but not necessarily class. Back home, she becomes an artifact. Her aloofness and her lavish garments are a veritable proclamation of the productivity of countless others. She becomes the commodity par excellence. As such, she can be ritually circulated from one male admirer to another.

It so happens that Belinha is engaged to Julio who turns out to be Roger's old friend and to whom Roger now owes his livelihood. Belinha's return makes possible Roger's and Julio's reunion. Their reunion is posited against domesticity. Whereas domesticity signals national conventions in the film, friendship and brotherhood transcend political borders. Furthermore friendship involves risk and adventure. Having fallen for Belinha, Roger has to diffuse the potential conflict. He will do so by opening new horizons for Julio. Couched in an already inverted vocabulary of national stereotypes, Roger resolves to let "nature" determine whom Belinha will marry. Julio adds "common sense" to the equation. The upshot of this rivalry is that Belinha is firmly reinserted in a patriarchal economy. Safely ensconced, she now derives her value through the exchange that she makes possible—the bonding between two men.

At the beginning of the Rio section, after the series of postcards, the camera focuses on Roger dressing in the presence of Julio. While the camera lingers on Roger as an object of desire, the conversation revolves around Roger having met Belinha. In "Women on the Market," Luce Irigaray proposes that woman is the material alibi for the desires for relations among men. The symbolic order that is sustained through homoeroticism prohibits the direct expression of that desire, obliging it to assume the censored and circuitous form of heterosexual exchange, or what Irigary describes as the homosocial. In this dressing room sequence, the film acknowledges and displaces the homoerotic onto the homosocial. The competition for Belinha's heart becomes a friendly affair, climaxing in an elaborate aerial musical display as part of the opening of the Hotel Atlantico owned by Belinha's father, Senhor Rezende.

Before the hotel can open, the forces of an earlier form of imperialism must be vanquished. Dark shadows, pertaining to members of a Greek gambling syndicate based in Monte Carlo, try to prevent the opening of the hotel by bribing the mayor to delay the issuing of an entertainment permit. This subplot highlights and simultaneously brackets the economic stakes at play. As shadows, the villains are figures out of animated films. Given the early imagery surrounding the Swiss hotel manager, I cannot help recalling Freud's notion that representation is a cannibalistic discourse. At this late point in the film a consensus has been built around the need to give up and replace cultural allegiances underwritten by European values that Hollywood can poke fun at its own constructions. Nonetheless, historians of the period argue convincingly that the FDR's Good Neighbor policy is an expression of United States isolationism. Government policy makers feared the formation of trading blocks in other parts of the world. The policy's security issues reflect apprehensions that Latin America would be penetrated and taken over by Germany and Japan. Of all the countries Brazil was the most vulnerable because of German investment.[10] As a terrain of international intrigue, Rio is no historical accident either.

Good-neighbor Roger outwits the shadows. He rises to the occasion and circumvents the entertainment ban by concocting an aerial show over the hotel, reminiscent of a military invasion. Instead of bombs, the planes deliver a payload of chorus girls. Rogers cinematically delivers Ziegfeld Broadway to Brazil. The aerial show assures the successful hotel opening. In gratitude Belinha's father sends Roger a written note thanking him for saving him from bankruptcy and public humiliation. The hotel's success will make possible his daughter's marriage . . . to Julio, it is assumed. Despite Roger's ingenuity, Brazilian common sense embodied by the father seems to have won.

While Roger concocts the film's most theatrical moment, he turns over the aerial extravaganza to Julio. Aware that his ingenuity removes the last obstacle between the Brazilian lovers, Roger decides to catch the next flight to Buenos Aires. Julio has no recourse but to assume command. In mid-flight, Julio observes through his binoculars Roger's farewell kisses. Julio interprets the kisses as nature taking its course. Hence once the aerial show is over, he grabs Belinha and rushes to catch the Buenos Aires flight, calming her by promising to marry her. As it turns out, he is not the groom. Airborne, he literally gives her away to Roger. In feigning marriage, Julio cements the homosocial bond, his friendship with Roger. The film's ending shots are of Julio parachuting back to Rio, back to the modern public sphere, symbolized by the Hotel Atlantico.[11]

Among the benefits accrued by the denizens of the modern is the idea that anyone can enter and function in the public sphere with dignity. During her opening number, Honey reminds the audience of exactly the opposite. According to the lyrics, the price for being modern is losing one's dignity. Some of her lines are: "Music makes me a sinner, dancing is my crime, Music makes me lose my dignity." Thus does this musical that casts her as the dumb, blond chorus girl. Since the film constantly aligns immobile figures with the past, her characterization accentuates the film's contradictory celebration of mobility. Honey and her cohorts dazzle the Brazilians because of their aerial performance. They operate above the ground, defying the laws of gravity. These flying bodies make it difficult to note differences in identification processes along lines other than traditional/modern despite Mizejewski claim that Hollywood's adaptation of Ziegfeld Broadway was "inevitably gendered concepts, the visual semantics of female bodies performing as patterns for a presumed male camera/eye" (143). The sequence sustains the film's project to endorse identification and belonging. Julio's gift is part of this projection.

When Julio gives Belinha to Roger, he suffers the same filmic fate as Honey. He too loses his dignity. Students of machismo have theorized that in the colonial contract the reward for male acquiescence to the will of the conqueror was his socially enforced superiority over and dominance of the female. In the Good Neighbor era, I would propose that the reward for feigning masculinity is mobility. It is not so much that the mobility projected by Hollywood is inherently more democratic, but it certainly represents a more extensive and imaginative sense of the possible. While the film hails movement as liberative, these pages disclose how movement is still socially structured. Free choice in love is unpredictable and arbitrary only in appearance: Belinha and Roger's marriage coerces desires. The plot's complexities are reduced to a singular goal: to be assimilated into the public sphere, to be modern, to be *Americans*. Border crossings are permissible as long as they can be contained. Through the staged musical competitions, the film works hard to create a consensus around this horizon of possibility.[12]

So far my observations could be brought to bear on the side of the homogenization argument in terms of global interactions. Before concluding, I want to note that at the level of music the film anticipates if not contributes to the adoption of the *samba* as the national dance in Brazil. The *samba* had quickly spread as a form of popular music throughout Brazil's working class with the introduction of the radio in the late 1920s. The original "*samba de morro*" evolved into a mellower *samba* and was adopted by the middle sectors of Brazilian society in the late thirties in opposition to the upper class's infatuation with the fox trot. Within the film, this cultural struggle is packaged as pure spectacle.

When Ginger and Fred arrive in Rio, they and the members of The Yankee Clipper band check out the local competition. In a dazzling musical sequence, they find out that the local community prefers the *carioca* to the fox trot. Although it has been argued that the upshot of this sequence is the Americanization of the *carioca* first by the fact that the *carioca* is sung by the Afro-American singer Etta Moten, and then interpreted by Fred and Ginger, the narrative sequence has a black dance troupe replicate Fred and Honey's performance. This sequence, in turn, gives way to a sequence in a very exclusive and expensive Rio nightclub where Del Rio and Astaire dance "Orchids in the Moonlight." For the Brazilian audience, the dynamic of this juxtaposition might be enlarging the gulf between social classes. Not only does this film intervene in an emerging cultural class struggle; but also it paves the way via the *carioca* for the fad of the *samba* in the States culminating with the Carmen Miranda star text. While Miranda was an effervescent vision of what awaited anyone who flew down to Rio, at home, she was controversial, not least because of her popularity in the United States. Until 1967 when the movement *Tropicalismo* appropriated her as one of its central figures, Carmen Miranda was a cause for both national pride and shame.[13]

Carmen Miranda's Hollywood debut was in 1940 in another flying film, *Down Argentina Way*, which restages *Flying Down to Rio*. Plot-wise, Carmen Miranda role exceeds her star billing.[14] She has a cameo role as a singer in the nightclub that the protagonists visit. The same sequence functions as the backdrop for the opening credits, announcing Hollywood's "success" in interpellating Latin America as spectacle. This forties' film is a shifter or marker of Hollywood's recognition of how cultural markets operate. As I have argued above, the cultural commodity Hollywood projects is a lifestyle, associated with modern technology that by the late thirties/early forties was replacing the traditional European lifestyle that had until then dominated the "upper-class" marketplace. In terms of *Down Argentina Way*, the new impediment is folk culture, whose foreignness is rendered harmless by Carmen Miranda's excess. The quotation marks around *success* are a reminder that hegemonic projects are rarely completed, always shifting in relation to changing economic, technological and social formations. This discourse, nonetheless, would quickly become a grid of stereotypes that would allow a particular image of Latin America to filter into the United States consciousness and against which we have to read such recent films as *La Bamba*, *The Perez Family*, and *Lone Star*, to which I will briefly turn as a conclusion.

Under the guise of the autobiography of the first successful Latino crossover pop-artist, the director Luis Valdez feigns the autobiographical in order to see Latinos as others see them, only more so. Ritchie Valenz's premature death undermines the rags-to-riches Hollywood success story that the film apparently endorses as a way out of the barrio. Like Julio, Ritchie's success comes at a price. He changes his name. His death, however, blocks any easy identification with the cinematic hero. Even the film's title indicates a certain distance from its subject. Ritchie's death is meaningful if others do not have to become a spectacle, which within the film they do. The most enduring scene of the film, maybe, is the end where Ritchie's brother stands on the bridge screaming while the song *Goodnight My Love* by Los Lobos plays. While the song "La Bamba" endures as a mark of resistance to cultural assimilation, the staged grief compromises the film's attempt to blow up the grid that constructs *Latinidad*.[15]

Drawing on the similar mechanisms of parody and counterfeiting, the directors Mira Nair and John Sayles also foreground the transformative cultural agency of the subaltern. In *The Perez Family* by Nair, Marisa Tomei plays a Cuban, headed for America, head filled with dreams of movies. While her Carmen Miranda outfits articulate her apparent acceptance of Hollywood's identity grid, her chances to obtain a green card depend on her familial status. The film records her attempts to secure a family. She finally succeeds by counterfeiting a family, thus parodying one of the favorite images of (conservative) 1990s politicians: a pregnant human being crossing the border to have her child born an American citizen, as if America were the sole property of the United States imaginary.

While *The Perez Family* counterfeits the family, *Lone Star* deconstructs it by positing incest as the ground from which a new border romance can be imagined.[16] In Sayles's film, incest is not blindly enacted, rather it is willfully forgotten by its protagonists. In so doing, they voice the film's central remark: "Blood only means what you let it." Defining blood involves forgetting a linear history in favor of a hybrid past in which personal and national stories commingle. These fluid stories do not function as the foundational formations required by school textbooks. What replaces the linear high-school history in the act of forgetting is a sense of the past wherein they can define (or describe) history based on their present situation (an incestuous relationship). Sayles's protagonists consciously forget in front of an abandoned drive-in screen.

The blank screen underscores how cinematic technologies have in the most profound, socially and yet personal way transformed us as subjects. Simultaneously, the screen's blankness invites our complicity in formulating new spatial, temporal and bodily investments. These investments are always historically informed not only by changes in the technologies of representation but also by the political, economic and social context, and thus always both co-constitute and express cultural values. By exploiting Hollywood's grid of *Latinidad* to which *Flying Down to Rio* contributed so greatly, these three films endow a modicum of dignity to their respective protagonists.

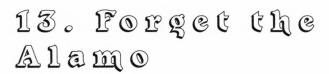

13. Forget the Alamo

Reading the Ethics of Style in John Sayles's *Lone Star*

—*Todd F. Davis and Kenneth Womack*[1]

"Blood only means what you let it."

—John Sayles, *Lone Star* (90)

In an editorial of 26 March 1997, Linda Chavez, the President of the Center for Equal Opportunity and a nationally syndicated columnist, laments Hollywood's subtle "chipping away at the incest taboo," arguing that John Sayles's 1996 film, *Lone Star*, advocates incest as "just another alternative life style choice." While Chavez derides the film as a "boring, politically correct saga about prejudice and murder in a small Texas town," her critique of Sayles's narrative neglects the tremendous import of incest as a metaphor for the history of ethnic struggle in Frontera, Texas, *Lone Star*'s fictive cultural battleground ("Kiss" 25).[2] Similarly, Laura Miller of *Salon Magazine* ridicules *Lone Star* as "a sort of Frankenstein's monster cobbled together from dozens of garden-variety movie clichés and ordered by its creator to deliver a moral of bland multiculturalism" (3).[3] As with

Chavez, Miller seems loathe to recognize Sayles's deliberate narrative design and his express interest in commenting upon the fractious cultural dilemmas of our past and their often silent impact upon the present. In *Lone Star*, Sayles skillfully exploits the incest taboo as the vehicle for his analysis of the interconnected ethnic threads that constitute contemporary American life and the often uneasy relationships that continue to exist between the races. Sayles's incest metaphor also provides the writer and filmmaker with a prescient means for exploring the ways in which our shared history impinges upon the ethical choices that confront us in the present. In short, Sayles's parable of intercultural incest allows him to cross a variety of ethnic borders as he considers the conflicted and shifting notions of identity that confront *Lone Star*'s array of characters.

Sayles constructs his ethical examination of Frontera's historical and present-day cultural dilemmas by virtue of an arresting and carefully plotted visual style. As Martha C. Nussbaum notes, an artist's sense of style—whether visual, literary, or otherwise—often functions as a means for rendering ethical judgments. In *Love's Knowledge: Essays on Philosophy and Literature*, Nussbaum argues that "form and style are not incidental features. A view of life is *told*. The telling itself—the selection of genre, formal structures, sentences, vocabulary, of the whole manner of addressing the reader's sense of life—all of this expresses a sense of life and of value, a sense of what matters and what does not, of what learning and communicating are, of life's relations and connections," she writes; "life is never simply *presented* by a text; it is always *represented as* something" (5). In *Lone Star*, Sayles employs a combination of camera techniques and editing maneuvers as his dramatic means for commenting upon the nature of Frontera's shared sense of culture and community. By using a series of flashbacks and flash-forwards, Sayles highlights the sociological disjunctions between Frontera's segregated past and its relationship to the ethnic tensions that plague the border town's historical present.

Sayles produces *Lone Star*'s striking visual style through his careful manipulation of the audience's sense of time and place. By altering our traditional understandings of temporality and setting, Sayles succeeds in demonstrating the ethical interconnections between the past and the present. In *Narrative Discourse: An Essay in Method*, the French rhetorician Gérard Genette offers a useful mechanism for exploring the particular narratological elements that establish style and tempo within a literary work, in Genette's case, Proust's *À la recherche du temps perdu*. These narrative movements—specifically, summary, ellipsis, descriptive pause, and scene—reveal the stylistic foundations that produce the overall impression that a given narrative evokes. Such movements establish a tempo within a text, and their efficacy can be measured by the effects they create within that narrative. With *Lone Star*, the application of Genette's narrative principles usefully demonstrates the moral impact of Sayles's visual style, as well as of his strategic, ethically motivated tampering with traditional conceptions of time and place. Genette's narratological schema also underscores the manner in which the narrative elements inherent in Sayles's film function as a means for considering the "disruptive power" of history, in the words of Richard Schickel, and its remarkable impact upon the present when the past remains obscured by a veil of silence (95).

Yet the application of Genette's theories of narrative discourse to film calls into question many of the rhetorician's arguments regarding temporality and textual duration. In contrast to the variable nature of the reading experience, the cinema confronts its audience with a markedly different, more controlled form of narrative consumption. Simply put, the notion of screen time differs dramatically from reading time because film—at least under normal, theatrical viewing conditions—never stops rolling; the conditions of cinema strictly control narrative duration, itself a more elastic and mutable concept during the reading experience. "Just as we cannot choose to skip around in a film or go back and rewatch a portion," David Bordwell observes in *Narration in the Fiction Film*, "so we cannot control how long the narration takes to unfold. This [limitation] is of capital importance for filmic construction and comprehension" (80). In short, projection time governs the audience's reception of film narrative. While Genette's theories of discourse prove revelatory when applied to the cinematic experience, a stylistic reading of film demands consideration of the various narrative properties specific to film as a storytelling genre. As Edward Branigan notes in *Narrative Comprehension and Film*, "By linking style to the fundamental time of projection, style becomes a basic ingredient of cinema—one of the ways in which the medium controls narration and the spectator's perception of plot and story" (149).

Although understanding the constraints of projection time highlights the inherent stylistic differences between filmic and literary narratives, the notion of cinematic implied authorship demonstrates the decidedly similar function of authority in each medium. While the contingency of the pro-jector seems to negate some of the value of Genette's theories to film study, particularly his notion of the descriptive pause, understanding the role of authorship in film underscores the cinematic relevance of his theories regarding summary, ellipsis, and scene. "Films, like novels," Seymour Chatman argues in *Coming to Terms: The Rhetoric of Narrative in Fiction and Film*, "present phenomena that cannot otherwise be accounted for, such as the discrepancy between what the cinematic narrator presents and what the film as a whole implies" (130–31). For this reason, as consumers of film narrative—as with literary texts—we depend upon a given film's implied author for the manner in which we consume the cinematic experience.[4] Simply put, we perceive what implied authors or narrators perceive; we often share in their speculations about the narrative's possible outcomes, as well as in their emotional responses to the events that they encounter on the screen. The cinematic narrative's principal focalizer essentially oper-ates in this sense, then, as the director's alter ego, the character through whom the audience experiences the film's story, plot, and dialogue.

In *Lone Star*, Sayles's narrative traces the multicultural progress of Rio County by following Sheriff Sam Deeds (Chris Cooper)—both the son of Frontera's former and legendary sheriff, Buddy Deeds (Matthew McConaughey), and the film's implied narrator—in his investigation of the apparent murder of his father's misanthropic predecessor, Charley Wade (Kris Kristofferson). In the film, the specter of his celebrated father's local mystique haunts Sam as he begins to discover the mysterious past shared by Frontera's at-once segregated and interconnected Anglo, Hispanic, African-American, and Native-American communities. While Sayles uses the conventional stylistics of the murder mystery to establish the frame of the story, his true search remains clear: Frontera, once a town on the margin of Anglo-American expansion, now resides on the frontier of Ameri-can multiculturalism. As with many border towns in the United States, Frontera's limits of demarcation seem arbitrary in nature. Those who live in town share a heritage and a history that binds them to one another in unexpected, and, at times, shocking ways; because of the bonds of history, Sayles seems to argue in *Lone Star*, it is often difficult facilely to sort out the good from the bad, the right from the wrong. Sayles further complicates the intersections of race and class via Frontera's military base, which affords his narrative with the historical precedence of protectionism that permeates much of the thinking in Frontera and in America in general. The presence of the military base also allows Sayles to introduce a number of African-American characters into Frontera's predominantly Anglo and Hispanic multicultural mélange. Together, these aspects of *Lone Star* furnish the director with a microcosm of race in the United States, as well as an element of flux, for those who live on the base are not rooted in Frontera's past in the same ways as the locals.

Early in the film, Sayles establishes Sam Deeds as *Lone Star*'s principal "focalizer." Because he represents the law, his search—while personal in some regards—touches the lives and locations of virtually all of the characters. Shlomith Rimmon-Kenan explains that "focalization has both a subject and an object. The subject (the 'focalizer') is the agent whose perception orients the presentation, whereas the object (the 'focalized') is what the focalizer perceives" (74). In many ways, Sam serves as the moral or ethical compass of the film; his perceptions of Frontera and its inhabitants certainly orient the viewer to the landscape of intersecting cultures while also allowing for a form of mediation. Because Sam appears to be a man of reasonable actions and reasonable conclusions, he creates a sense of reserved judgment that in turn permits the viewer to watch and wait. Sayles exploits the conventions of the murder mystery in *Lone Star* as a means for heightening his audience's curiosity about the puzzling events of Frontera's past; as the film's literal detective, Sam leads us on a quest for the truth—not only about the identity of Wade's killer, but also about the truth of Frontera's cultural history. As David Bordwell and Kristin Thompson note, "It is the detective's job to disclose, at the end, the missing causes—to name the killer, explain the motive, and reveal the method" (69). Transcending the genre, Sayles's murder mystery does not push the viewer toward a verdict; rather, Sayles seems more intent on challenging the viewer to deliberate over the affairs of Frontera instead of merely judging them. By asking his audience to consider the nearly unreconcilable conflicts inherent in Frontera's labyrinthine cultural fabric, Sayles rather explicitly eschews the "bland multiculturalism" and one-dimensional earnestness of which critics such as Miller speak.

In this fashion, Sayles narrates much of *Lone Star*—especially Sam's own uneasy relationship with his father and with the past—through the use of summary.[5] What makes *Lone Star* of interest stylistically is the fact that Sayles actually uses summary as more than simple connective tissue. While Sayles employs summary in order to underscore the importance of other moments in the film that take place in the historical present, the summary scenes, nonetheless, transcend their role as mere background. In effect, by placing more weight upon summary than is customary, Sayles suggests the ethical portent of history and its intimate relationship with the present.[6] To this end, Sayles projects Sam, as "listener," into several summary scenes by using ellipsis, a narrative element that highlights the connections between the past and present, elucidating the shared interstices of the Frontera community. In his study of narrative discourse, Genette establishes two forms of ellipsis, explicit and implicit. Explicit ellipses clearly indicate a lapse of time, according to Genette, while implicit ellipses suggest a more indefinite time-lapse and can only be inferred by the reader based upon a gap in a given narrative's continuity (106–09). Most often using explicit ellipses, Sayles signals such transitions in *Lone Star* by drawing the viewer's eye toward details of historical significance. First panning either left or right, up or down, Sayles then uses a form of the elliptic cut to connote a shift in time, and, in certain instances, a shift in place as well. Bordwell and Thompson define this process generally as elliptical editing, which consists of "shot transitions that omit parts of an event, causing an *ellipsis* in plot and story duration" (260).

The first instance of explicit ellipsis occurs early in the film in the Café Santa Barbara. There, Hollis Pogue (Clifton James), former deputy and current mayor of Frontera, holds forth to a court of "two good old boys" on the legendary subject of Buddy—whom he hopes to honor with the naming of a park and the commissioning of a statue.[7] Before Sayles shifts his narrative into the past through the stylistic device of ellipsis, he allows Sam to engage Fenton (Tony Frank), one of the good old boys listening to Hollis, in a dialogue about the commemoration in the present. Fenton is enraged because, as he puts it, "every other damn thing in the country is called after Martin Luther King; they can't let our side have one measly park." Pointing out that the other possibility for the park commemoration concerned a Mexican-American youth who was killed in the Gulf War, not an African-American, Sam goads Fenton into a more animated racist diatribe. In response to Fenton and Sam, Hollis suggests that "the Mexicans that *know*, that *remember*, understand what Buddy was for their people." At this juncture, Fenton entreats Hollis to tell the story of how Buddy came to be sheriff in 1957. Although at first Hollis demurs because "everybody heard that story a million times," he eventually agrees when Sam says he wants to hear Hollis's "version of it." At each point in the film when Sayles shifts, through ellipsis, from the present into the recounted past, he purposively demonstrates that what we are receiving is a "version" of history. Sayles's use of summary prods the viewer toward an understanding that history is personal, political, and, perhaps most important, contextual; his decision to use the generic conventions of the murder mystery, moreover, supports the idea that the truth of the past is always shifting in relation to the vantage point of the observer. While many readers might struggle with the idea that history shifts depending on context, few would deny that a murder investigation involves finding clues within the stories of witnesses and suspects, that the objective act of the crime is lost to the past and may only be discovered through the myriad tales of those who live on. In *Lone Star*, we journey through ellipsis into summary so that not only the story which the silence of historical memory seeks to avoid may be heard, but, as *Lone Star*'s conclusion reveals, that all stories inevitably impinge upon one another's borders.

While Genette's theory originates with written narratives, the principles of ellipsis and summary offer insight into film as well. In this case, the film cut—the most common transition between shots—functions in film in a manner similar to an ellipsis in print narrative. Sayles uses the traditional cut in *Lone Star* to great effect in his visual narration of Frontera's multicultural tableau. For instance, the film opens with three simple cuts that establish the army base, Pilar Cruz's school, and Mercedes Cruz's café as important settings for the story. Sayles chooses, however, to use elliptical editing—which he achieves with tracking shots—at several strategic points in the film to emphasize the interconnections within Frontera's many different histories, the ways in which the past and the present preside over the actions of those living in the here and now. In the first instance of elliptical editing, Hollis begins his version of the story about the night that Buddy became sheriff. As the ellipsis begins and Hollis's story shifts into summary, the camera moves from the faces of the men who are gathered around the restaurant table in the present moment to a tight focus on the tortilla basket that rests in the center of the table. Sayles cues the audience to the shift in time by highlighting the basket's plastic construction in the present in contrast to its straw fabrication in the past. Far more subtle than a superimposed date on the screen, this technique not only emphasizes the fluidity and consequence of time's passage; it also serves as the means via which Sayles symbolically conflates Frontera's sense of cultural past and present.

Hollis's story serves as a striking visual introduction to Buddy's character and creates a moment in which we may observe Sam's reactions to the looming presence of his dead father. One of the ancillary themes running through *Lone Star* concerns the relationship between fathers and sons. When Frontera's citizenry often remind Sam in direct and indirect ways that there will never be another sheriff like Buddy, they imply that Sam will never live up to the standards of his father. In a corollary story, Colonel Del Payne (Joe Morton), the new commander of the army base, struggles both with the forty-year divide that rests between himself and his father, Otis Payne (Ron Canada), owner of "Big O's," the only bar in town where African-Americans feel welcome, and with the increasing separation that grows between himself and Chet (Eddie Robinson), his high-school aged son. Sayles emphasizes the significance of knowing the past through interpersonal relationship as he explores the dynamic within these families. The notion that knowledge comes through such relationships is introduced early in the film at the school board meeting where angry parents argue about the multicultural pedagogy that Pilar (Elizabeth Peña) employs in her history courses. The assembled parents challenge her current teaching methodology because she supplements the approved textbook with lessons that attempt to expose students to several different perspectives of a single historical event, a technique replicated by Sayles himself as he offers multiple perspectives in the narrative construction of *Lone Star*. The meeting exposes the divisions in the community that have evolved over time because of the lack of intercultural relationship and communication among Frontera's citizenry. As with Sam or Del or Chet—whose personal lives have been separated by anger and misunderstanding—the community as a whole can come to no true understanding of its many histories, of its shifting sense of cultural identity, without the ability to listen to one another in human relationships.

On one level, by making a film like *Lone Star* Sayles encourages his audience to engage in ethical debate with the very problems that threaten his characters. Through the compelling form of the murder mystery, Sayles draws the audience into a relationship of desire for the knowledge of what actually transpired at the scene of the crime, but, as a result of that knowledge, he presents us with a story that transcends generic boundaries and moves us into closer relationship with the concerns of the other cultures he introduces in the film. In "Film and Cultural Identity," Rey Chow explains that because "cultural identity is something that always finds an anchor in specific media of representation, it is easy to see why the modes of illusory presence made possible by film have become such strong contenders in the controversial negotiations for cultural identity; film has always been, since its inception, a *transcultural* phenomenon," Chow contends, "having as it does the capacity to transcend 'culture'—to create modes of fascination which are readily accessible and which engage audiences in ways independent of their linguistic and cultural specificities" (169, 174). Without the relationship that Sayles creates via the murder mystery, however, the transcultural experience that *Lone Star* offers would not carry the same ethical import. Because Sayles draws his characters together naturally through Sam's detective work, their lives and histories commingle in an authentic fashion, compelling the audience toward a deeper understanding of race and family. As with his earlier films such as *Brother from Another Planet* (1984) and *City of Hope* (1991), Sayles establishes cultural metaphors in *Lone Star* in order to highlight the deeper interconnections that define our shared sense of humanity. As we discover in the film's startling conclusion, Sayles's primary concern—although we become involved with the very real families that populate Frontera—is that we come to a knowledge of the universal family of humanity, an idea, he suggests, that ultimately binds us to one another.

Yet Sayles's films inevitably recognize that coming to an understanding of the nuances of interpersonal connection often exacts a painful price. In effect, as we move through the stories of characters whose lives were touched by Buddy, we begin to recognize that Sam's efforts at solving the murder of Wade indicate a cultural shift that many in Frontera simply don't wish to make. In his review of *Lone Star*, Schickel suggests that "the silence of [Wade's] grave symbolizes a larger and more conspiratorial silence afflicting Frontera. . . . Sayles wants us to count the costs of silence too—in the baleful distortions it imposes on the people who keep it, in the damage it eventually does to innocents like Sam and Pilar when they are not let in on the secret it shrouds. Above all," Schickel continues, Sayles "wants us to understand that when we deny history we grant it a more disruptive power" (95). The cultural shift that must occur in Frontera involves the embrace of histories, not the denial of history. In the past, when Frontera was a town ruled by Anglos, order was founded upon a single ethnic narrative, and Buddy not only helped author that narrative but also worked hard to enforce it. While he certainly did not use the sadistic measures of his predecessor, the desire for a peace founded upon a single narrative remained. Not surprisingly—as we see in the stories told in visual summary by Minnie or Big O or Chucho—the African-American and Hispanic communities did not seek to disrupt Buddy's narrative or abolish his rule as sheriff. The conditions they lived under during Buddy's tenure were far more amenable than those during the tyranny of Wade. But at the current juncture in Frontera's history, the next generation is no longer satisfied by the single historical narrative embraced by the town's elders, and, because of this turn away from a single organizing myth of the good Buddy Deeds and the evil Charley Wade, we witness the disruptions at the school as Pilar attempts to demonstrate the diversity and complexity of history or the revelation encountered by Del as the young female private in his command explains to him that she is in the army because "this is one of the best deals they [the white majority] offer."

The use of visual summary, and, in some instances, descriptive pause, also provides Sayles with a means for imbuing the setting of *Lone Star* with a striking sense of the various ethnic figures who surround greater Frontera—from the Mexicans who live just beyond the nearby river's watery borders to the Native Americans selling cultural artifacts on the outskirts of town and the Texans themselves, who function as modern caricatures of mythic Western archetypes from a bygone era. Sayles allows his audience to encounter these different cultural factions by placing Mexican, Native-American, and Texan characters, respectively, in the path of Sam's murder investigation. While attempting to learn about the circumstances of the death of Eladio Cruz (Gilbert R. Cuellar, Jr.) during Wade's tenure as sheriff, Sam visits Chucho (Tony Amendola), a former Texas resident and the current owner of a tire repair shop, in the Mexican border town of Ciudad León. Known locally as the *Rey de las Llantas* ("King of the Tires"), Chucho narrates the events surrounding Wade's cold-blooded murder of Eladio by way of summary, while also musing about the "invisible line" that divides Mexico and the United States. This invisible line not only divides those two countries, but also the past and the present, imbuing the boundary with both geographical and historical significance. Hoping to learn more about his father's past, Sam later visits Wesley Birdsong (Gordon Tootoosis) at the Native American's roadside stand. During their ensuing conversation, Wesley sifts through a variety of cultural artifacts, from a longhorn skull and a wooden replica of the Alamo that also functions as a radio to a rattlesnake skin and souvenir buffalo chips. Through a series of descriptive pauses, Wesley informs Sam about Buddy's restless past, as well as about the former sheriff's extramarital relationship with a mystery Frontera woman. According to Genette, descriptive pauses occur when the author withdraws from the diegesis, or story, to describe a scene that the reader and other characters in the passage are not currently viewing (99–102). In this manner, Wesley—as he pauses to examine the found objects of Frontera's past and narrates the events of Buddy's youth—provides Sam with valuable insight into his father's personal history.[8] The dusty, unsold contents of the Native American's roadside stand also signal the viewer about the ephemeral nature of Texas's Western past and the declining value of that past in the state's shifting multicultural present.

Finally, Sam's encounter with his manic-depressive ex-wife offers valuable visual clues about the fate of the archetypal Texan in the modern world. Once a cultural icon of Western life and values, the Texan—represented by the personage of Bunny (Frances McDormand), Sam's former wife—now struggles to find a sense of identity as the exaggerated caricature of the sports fanatic. Disparaged by her father for being too "high strung," Bunny sits in a living room that functions as a virtual museum of Texas sports memorabilia. Wearing a Houston Oilers sweatshirt and a Dallas Cowboys hat and sitting in front of a big-screen television, Bunny perches on a couch surrounded by signed footballs, team posters, and videocassettes of Texas professional and college football games. Bunny's obsession with the world of Texas sports manifests itself in her wide-ranging knowledge of football statistics, even including such sports ephemera as the weight-lifting abilities of local high-school football players and the nuances of the professional football draft. Yet, as with Chucho and Wesley before her, Bunny functions as but one more piece of the multicultural puzzle that confronts Sam as he searches for Wade's killer.[9]

In order to illuminate further the ethical nature of Sayles's use of visual summary, we must first examine the narratological element that Genette refers to as scene and how scene in *Lone Star* pushes Sam and Pilar toward radical insights about their love and their relationship to the community of Frontera. Although the most startling revelations in the film occur in summary passages, as an audience we remain concerned about the effect of these revelations on the characters in the present. A scene most often occurs in dialogue, says Genette, and "realizes conventionally the equality of time between narrative and story" (94). Sayles skillfully uses summary to comment on such scenes in his visual narrative, and their juxtaposition in *Lone Star* is loaded with ethical import. Sayles concentrates the film's most dramatic energy in three scenes involving Frontera's painful, yet ultimately remedial, excavation of its monocultural past. In the first scene, Sayles narrates Mercedes's arrival in Texas and her first meeting with Eladio, her future husband, using a brief visual summary that provides a flashback to 1945 of Mercedes crossing the Rio Grande from Mexico to Texas by moonlight.[10] Sayles carefully juxtaposes this summary with a scene depicting Enrique (Richard Coca), one of the employees in Mercedes's restaurant, begging her to help him care for his girlfriend, who has broken her leg while illegally entering Texas. When Enrique confronts her with his dilemma,

Mercedes instinctively decides to call the border patrol, for she prides herself on only hiring legal immigrants, whom she admonishes to speak English—"This is the United States," she recites to the employees of the Café Santa Barbara, and "we speak English." Yet Enrique's situation reminds her of her own initial passage to Texas, and Mercedes eventually chooses to assist Enrique in his plight without notifying the border patrol. By deciding to act on Enrique's behalf and implicitly sanction his girl-friend's illegal entry into Texas, Mercedes opts to embrace, rather than redact, her own personal history.

Sam comes to a similar conclusion about Frontera's jaded cultural past when he finally discovers the identity of Wade's killer. As the narrative of *Lone Star* seems to reach its dramatic apex, Sam confronts Hollis and Otis late one night at Big O's, the last place where anyone ever saw Wade alive. As Otis begins to narrate the events of that fateful evening, the camera pans from the present into the past through the bar's back room, where we suddenly see a much younger Otis engaged in an intense card game with four other African-American youths. Interrupted by Wade, Otis's after-hours guests scatter, leaving him alone to face the sadistic sheriff. As Wade prepares to shoot Otis at point-blank range, Hollis, the sheriff's ever-present deputy and the witness to his numerous human atrocities, fires upon his superior just as the shadowy figure of Buddy enters the bar. Fearing for Hollis's safety if the truth of Wade's death ever emerged, Otis, Hollis, and Buddy decide to allow legend to narrate the tale of the late sheriff's disap-pearance. As "time went on," Otis explains to Sam, "people liked the story that we told better than anything the truth might have been." Yet with the identity of Wade's killer finally revealed, Sam chooses to ignore the literal truth of history and let Buddy's role in the popular story of Wade's death endure. "Buddy's a goddamn legend," Sam concludes; "he can handle it." Again, as with Mercedes before him, Sam—through the visual auspices of Sayles's narratological summary—allows history to repeat itself rather than correct the fraudulent narrative of the past. By letting Buddy's legendary deeds on behalf of Frontera survive, Sam embraces, rather than disavows, the border town's ethnically beleaguered past.

While the knowledge of his father's actual role in the disappearance of Wade provides Sam with some sense of conclusion to the murder investigation that he conducts throughout *Lone Star*'s narrative, his close inspection of Frontera's past confronts him with several alarming questions about his personal heritage. During the course of his forensic study of Frontera's cultural past, Sam rekindles a romantic relationship with Pilar that finds its origins in their teenage years. Sayles employs summary as a means for informing the audience about their romantic past and the sudden, dramatic demise of their relationship at the hands of Buddy. In one instance, Pilar laments—rather ironically, considering her enduring feelings for Sam in the present—that "nobody stays in love for twenty-three years." Sayles segues from Pilar's words in the present to a 1972 summary scene at a drive-in movie theater, where we witness Buddy and Hollis in the act of surprising the half-clothed Sam and Pilar in their car. As the sheriff and his deputy separate the couple and begin taking them back to their respective homes, the crowded drive-in erupts in a round of car horns and brightly lit headlights. Sayles skillfully shifts from his summary of the past into a present-day scene depicting Sam alone at the abandoned drive-in theater, sitting on the hood of his squad car and staring at the broken-down movie screen.

Sayles later contrasts the image of Sam's lonely vigil at the drive-in theater with the meeting between Sam and Pilar at the drive-in that closes the film and also provides the impetus for Chavez's strident critique of *Lone Star*. For the first time in his narrative, Sayles chooses to dispense with his summary of the past and confront his characters in a mimetic scene that boldly and completely interacts with the present, with the here and now of Frontera.[11] As Sam reveals the identity of Buddy's mystery woman as Mercedes Cruz—and, in the process, finally explains the intensity of the connection that they shared for so many years—Pilar reacts to the silence that suddenly and conspicuously lies between them: "So that's it?" she asks; "you're not going to want to be with me anymore? I'm not having any more children," she continues, and "I can't get pregnant again, if that's what the rule is about." With the narrative of Frontera's past once again confronting them in the present, Sam and Pilar decide to "start from scratch:" "Everything that went before, all that stuff, that history," Pilar remarks, "the hell with it." As the couple stare at the blank tableau of their future in the image of the abandoned drive-in's dilapidated movie screen, Pilar confidently urges Sam—indeed, Frontera's entire populace—to "forget the Alamo." Sayles shatters the visual silence of the screen with the optimistic strains of Patsy Montana's 1935 hit, "I Want to Be a Cowboy's Sweetheart."[12] Through his depiction of Sam and Pilar in the act not only of reconfiguring their shared past together but also of assenting to their incestual relationship, Sayles once again demonstrates the manner in which his characters opt to revise the narratives of the past—to allow history to repeat itself while simultaneously reviving their love for each other—in order to facilitate senses of community and interpersonal connection, elements of humanity previously denied to them by Frontera's culturally fractured past.

By constructing his visual rendering of the interconnections between the past and present communities of Frontera, Sayles succeeds in fashioning the elaborate incestual cultural metaphor that so troubles Chavez. In *Lone Star*, Sayles reminds us about the tremendous pull that the past exerts upon our lives in the present, as well as about the necessity of reading contextually the narratives of the past in order to glimpse the possibilities of the future. In her introduction to the anthology *Two Worlds Walking: Short Stories, Essays and Poetry by Writers with Mixed Heritages*, Diane Glancy claims that in America there is a movement toward wholeness based on our diversity, that we need to examine "the worlds that walk within us," to recognize the "new order of migration, in which *the going* is the journey itself, rather than arrival at a *destination*" (xi). By allowing his characters to embark finally on the journey of Frontera's future, Sayles confronts the denizens of the border town with the need to cross the ethnic borders that divide them and to establish and maintain a genuine sense of community, an aspect of humanity withheld from them previously both because of the tyranny of Wade and because of the rigidity of the cultural narrative authored by Buddy. While Sam's murder investigation never results in an arrest, trial by jury, or verdict, his search for the truth—even as he chooses to embrace the narrative of the past—reveals the value of community to Frontera's endurance and cultural health. As Julie D. Balzekas, an executive committee member of the Joint Center for Poverty Research, reminds us, "Responsible behavior is at the core of all moral teachings—in fact, one could argue that those lessons of responsibility most essential to the healthy functioning of a culture become the morals of that group" (14). Finally recognizing themselves as a community of disparate cultures with a shared sense of history, the citizens of Frontera under Sam Deeds's watch succeed in accepting the responsibility for their past, their present, and, ultimately, their future.

Imbuing *Lone Star* with a carefully constructed incestual metaphor—as opposed to the incest taboo that Chavez laments—allows Sayles to underscore the ethical force of his screenplay, a narrative that achieves its moral aims through Sayles's skillful use of visual style. "Style itself makes its claims, expresses its own sense of what matters," Nussbaum remarks. "Literary form is not separable from philosophical content, but is, itself, a part of content—an integral part, then, of the search for and the statement of truth" (3). In this way, style functions essentially as an ethical construct, as a vehicle for Sayles's considerable cultural and ethical arguments. Reading *Lone Star* in terms of Genette's narratological elements reveals the manner in which Sayles's film succeeds as a dramatic rejoinder to the cultural dilemmas that mark our past, as well as a genuine vision of American life and the shifting sense of identity that defines our contemporary value systems. "The urge to find one's place, to create and feel the comfort of community, is the abiding American story," Edward Guthmann observes. "Whereas European, African, and Asian cultures are marked by diaspora— by parents losing their children and populations struggling to preserve tradition and continuity—the American story is one of improvising an identity" (D1). In *Lone Star*, Sayles narrates an essentially American story, for his characters not only struggle to embrace the competing narratives that mark our past, but also attempt to improvise the stories that will decide the course of our shared cultural future.

Notes

Introduction

1. For a fuller overview of some of these influences on and precursors of exile and diaspora film criticism, see Hamid Naficy, *An Accented Cinema*, chapter 1. The bibliography at the end of *Moving Pictures/Migrating Identities* contains a sampling of relevant works by the authors mentioned.

2. For a detailed analysis of Frears' use of glass and spatial relations in this film, see Kaleta 216–39.

3. For a critical analysis of the relationship between the nation-state, transnationalism and diaspora cultures, see Appadurai; Jameson and Miyoshi; Wilson and Dissanayake.

2. Traversing the Screen Politics of Migration

1. Koller remarked in the ensuing days of whirlwind press interviews in Los Angeles, "I never expected to win. We all thought 'Cyrano' was going to win . . . If I had been the judge of it all, I would have given the award to [Michael Verhoeven's] *The Nasty Girl*" (Stack E2).

2. Koller surmised, "We had limited finances to advertise the film, which is always the case, but I think with this film there was another reason: maybe it hit a little too close to home" (Thomas F17).

3. The list of such films is too numerous to include, but a few more prominent titles, some of which remain accessible through international distributors today, include Rainer Werner Fassbinder's *Angst Essen Seele Auf* (1973), Christian Ziewer's *I See This Land from Afar* (1977), Werner Schroeter's *Palermo or Wolfsburg* (1979), Erika Runge's *Lisa and Tschepo: A Love Story*, (1981), Jan Schütte's *Dragon Chow* (1987), and Hark Böhm's *Yasemin* (1987).

4. Indeed, even in the instance of foreign nationals producing films in West Germany, such as Tevfik Baser—perhaps best known for his *40 Square Meters in Germany* (1986)—criticism has been exerted by his own countrymen abroad that he was too willing to secure his own directorial success by corroborating preconceived notions harbored by the Germans about the status of women in Turkish culture.

5. Some of the more canonicized texts that constitute the genre discussion in film criticism include: Altman 1987 and 1999, Schatz 1981, Wood 1977, Braudy 1976.

6. I am thinking of Foucault's discussion in "The Discourse of Language," appended to *The Archaeology of Knowledge*, in which he begins the retreat from his prior methodological position of treating discourse as completely self-contained, self-regulating and ahistorical. In effect, this is the point at which the notion of genealogy, of institutional or socially-interested

power relations that inform and transform discursive formations over time, begins to surface, herein anticipating the performative exegesis of *Discipline and Punish*.

7. In "The Discourse on Language" he identifies "exteriority" as one of four operative strategies or principles of his methodology. It is a strategy that stands in contradistinction to psychoanalysis and Marxism, which seek deeper meanings or truths hidden in discourse, read as symptom of repressed realities. Foucault assumes a formalist or structuralist stance, taking the surface of discourse itself, "its appearance and its regularity" (229), as the fundamental reality rather than seeking transhistorical truths that discourse functions to mask.

8. Annette Kuhn (1988) utilizes this line of Foucauldian reasoning to quite convincing effect with regard to early British cinema.

9. In the early 1990s, the American share of the European cinema market was topping 75%, while the foreign share of U.S. box-office earnings hovered at a mere 2% (Morley & Robins 18).

10. In an interview with Sheila Johnston, Koller explains, "The Kurdish community in Switzerland was frustrated that their story wasn't at the center of the film. But my Turkish partners told me what could happen to everybody involved if we had done that. Because the Kurdish language was not officially accepted in Turkey, we would have not got permission to make the film there and the crew would probably have faced problems after the shoot" ("The Incredible Journey" 19).

11. In "Different Spaces," Foucault describes the spatial implications of the mirror, his discussion evidently informed by Lacan: ". . . between utopias and these utterly different emplacements, these heterotopias, there must be a kind of mixed, intermediate experience, that would be the mirror. The mirror is a utopia after all, since it is a placeless place. In the mirror I see myself where I am not, in an unreal space that opens up virtually behind the surface; I am over there where I am not, a kind of shadow that gives me my own visibility, that enables me to look at myself there where I am absent—a mirror utopia. But it is also a heterotopia in that the mirror really exists, in that it has a sort of return effect on the place that I occupy. Due to the mirror, I discover myself absent at the place where I am, since I see myself over there. From that gaze which settles on me, as it were, I come back to myself and I begin once more to direct my eyes toward myself and to reconstitute myself there where I am. The mirror functions as a heterotopia in the sense that it makes this place I occupy at the moment I look at myself in the glass both utterly real, connected with the entire space surrounding it, and utterly unreal—since, to be perceived, it is obliged to go by way of that virtual point which is over there" (*Aesthetics* 178–79).

3. Traveling Pictures from a Turkish Daughter

1. See Barthes and also Foucault, "What is an Author?"; on the autobiographical practices by women, see Smith.

2. I have borrowed this term from Sheila Petty's book title *The Archaelogy of Origin: Transnational Visions of Africa in a Borderless Cinema*; see also Kosta, *Recasting Autobiography*, and Ella Shohat and Robert Stam.

3. For more information about the director see Löwisch.

4. Two interesting short films are *Per Luftpost* (*By Airmail*, 1992) and *Unberührt* (*Untouched*, 1993) which problematize the situation of Turkish teenage girls in Germany. Derin's latest feature film is *Zwischen den Sternen* (*Between the Stars*, 2001).

5. In her autobiographical analysis, Jutta Brückner reconstructs the years between 1953 and 1956 in Germany and describes how women's identity was constructed within the

given framework of cultural and political discourses; also see Kosta, "Representing Female Sexuality."

6. This title is borrowed from the German film festival "Women Behind the Camera: Contemporary Filmmakers in Multicultural Germany" that I organized at Wellesley College in March 2002; see http://www.wellesley.edu/German/filmfestival. The proliferation of films by minority women in Germany in recent years includes works by Angeliki Antoniou, Hatice Ayten, Serap Berrakkarasu, Delia Castaeira, Wanjiru Kinyanjui, Branwen Okpako, Ayse Polat, Sema Poyraz, Miriam Pucitta, and Yesim Ustaoglu.

7. Here I would like to refer to Christopher Clark's discussion of the internationally acclaimed German film *Lola rennt* (*Run Lola Run*, Germany, 1999) by filmmaker Tom Tykwer. Clark's interpretation is based on Margit Sinka's observations on the portrayal of Berlin in *Lola Rennt*. According to Clark, Tykwer "fuses Berlin together in order to present a vision of optimistic and dynamic young Germans" (15). However, the film excludes references to the existence of a minority culture in Berlin, and the representations of nuns perpetuates the idea of a homogenous (Christian) society in German cinema. See also Sinka.

8. Sheila Petty refers in her discussion of black experience in diasporas to the work of Paul Gilroy, Renaldo Walcott, and James Clifford who propose from different perspectives a connection between diaspora and origin (6).

9. In his extraordinary article "Leaving Home: Film, Migration, and the Urban Experience," Kaes demonstrates how the train sequence at the beginning of Ruttmann's film symbolizes the arrival of millions of migrants in Berlin. Within the context of transnational migration, Kaes interprets this opening scene as "the dislocation of millions of people in the decades before and after the turn of the century," and states further: "The film's opening sequence [. . .] suggests both the birth and separation and the undeniable experience of a primary loss. For the fateful transition from the countryside into the metropolis, the film finds images of a racing train, edited so as to heighten the dynamics and, at the same time, increase the disorientation. We see no passengers in the train, no human faces, only the gigantic impersonal machine that transports us, the viewers, into the city, recalling the sense of displacement migrants and immigrants . . . felt after deciding to leave behind their origins, their childhood, their sense of belonging, their community, their *Heimat*" (79–192).

10. This quote is spoken originally in Turkish. For this article, I have used the translation from the subtitles of the English version of Derin's *Ben annemin kiziyim*.

11. The best known examples are the films of Helma Sanders-Brahm's *Shirins Hochzeit* (*Shirin's Wedding*, 1975), Peter Keglevic's *Zu Haus unter Fremden* (1979), Tevfik Baser's *40 qm Deutschland* (*40 square meters of Germany*, 1985) and *Abschied vom falschen Paradies* (*Goodbye to a false paradise*, 1988), Hark Bohm's *Yasemin* (1987/88).

12. See Beverly and his discussion of Rigoberta Menchu's testimonial text.

13. Friedman concentrates in her critical essay on women's authobiography on the work of feminist theorists Sheila Rowbotham and Nancy Chodorow. Both works are building on Lacan's metaphor of mirrors and Simone de Beauvoir's *The Second Sex* and show how women existing at the margins of culture develop a "new consciousness" if they do not recognize themselves in the reflections of cultural representation.

14. This well-known modern version is sung by the female Turkish pop singer Sezen Aksu. In the documentary, this song is presented through nondiegetic sound.

15. The presented images by Derin also relate to the work of filmmaker and theoretician Trinh T. Minh-ha who discusses in her documentary *Surname Viet Given Name Nam* (1989) the context that shaped Vietnamese women's consciousness both in Viet Nam and in the United States. Interestingly, both documentaries examine the difficulties of representation

and the cultural images that served as role models for female identification in Turkish and Vietnamese culture; see Minh-ha.

16. Seyhan Derin. Personal interview. 30 March 2000.

4. Solidarity and Exile

1. Friedrichsmeyer et. al., Introduction 18, 24–25, and Sieg, "Ethnic Drag and National Identity: Multicultural Crises, Crossings and Interventions" 301.

2. West German film has produced a large number of films dealing with the Third World and especially Latin America, from the political (*Aus der Ferne sehe ich dieses Land* or *Es herrscht Ruhe im Lande*), to the autobiographical (*Malou*), to the fantastic (*Aguirre, Fitzcarraldo, Blauäugig*). The GDR's production is more limited, but also has some scope: Rainer Simon's co-production with ZDF, *Die Besteigung des Chimborazo* treated the excursions of Alexander von Humboldt; while Heynowski and Scheumann, in one of several films about Chile, posed as West German documentarists to expose the dictatorial practices of the Pinochet regime (*Ich war, ich bin, ich werde sein*, 1974). The only other film to dramatize the fate of Latin American exiles in the GDR, however, is *Isabel auf der Treppe* (Waltraud Lewin, 1984), which is based on a more straightforward tone of sympathy for the plight of refugees in need of help. In this context, the dramatic complexity of *Blonder Tango* stands out.

3. As Barnett's book indicates, among East European states only Romania came close to the GDR in Third World activity.

4. See the official documents: *Gegen Rassismus, Apartheid und Kolonialismus. Dokumente der DDR 1977–1982; Gegen Rassismus, Apartheid und Kolonialismus. Dokumente der DDR 1949–1977;* and Barnett's analysis, chapter 2.

5. See Lamm and Kupper 55–56. Examples of the contempt for Third World movements not in the GDR mold include remarks by Markus Wolf, the GDR's chief of foreign espionage (Wolf 258–59). Gilbert Ofodile of Nigeria wrote in a West German publication of the 1960s that he and other African students were photographed as visiting dignitaries for the GDR press, but their political views were not solicited if they deviated from the Leninist model.

6. The abstract value of Chile should not trivialize the biographical reality at the basis of this film's narrative, however, since both screenwriter and lead actor are indeed living examples of the abstract solidarity the GDR promoted. And Chile even provided the final haven to the GDR's deposed head of state Erich Honecker until his death in 1994.

7. Translations of the film dialogue are my own.

8. For a longer analysis of this scene and *I was 19*, see my article "From Anti-Fascism to Gegenwartsfilm: Konrad Wolf."

9. Here he again echoes Vadim in Konrad Wolf's *I was 19*: "Goethe and Auschwitz, two German words in every language. How can I make the children understand that?"

10. On Joseph Schmidt, see the biography by Gertrud and Karl Ney-Nowotny and the compact disk recording of Schmidt, *Deutsche und Englische Soundtracks/Soundtracks from German and English Films*.

5. *Servus Deutschland*

1. An abbreviated version of this article was presented at the *Jahrhundertwenden* centenary celebration of the University of Cincinnati's Department of Germanic Languages and Literatures. Special thanks to the Charles Phelps Taft Memorial Fund and the Max Kade Foundation for support on this project. Also I am grateful to Ramón Soto-Crespo and Susan Gustafson for helpful comments and suggestions.

2. In recent years, filmmakers such as Fatih Akin (*Kurz und Schmerzlos*) and Yüksel Yavuz (*Aprilkinder*) have released films dealing with the immigrant experience to great critical acclaim. See Hamdorf 44–45.

3. The much analyzed term "Heimat" has no real English equivalent. I will use it here in the same way as that offered by Ina-Marie Greverus and Michael Geisler. Perhaps the best definition of Heimat is one which Geisler quotes from Greverus, *Auf der Suche nach Heimat*: "an individual's emotional affinity to a socio-cultural region, which provides, or appears to provide, a sense of identity, security, and of taking an active part in defining one's own lifestyle" (42). See also Greverus's "The 'Heimat' Problem," and Ecker.

4. For an overview of the NGC, see Elsaesser's seminal study *New German Cinema* and Anton Kaes' *From Hitler to Heimat*.

5. The protagonists in the films under discussion offer a contrast to German literary pictures of exile and immigration wherein "Heimat" is often idealized through a desire to return home; see Ecker 26–27.

6. The weekly news magazine *Der Spiegel* devoted its cover story to this debate in its issue of 11 January, 1999. Many articles addressing the topic appeared in daily and weekly papers before, during and after the elections. The Social Democrats promised to change the citizenship during their campaign.

7. See Pflaum and Prinzler who make this point as well (100).

8. Davidson uses the generally accepted designation of the NGC as the period of German filmmaking from 1962–1989, beginning with the Oberhausen Manifesto and ending with the fall of the Berlin Wall.

9. See, for example, *New German Critique* (1985), which devoted an entire issue to new discourses of "Heimat," including Miriam Hansen's "Dossier on *Heimat*," republished in Ginsberg and Thompson, who devote an entire section to the Heimat debate. See also Kaes for an extensive analysis of the discourse of history in the NGC.

10. While "Trauerarbeit" was an important step in the *Vergangenheitsbewältigung* (coming to terms with the past) in the post-war era, many intellectuals debated the degree to which it had been carried out among the populace. This issue arose again in 1990, after the unification of East and West Germany, when the degree to which East Germans had undergone the necessary "Trauerarbeit" was called into question; see here especially Santer.

11. For an analysis of the development of the concepts of exile and nomadism (homelessness), see Peters.

12. Freud distinguishes mourning from melancholy, which is the pathological version of the former, characterized and distinguished primarily by the lack of self-regard and self-esteem, and, as we shall see, is in certain cases characteristic of the cinematic treatment of exiles.

13. Levin cites Donald Bogle's study of the representation of the African-American entertainer in the cinema. See Levin 124. He argues that Jasmin becomes a sort of "Über-other" whereby Brenda is then relegated to "unter-other" and by the film's conclusion Brenda has lost the control she once had of the café (124).

14. Davidson even suggests that certain ambiguities in the film even lead to questions about the relationship between Brenda and Jasmin, whereby the women's sexual identity is re-defined as well (100). The role of sexual identity in one's overall conception of self will play a major role in Adlon's 1991 film *Salmonberries*, discussed here later.

15. "Kotz" carries, of course, the additional vulgar meaning in German of "vomit." Julia Kristeva counts vomit among aspects of the abject, which like other polluting objects, "stand[s] for the danger to identity that comes from without" (*Powers of Horror* 71). While it is both a part of the self yet rejected by the self (in a means of self-defense), it is crucial in identity formation and self-actualization: "it is thus that *they* see that 'I' am in the process of

becoming an other at the expense of my own death. During the course in which 'I' become, I give birth to myself amid the violence of sobs, of vomit" (3).

16. O'Sickey compares Roswitha's collecting of salmonberries and her constant re-arrangement of the jars to Freud's analysis in *Beyond the Pleasure Principle* of the *fort/da* games that children play which constitute a device to help overcome a painful loss. Similarly, she argues, Kotz plays this game in her continual re-telling of her origins in an attempt to heal the loss of her mother and father but also, I would argue, to heal the separation and isolation from society which she experiences. As only a half-Inupiaq native, she is an outsider in her own homeland for she fits into neither the native nor the Western community in town.

17. For simplicity's sake, I have translated and paraphrased all quotes from the film if not otherwise noted.

18. For a discussion of the rise of multicultural German films, see Trumpener 733–43.

6. The Desire of the Other

1. A version of this essay appeared in *Romance Languages Annual* XI (2000) .

2. Today "the other" has become a prolific site of theories of knowledge and politics. The original premise of "knowing the other," demystified and translated into "speaking about/for the other" as a result of a wide range of critical theories and postcolonial studies (from Claude Lévy-Strauss's relativism, to Hamid Naficy's "haggling" and "counterhailing," to Maria Lugones' "spatialized linguistic resistance"), is now a question of negotiated transcultural discourses on agency—the possibility of "speaking nearby" (Trinh Minh-ha 101). For a recent exploration of power, desire and "looking relations," see E. Ann Kaplan, specifically her chapter "Travelling Postcolonialists and Women of Color."

3. See also Detassis 21, 25; Volpi 150, 152; Gili 28–29, Crowdus and Porton 8. In all these interviews, this use of the other was left unproblematized. All translations, unless otherwise noted, are mine.

4. On the importance of the metaphor of travel in Western metaphysics, see Caren Kaplan, especially the chapter "Traveling Theorists," which offers an exhaustive account of postcolonial studies on the subject.

5. I owe this accurate description to one of my film students, Estée Pierce.

6. On the historical relationship between fascist Italy and Albania in 1939, see Vitti 252–53.

7. On "the importance of a piece of bread," see Amelio's comments in Crowdus and Porton 6.

8. There exists here, in the interaction between the desiring Albanian subject and Gino—who is expected to act as its guarantor—a dimension for the most part disavowed by the film. This return of desire, or counter-desire elicits in Gino a barely articulated moment of colonial anxiety, of fear of contamination—the other half of the colonial's heterogeneous project of domination and consumption. On this, see Homi Bhabha, "The Other Question" 25–28.

9. But whose perception is this? Amelio's own diaries reveal that, among multiple narratives, it is *this* kind of story and *this* kind of pain that held his interest (Detassis 27, 30, 62).

10. On Amelio's critique of consumerist capitalism, see Vitti 253, 260 note 18, and 261 note 24. Pier Paolo Pasolini, following Marcuse, fought a bitter fight against American-style neo-capitalism and its ruinous effects in the 1960s on the Italian social imaginary (indeed on the historical social classes), which, through the manufacturing of false consumer desire, brought about the loss of traditional cultural differences. He called this socio-cultural homogenization an "anthropological revolution" or mutation (*Scritti corsari* 46–52, 66–77),

and he denounced television as not only the most pernicious tool of the new power, but as the very site of production of repressive power (*Scritti corsari* 30). In a talk delivered at a Festa dell'Unità in the summer of 1974 (now "Il genocidio" in *Scritti corsari* 277–83), Pasolini blamed television, among other means of mass-communication, for "cultural genocide" (282). On Pasolini's "historical pessimism," see also Greene 177–81.

11. At the end of the film, in his madness, Michele slips again into yet another past, that of an imagined emigration to America: "I want to be awake when we arrive in New York."

12. Cinemascope, Amelio writes, is "an 'epic' format, which has very little to do with the real, and even less with innocence" (Detassis 40). In another instance, he said, "I chose cinemascope to underline that this was a 'foreign' gaze, not Albanian . . . (given the Italian tradition of the genre film) . . . I wanted to immediately announce my belonging to another film culture" (Volpi 153).

13. On the relation between knowledge (gnosis) and a historically normative doxa (opinion) in Western anthropological discourse on Africa, see Mudimbe.

14. There is a recent proliferation in the West, but especially in Italy, of films on the Balkans and on the former Iron-curtain countries in general: in Italy, Carlo Mazzacurati's *Il Toro* (1994) and *Vesna va veloce* (1996), Maurizio Zaccaro's *Il carniere* (1997), Armando Manni's *Elvjis and Merylin* (1997), Mario Martone's *Teatro di guerra* (1998). In France, there seem to be only a few such films, e.g., Jean-Luc Godard's *Forever Mozart* (1996), a fiction film, and Marcel Ophuls' *War Correspondent: The Troubles We've Seen* (1994), a postmodern documentary. To my knowledge, there are no fiction films on the Balkans produced in Germany. On the other hand, a counter phenomenon seems to be taking place, that of indifference, as film critic Dina Iordanova writes, attributing the complacency of Western media to deeply entrenched institutionalized consumerism (884).

15. On Pasolini's distinction between naturalism and realism, see Marcus 245–49, Viano 165, Greene 40–44, and Gordon 211–13.

16. But Amelio too performs an unconscious slippage towards a more blameworthy, and more imaginary than la Callas, agent of hypocritical good works: he would have felt "like those ladies who when distributing candy in the slums, leave the fur-coat at home" (Sesti 57).

17. Although these films are to be placed in the avant-garde, rather than commercial cinema, as Amelio's film is, I believe that their perspective is relevant to the dynamic of privilege and appropriation that has been the focus of my analysis.

18. In this essay I only discuss certain aspects of Godard's film. A more complex analysis will be part of my essay "Sarajevo: Notes for a Balkan Mythos," to appear in the anthology *Screening the Balkans: From West to East/From East to West*, edited by Aine O'Healy and myself.

19. See Narayan for a critical examination of the concepts of "epistemic privilege" and "epistemic advantage" possessed by oppressed groups.

20. For a critique of similar positions of detachment in post-Foucauldian French thought, see Wheeler, who brings Rorty's neo-humanism to bear on Baudrillard and Lyotard; and Scarry, whose study of the materiality of pain, though not concerned with identity-politics, remains one of the most significant contributions to this issue.

7. Voices Unveiled

1. The term "public culture" was originally proposed in 1988 by Arjun Appadurai in the essay, "Why Public Culture?" Appadurai sought to replace terms extant in history and anthropology such as "popular," "folk," or "traditional" culture with a concept better suited to the cosmopolitan cultural processes of today's world. Reference to *French* public culture draws attention to the ways such processes are still often shaped by a national discourse in spite of

the increasingly transnational nature of much news media and information technology. We follow Sherry Ortner's use of the term in her analysis of public representations of Generation X in the United States:

> By "public culture" I mean all the bodies of images, claims, and representations created to speak to and about the actual people who live in the United States: all of the products of art and entertainment (film, television, books, and so on), as well as all of the texts of information and analysis (all forms of journalism and academic production). "Public culture" includes all the products of what is commonly called the "media," but much more as well (414).

Here we are concerned with the national public discourse on issues of immigration in France and the contribution of Benguigui's film to it.

2. Except for an outburst of shared laughter in the scene where Khira Allam cannot recall Enrico Macias' name, the filmmaker's voice is unheard. The abstract narrator of the film is plural.

3. Among Parmar's films on women are two short subjects: *Sari Red* (1988, 12 minutes) on the racist murder of an Indian woman in the United Kingdom in 1985, and *Khush* (1991, 24 minutes) on the taboo topic of homosexuality in India; and a long feature film on African-American feminims: *A Place of Rage* (1991).

4. Beur: mot désignant une substance alimentaire grasse et onctueuse (voir Petit Robert). De plus en plus écrit de cette façon par les journalistes (grosse faute d'orthographe! Cf. *La Disparition* de G. Perec). Voudrait maintenant désigner une population issue de l'immigration maghrébine . . . on a eu *Pain et Chocolat* . . . manquait le Beur. Décidément, l'immigration, ça se mange bien au petit-déjeuner! (Begag 10–11).

5. E.g. *C'est Madame la France que tu préfères* (1981), *Le départ du père* (1985) (Cf. Mireille Rosello's list of thirty films by Beur or Arab directors, in Sherzer 148–49).

8. More Than Meets the Eye

1. All translations from the French are my own, unless otherwise indicated.

2. Claire Denis also sees colonialist women as representative of France: "The lives of the women who were our mothers all had one thing in common . . . These women found themselves in an incredibly violent situation. They represented the French nation in a dump where no one gave a damn" (qtd. in Strauss 32).

3. Denis justifies this portion of the film on political grounds alone: "[I] wanted there to be at least one image of present-day Africa. I didn't want to portray Africa only in the past as if when colonization ended, someone said '*It's the end of an empire, this world is finished*.' Even if Africa has economic problems, it still exists and you have to show it" (qtd. in Strauss 31). Without questioning the sincerity of Denis's intentions, the frame story of *Chocolat* also serves more purely literary functions.

4. Sante writes: "In one of the film's throwaway allusions, the American, originally named William Park, has renamed himself Mungo, after his family's pre-slave name. The historical Mungo Park was one of the first Europeans to penetrate deep into the African interior. Claire Denis's accomplishment is something very similar: a profound journey of exploration." In fact, Mungo has not renamed himself and we do not know why he has been given this nickname; he tells France only that it is "a nickname they call me here."

5. Although I have no evidence that Denis ever read Mungo Park's *Travels in the Interior Districts of Africa*, I have no doubt that her use of his name is the result of conscious choice, given the general significance of naming in *Chocolat* and the clear suggestiveness of this name in particular. That not all viewers can be expected to recognize her allusion does not prevent it from enriching the text and our reading of it.

6. For example, Mungo's foreignness is suggested by the scene in which his son gives him a vocabulary lesson in a native language.

7. Park tends to be an engaged and curious observer but also a highly non-judgmental one. The original mission with which he was charged by the African Association had no purpose beyond that of travel itself; Park was asked to follow the Niger river to see where it might lead.

8. I quote selectively from the first chapter alone, in which the author successively "undertak[es] the voyage," "depart[s]," "arrives at Jillifree," "proceeds to Vintain," "proceeds up the river," "arrives at Dr. Laidley's," and "prepares to set out for the interior" (xi).

9. Hayden White argues that historical discourse consists "of the provisions of a plot structure for a sequence of events so that their nature as a comprehensible process is revealed by their figuration as a story of a particular kind" (58).

10. I don't think it really matters whether we choose to interpret the relationship between Aimée and Protée as potentially romantic or as explicitly and "only" sexual, although Denis understandably prefers the latter. Frantz Fanon has suggested that "colonial desire" functions differently for men and women and that "when a white woman accepts a black man there is automatically a romantic aspect" (qtd. in McClintock 362). Denis herself implicitly confirms this standard interpretation by her attempt to invert it: "Personally, this story is more interesting than most stories about Africa, which usually show that if the white woman wants sex with the black man, the black man is more than happy to have her" (qtd. in Reid 68, in English).

11. Compare, for example, the two passages that follow from Park's *Travels*. Marc contemplates philosophical and political questions from a poetic distance but also presumes to speak for the colonized "other." Park describes real events, which affect him personally, whether they take the form of comedy or pose a threat: (1) "They rallied me with a good deal of gaiety on different subjects; particularly upon the whiteness of my skin, and the prominency of my nose. They insisted that both were artificial. The first, they said, was produced when I was an infant, by dipping me in milk; and they insisted that my nose had been pinched every day, till it had acquired its present unsightly and unnatural conformation. On my part, without disputing my own deformity, I paid them many compliments on African beauty. I praised the glossy jet of their skins, and the lovely depression of their noses; but they said that flattery, or (as they emphatically termed it) *honey-mouth*, was not esteemed in Bondou" (56). (2) "They were very inquisitive, and examined my hair and skin with great attention; but affected to consider me as a sort of inferior being to themselves, and would knit their brows, and seemed to shudder when they looked at the whiteness of my skin" (138).

12. "Si le roi m'avait donné/Paris, sa grande ville,/Mais qu'il me fallait quitter/l'Amour de ma vie,/Je dirai au roi Henri/Reprenez votre Paris./J'aime mieux ma mie, au gué." "Ma mie" is a contraction for "mon amie" (m'amie), that is "la femme aimée." The association here, though oppositional in this context, between the beloved woman (literally named "Aimée) and the capital of France, can be seen to reinforce the symbolic connection between French women and national identity.

13. Given the importance of naming within the film, it does not seem insignificant that Marc, Luc, and Jon(athan), the three most prominent white men in the film, all representative in different ways of the abuses of colonialism and all in some sense infatuated with Aimée, mother of "France," should bear the names of three of the four books of the Gospel, particularly given the importance of the Catholic Church in helping France to define and carry out the "mission civilisatrice" of French colonialism in Africa. Luc, of course, is identified as a former seminarian, and Randall, whose wife has had an affair with him, ironically comments to Marc that "Monique thinks he's a saint."

14. Shohat and Stam see the "Prospero complex" as one example of the "infantiliza-tion trope" that works in a variety of ways to construct the colonized as primitive. France's relationship with Protée shows how tropes can travel within colonialist cinematic discourse. Borrowing here Shohat's and Stam's term for Shirley Temple in *The Littlest Rebel*, whose show of leadership over Bill Robinson "offers the cinematic *mise-en-scène* of this [infantilization] trope" (140), France also functions as a "powerful girl-child" in *Chocolat*. Shohat and Stam also note that the parallel tropes of "infantilization" and "eroticization" often appear together, and this too is the case in Denis's film. Critics have tended to ignore the extent to which France herself is explicitly gendered (she is a *girl*-child) and her relationship with Protée is explicitly eroticized; Kaplan, for example, describes what she nonetheless calls "the illicit liai-son" between Protée and France as "totally asexual" (163–64). France, more than Aimée, functions in a narrative of cross-racial romance, notably by the verbal (e.g., "Here's your share, my little chickadee" [*Voilà ton picotin, ma cocotte*]) and visual parallels that are estab-lished between France and Protée and Delpich and Thérèse.

15. The mythological origin of Protée's name has often been cited as a sign of the mul-tiple roles he plays within the film. There is another possibility, which seems particularly inter-esting in relation to the film as a whole. "*Protée*" also identifies an order of amphibians called Urodele whose ability to change the color of their skin suggests what Bhabha calls "the ambiva-lence of mimicry" within colonialism (qtd. in Kaplan 154); the body of the salamander, which appears white in the dark, becomes covered with black or brown spots when exposed to light.

9. Crossing the Border

1. See Roberts 64–101; for a discussion of agrarian secret societies see also Beames and Williams.

2. Jordan 17. There are some discrepancies between filmic dialogue and that of Jordan's screenplay; all other dialogue is transcribed from the film by the author.

3. I am grateful to my colleague Dr. Ann Kaegi for pointing out the colonial implica-tions of "Saracen."

4. For a study of the informal system of 'justice' operated by Sinn Fein/IRA in West Belfast see Hamill.

5. David Lloyd claims this concept of "nature" is essentialist and that both it and the film reinscribe stereotypes of nationalistic atavism (64–76).

6. Terry Byrne's reference (88) to the carnivalistic atmosphere has inspired this analysis.

7. I am grateful to Dr. Keith Spence for this point.

8. On the film's misogyny see Ayers and Edge.

9. For an interesting interpretation of the greenhouse see Hill 95–96.

10. For an interrogation of bourgeois feminism see Caryl Churchill, *Top Girls* (1982).

11. The concept of "blood sacrifice" emerges in the ideology of the proponents of the Easter Rising in 1916, paralleling the masculinist ideology of the early War Poets.

12. For an alternative reading of this see Boozer.

10. Egoyan's *Exotica*

Acknowledgments go to the students in my contemporary film history course at the University of Newcastle (Australia), for serving as a sounding board for some of the ideas pre-sented here, and to Ira Raja, for commmenting on an earlier draft.

1. Paul Coates notes that this doubled placement of the mirrors "clearly problematizes the legitimacy of any looking" (22). See Coates also for a further discussion of the ambiguous themes of protection and their relationship to voyeurism.

2. Egoyan interestingly uses similar terminology in an interview to describe the effects of the past on his own life, the way his "cultural baggage" made him feel insecure after moving to Toronto; see Naficy, "Accented Style" 189.

3. The spatial openness of these Edenic field sequences is in striking and largely refreshing contrast to the claustrophobic and cluttered feel of some of the present-day scenes, particularly those at the Exotica and at Zoe's and Thomas's offices, where the respective owners are literally and figuratively crowded by the past. This spatial motif bears out Naficy's interesting postulation of a claustrophobic tendency in exilic cinema, which articulates, among other things, a desire for security and "emplacement" in conjunction with a feeling of entrapment in unfamiliar surroundings ("Phobic Spaces"; see also discussion in relation to Egoyan's work in "Accented Style" 199–204).

4. Thomas's ritual of "hiring" ethnic dates on a regular basis to take to ballet performances makes for interesting comparison with the ritual that dictates the narrative structure of the director's preceding film, *Calendar* (1993). The protagonist of that film, a photographer played by Egoyan himself, hires a different ethnic woman to visit him at home each month (evidently on a kind of "date") and act out a scenario in which she excuses herself from their conversation in order to make an amorous phone call in her native tongue. This somewhat more tongue-in-cheek ritual, intercut with flashbacks to the events which precipitated the end of the protagonist's marriage, appears to function as a means of coming to terms with romantic/familial loss and ethnic alienation and desire—themes which also circulate in *Exotica.*

5. Egoyan comments on this imagery in Naficy, "Accented Style" 201–02, discussing as well how a sense of home requires a "collective projection," that is, "a number of people all believing the same thing at a certain time."

6. In contrast, the protagonist's disquiet in *Calendar* arises from his perception that his wife has begun to *deny* their shared past. "Why can't you refer to our history of each other?" he complains in a voiceover addressed to his spouse, adding (in terms evocative of exile), "You make me feel like a stranger. . . . You leave me stranded."

11. Mediating Worlds/Migrating Identities

1. For a historical overview of exile and diaspora, see Peters.

2. Shohat and Stam, *Unthinking Eurocentrism*; Lisa Lowe, *Immigrant Acts: On Asian American Cultural Politics*; Jun Xing, *Asian America Through the Lens: History, Representations and Identity.*

3. See Jun Xing (157–74) for an extended discussion of some of these works. The National Asian American Telecommunications Association sponsors and disseminates information about independent film and video works by Asian American directors and maintains a comprehensive website on the latest releases <http://www.naatanet.org>.

4. For a discussion of the importance of the sister bond in *Double Happiness*, see Rueschmann 86–91.

12. Feigning Marriage/Befriending Nations

1. See the Introduction to their collection of essays, *Tropicalizations: Transcultural Representations of Latinidad.* The volume portends to be "a discursive dialogism in which both dominant and marginal subjectivities are at once given voice and constantly relativized in an analysis that attempts to transcend the old binary of self/other" (1).

2. See Habermas or Taylor, especially chapter 5, "The Need for Recognition."

3. While I partake of López's project, I also focus on the kind of work the film does nationally, that is, how the film interpellates the U.S. audience into its value system.

4. Ending the occupation of Haiti was well under way when FDR came to power. Hollywood had a longer lead-time than my statement might suggest. I should also point out that when film scholars speak of the Good Neighbor policy movies, they refer to those that were financed by the United States government during the war years, in particular the propaganda films the Disney studio made.

5. For the complete statement, see Herring 913–14.

6. There is a vast bibliography on United States-Haiti relations. Dash, in his excellent study, outlines the above argument.

7. I am aware of the problematic conceptualization of Latin America as hybrid. The most interesting exposition of the question is Roberto Fernández Retamar's widely known essay, "Caliban: Notes Toward a Discussion of Culture in Our America." For a more recent look at Latin American identity, also see Chanady's volume of essays.

8. In her excellent history of the Ziegfeld Girl, for example, Mizejewski notes: "Even after immigration was stemmed by legislation, postwar racial tensions increased, so that stakes rose on the representation of the "public body" as a white one . . ." (11).

9. I am indebted to Mizejewski's authoritative study of how the chorus girl in her incarnation as the Ziegfeld Girl became the "All-American Girl."

10. I am indebted to David Rock's essay "War and Postwar Intersections" for this historical analysis. Despite its stated time frame, his volume on *Latin America in the 1940s* evaluates the policies and attitudes of the United States toward Latin America between the onset of the Great Depression and the beginning of the Cold War.

11. When different geopolitical needs emerge at the end of World War II, male rivalry will not coalesce in marriage. I am thinking of *Gilda* (1946), in which Hollywood travels once again to South America. This time the female protagonist Gilda, played by Rita Hayworth, will circulate between her rivals until she is no longer deemed necessary and will be eliminated at the end of the film. *Gilda's* ending forces one to wonder if Julio's jump will not end in oblivion. Once the threat of fascism is eliminated, Latin America will once again parachute out of history. Indeed, the United States concentrates on rebuilding Europe at the expense of Latin America. Here I am drawing on David Rock's analysis of United States foreign policy in the forties.

12. In passing, the first major debate in Latin America on the issue of hegemony, that is, the Gramscian notion that culture is a main strategic force in the gaining and maintaining of power, took place in the late twenties as a response in part to Haya de la Torre's populist organization APRA (*Alianza Popular Revolucionaria Americana*). In the early twenties, he gained prominence in Peru leading the campaign for the foundation of popular universities, designed to intervene in the cultural life of the working class. Exiled, he founded APRA in Mexico as a continental organization against United States imperialism, not against capitalism per se. Unlike his main Peruvian interlocutor Mariategui, Haya de la Torre believed that Latin America needed to achieve a sufficient degree of capitalist development to carry out the equivalent of the French revolution, that is, a bourgeois revolution needed capitalism. For him, it was a question of Latin America retaining national control over United States investments while rejecting cultural influences.

13. For a popular history of this divided legacy, see Caetano Veloso.

14. *Down Argentina Way* re-stages *Flying Down to Rio*, except that the romance is between an Argentine male rancher (Don Ameche) and a wealthy New York equestrian (Betty Grable). A long-standing feud between their fathers prevents them from doing business or anything else. How to overcome the parental obstacles occupies the rest of the film.

For purposes of my "homosocial" argument, the feud between fathers carries the residues of a homoerotic love. It so happens that the fathers where school chums in Paris, of all places. Their friendship ends in discord when the elder Crawford reveals to the school authorities that Quintana has eloped with a prostitute. Before anyone loses his dignity, the couple is apprehended.

15. Valenz's death coincides with the launching of the Alliance for Progress by President John F. Kennedy.

16. For a parallel argument, see the respective discussions of these films by Shapiro in the sections: "Interventions" (64–69) and "Conclusions: Unsecuring through Uncommon Sense" (120–26). I suspect we are both indebted to Jacques Derrida's writings on counterfeit money.

13. Forget the Alamo

1. An earlier version of this essay was published in *Style* 32.3 (1998).

2. It should hardly be surprising that Chavez proves to be equally critical of the initiatives of the multicultural project. In "Multiculturalism Is Driving Us Apart," Chavez argues that "the re-racialization of American society that is taking place in the name of multiculturalism is not a progressive movement, but a step backward to the America that existed before *Brown v. Board of Education* and the passage of major civil rights laws of the 1960s" (41).

3. As with Miller, Barbara Shulgasser seems unconvinced about the ethical imperatives that mark the narratives of Sayles's films: "You want to stay with him because Sayles really is on the side of morality, fairness, and sensible thinking," Shulgasser writes, and "you want his movies to be as entertaining and riveting as he is ethical and high-minded. But they just aren't" (D3).

4. In *Narration in the Fiction Film*, Bordwell describes the implied author of a given film as an "invisible puppeteer, not a speaker or visible presence but the omnipotent artistic figure behind the work." Because of the peculiar nature of the cinematic experience—and particularly because of the fact that in most films "we are seldom aware of being told something by an entity resembling a human being"—Bordwell questions the necessity of determining a film's implied authorship. "To give every film a narrator or implied author is to indulge in an anthropomorphic fiction," he writes (62). Yet in a film such as *Lone Star*, with its explicit cultural agenda, the character of Sam Deeds clearly functions as Sayles's alter ego and the cinematic vehicle through which he exerts his own "visible presence" upon the film.

5. Genette defines summary, in terms of his narratological schema, as those moments in a narrative that provide the background or history for later scenes. In fact, says Genette, "summary remained, up to the end of the nineteenth century, the most usual transition between two scenes, the 'background' against which scenes stand out, and thus the connective tissue par excellence of novelistic narrative" (97).

6. As Chatman observes in *Story and Discourse: Narrative Structure in Fiction and Film,* "The cinema has trouble with summary, and directors often result to gadgetry." In summary scenes, Chatman adds, "The discourse is briefer than the events depicted" (68–69). In *Lone Star*, Sayles constructs summary scenes by depicting Sam in the acts of "listening" to past events. By creating a series of flashbacks, Sayles provides his detective with a mechanism for assembling clues from the past in order to solve the mysteries that confront him in the present. A mere observer of such moments in the film, Sam never actively participates in the summary scenes' construction. Rather, Sam—along with the audience—witnesses the events as they unfold and purposefully withholds judgment about their significance until the film's conclusion.

7. The eventual statue itself functions as a microcosm of Frontera's monocultural past. In the screenplay, Sayles offers the following description of Frontera's memorial to Buddy Deeds: "The cloth drops to reveal a bas relief in brass set in a block of smooth limestone. A decent likeness of Buddy in uniform, his hands on the shoulder of a small Mexican-looking boy who stands beside him, eyes raised worshipfully" (57).

8. In effect, Sayles employs Wesley's analysis of the various objects in his roadside stand as a means for providing Sam—and indeed, the audience—with essentially nondiegetic material about past events taking place outside of *Lone Star*'s narrative space. In this way, the descriptive pause usefully applies to filmic narrative by fulfilling Sayles's desire to provide Sam and the audience with significant extra-textual information about Buddy's mysterious past.

9. In his review of *Lone Star*, Mick LaSalle fails to recognize Bunny's significant cultural import: "Frances McDormand has a bit as the sheriff's football-fanatic ex-wife," LaSalle writes, "a role that should have been left on the cutting-room floor. It's five minutes of McDormand, bug-eyed, rattling about football statistics" (D3).

10. In this instance, Sayles essentially merges Genette's notion of summary with his use of the traditional flashback scene. In *Lone Star*, summaries provide significant background material that Sam—the implied author and narrator—will later employ in his solution of the film's murder mystery. Yet such scenes also function as flashbacks because they allow us, in Branigan's words, to "see an actual, present memory image of the character" as he or she relives a past experience (176).

11. While much of *Lone Star*'s narrative essentially summarizes the past as Sam attempts to solve the detective story that undergirds the film, the mimetic scene at the drive-in signals a dramatic shift in the manner in which the audience consumes Sayles's narrative. Suddenly thrust into the present, viewers no longer interact with Frontera's history as they did throughout the rest of the film. The drive-in scene takes place in real time and without narratological intrusions from the past in the form of summaries or ellipses. As the film closes, this scene produces a startling visual and emotional effect on the audience by forcing us to consider fully Frontera's multicultural present, as well as "the way we live now," in the words of Roger Ebert (449).

12. Interestingly, Montana crossed several cultural barriers of her own, becoming the first female recording artist to enjoy a million-selling record. She later performed "I Want to Be a Cowboy's Sweetheart" as a duet with Smiley Burnette in *Colorado Sunset* (1937).

Bibliography

Abdi, Nidam. "L'immigration racontée de vives voix" in *Libération*, Feb. 4, 1998.

Accad, Évelyne. *Sexuality and War: Literary Masks of the Middle East*. New York: New York University Press, 1990.

Addiss, Stephen. *Japanese Ghosts and Demons: Art of the Supernatural*. New York: Braziller, 1985.

Altman, Rick. "A Semantic/Syntactic Approach to Film Genre." *Cinema Journal* 23.3 (1984): 6–18.

————. *Film/Genre*. London: BFI, 1999.

Anderson, Benedict. *Imagined Communities: Reflections on the Origin and Spread of Nationalism*. Rev. ed. London: Verso, 1991.

Angel. Dir. Neil Jordan. Perf. Stephen Rea, Marie Kean, Ray McAnally, Donal McCann and Honor Heffernan. FilmFour, 1982.

Anzaldúa, Gloria. *Borderlands/La Frontera*. San Francisco: Spinsters/Aunt Lute Foundation, 1987.

Appadurai, Arjun. *Modernity at Large: Cultural Dimensions of Globalization*. Minneapolis and London: University of Minnesota Press, 1996.

————. "Putting Hierarchy in its Place." *Cultural Anthropology* 3.1 (1988): 36–49.

————. "Why Public Culture?" *Public Culture Bulletin*, 1.1 (Fall 1988): 5–9.

Ayers, Kathyrn M. "The only good woman, isn't a woman at all: *The Crying Game* and the politics of misogyny." *Women's Studies International Forum* 20.2: (Mar–Apr 1997): 329–35.

Bakhtin, Mikhail. *Rabelais and His World*. Trans. Helene Iswolsky. Cambridge, Massachusetts: M.I.T. P, 1968.

Balzekas, Julie D. "Loss of Taboos." Letter. *Chicago Tribune* 31 March 1997: 14.

Barker, Francis, et al., ed. *Europe and Its Others: Proceedings of the Essex Conference on the Sociology of Literature*. Vol. 1. Colchester: University of Essex Press, 1985.

Barlet, Olivier. "Entretien: Yamina Benguigui." *Africultures*. November 1997: 36–41.

Barnett, Thomas P. M. *Romanian and East German Policies in the Third World: Comparing the Strategies of Ceausescu and Honecker*. Westport, CT/London: Praeger, 1992.

Barthes, Roland. "The Death of the Author." *Image Music Text*. Trans. Stephen Heath. London: Fontana, 1977.

Baske, Siegfried, and Gottfried Zieger, eds. *Die Dritte Welt und die beiden Staaten in Deutschland*. Asperg b. Stuttgart: Edition Meyn, 1983.

Beames, Michael. *Peasants and Power: The Whiteboys and Their Control in Pre-Famine Ireland*. Sussex: Harvester Press; New York: St Martin's, 1983.

Begag, Azouz, and Abdellatif Chaouite. *Ecarts d'identité*. Paris: Seuil, 1990.

Belghoul, Farida. *Georgette!* Paris: Barrault, 1986.

Ben annemin kiziyim-I'm My Mother's Daughter, dir. Seyhan Derin, perf. Durkadin Derin, Zahire Cebeci, Elif Öztürk, and Seyhan Derin. Turkish/German OV with Engl. Subtitles. Germany, Turkey: European Union, 1996.

Benguigui, Yamina. *Femmes D'Islam.* Paris: Albin Michel, 1996.

———. *Mémoires d'immigrés. L'héritage maghrébin.* Un film documentaire de Yamina Benguigui. Paris: Canal Plus, 1997.

———. *Mémoires d'immigrés. L'héritage maghrébin.* Paris: Albin Michel, Canal Plus Éditions, 1997.

Berger, John. *Keeping a Rendezvous.* Penguin, 1992.

Bergman, Andrew. *We're in the Money: Depression America and its Films.* New York: New York University Press, 1971.

Bernstein, Richard. "Journey of Hope." *The New York Times* 21 April 1991: sec. 2, col. 5: 16.

Beverly, John. *Subalternity and Representation: Arguments in Cultural Theory.* Durham, London: Duke University Press, 1999.

Bhabha, Homi K. *The Location of Culture.* New York: Routledge, 1994.

———, ed. *Nation and Narration.* London; New York: Routledge, 1990.

———. "Of Mimicry and Men." *October* 28 (1984): 125–33.

———. "The Other Question . . ." *Screen* 24:6 (1983): 19–36.

———. "Signs Taken for Wonders: Questions of Ambivalence and Authority under a Tree outside Delhi, May 1817." *The Locations of Culture.* London: Routledge, 1994: 102–22.

———. "Unpacking my library . . . again." *The Post-Colonial Question: Common Skies, Divided Horizons.* Ed. Iain Chambers and Lidia Curti. New York: Routledge, 1996.

Bloemertz, Stephan. *Die Tageszeitung* 13 June 1999: 16.

Blonder Tango, DEFA Studios für Spielfilme 1986, distributed by Progress Film-Verleih.

Blythe, Martin. *Naming the Other: Images of the Maori in New Zealand Film and Television.* Metuchen, New Jersey and London: Scarecrow, 1994.

Boozer, Jack Jr. "Bending Phallic Patriarchy in *The Crying Game.*" *Journal of Popular Film & Television* 22.4 (Winter 95): 172–80.

Bordwell, David, and Kristin Thompson. *Film Art: An Introduction.* 4th ed. New York: McGraw-Hill, 1993.

Bordwell, David. *Narration in the Fiction Film.* Madison: University of Wisconsin Press, 1985.

Brah, Avtar. *Cartographies of Diaspora: Contesting Identities.* New York: Routledge, 1996.

Branigan, Edward. *Narrative Comprehension and Film.* London: Routledge, 1992.

Braudy, Leo. *The World in a Frame.* New York: Doubleday, 1976.

Butler, Judith. *Gender Trouble: Feminism and the Subversion of Identity.* New York and London: Routledge, 1990.

Byg, Barton. "From Anti-Fascism to Gegenwartsfilm: Konrad Wolf." *Studies in GDR Culture and Society* 5. Ed. Margy Gerber et al. Lanham, MD: University Press of America, 1985: 115–24.

Byrne, Terry. *Power in the Eye: An Introduction to Contemporary Irish Film.* Lanham, MD & London: Scarecrow, 1997.

Carr, Jay. "Koller's Trip to the Oscars was a Journey of Success." *The Boston Globe.* 12 May 1991: B6.

Caughie, John. "The Logic of Convergence." *Big Picture/Small Screen: The Relations Between Film and Television.* Eds. John Hill and Martin McLoone. University of Luton Press, 1998: 215–23.

A Century of Cinema. Series for BFI/TV Productions Channel 4, 1994–96.

Chambers, Iain. *Migrancy Culture Identity.* London; New York: Routledge, 1994.

Chanady, Amaryll, ed. *Latin American Identity and Constructions of Difference.* Minneapolis: University of Minnesota Press, 1994.

Charity, Tom. "Behind the Mountains." 1.3 (July 1991): 5.

Chatman, Seymour. *Coming to Terms: The Rhetoric of Narrative in Fiction and Film*. Ithaca: Cornell University Press, 1990.

———. *Story and Discourse: Narrative Structure in Fiction and Film*. Ithaca: Cornell University Press, 1978.

Chavez, Linda. "Kiss and Tell." *Chicago Tribune* 26 March 1997: 25.

———. "Multiculturalism Is Driving Us Apart." *USA Today: The Magazine of the American Scene* 124 (May 1996): 39–41.

Chow, Rey. "Film and Cultural Identity." *The Oxford Guide to Film Studies*. Ed. John Hill and Pamela Church Gibson. Oxford: Oxford University Press, 1998: 169–75.

———. *Writing Diaspora: Tactics of Intervention in Contemporary Cultural Studies*. Bloomington: Indiana University Press, 1993.

Christie, Ian. "As Others See Us: British Film-making and Europe in the 90s." *British Cinema of the 90s*. Ed. Robert Murphy. London: BFI, 2000: 68–79.

Clark, Christopher. "Transculturalism, Transe Sexuality, and Turkish Germany: Kutlug Ataman's *Lola and Billy the Kid* and *Salon Oriental*." *Sexuality and Alterity in German Literature, Film, and Performance, 1968–2000*. Diss. Cornell University, 2001.

Clark, Katerina, and Michael Holquist. *Mikhail Bakhtin*. Cambridge, Massachusetts: Harvard University Press, 1984.

Clark, Samuel, and James S. Donnelly, eds. *Irish Peasants: Violence & Political Unrest 1780–1914*. Dublin: Gill and Macmillan, 1983.

Clifford, James. "Diasporas." *Cultural Anthropology* 9.3: 302–38.

———. *Routes: Travel and Translation in the late 20th Century*. Cambridge, MA: Harvard University Press, 1997.

Coates, Paul. "Protecting the Exotic: Atom Egoyan and Fantasy." *Canadian Journal of Film Studies* 6.2 (1997): 21–33.

Cohen, Abner. *Masquerade Politics: Explorations in the Structure of Urban Cultural Movements*. Oxford and Providence: Berg, 1993.

Cook, Pam. "Approaching the Work of Dorothy Arzner." *Feminism and Film Theory*. Ed. Constance Penley. New York: Routledge, 1988: 46–56.

Crowdus, Gary, and Richard Porton. "Beyond Neorealism: Preserving a Cinema of Social Conscience: An Interview with Gianni Amelio." *Cinéaste* 21:4 (1995): 6–13.

The Crying Game. Dir. Neil Jordan. Perf. Stephen Rea, Miranda Richardson, Forest Whitaker; Jaye Davidson and Adrian Dunbar. Polygram, 1992.

Dash, J. Michael. *Haiti and the United States: National Stereotypes and the Literary Imagination*. New York: St. Martin's, 1988.

Daughters of the Dust, dir. Julie Dash, perf. Adisa Anderson, Barbara-O, Cheryl Lynn Bruce, Cora Lee Day, Geraldine Dunston, Vertamae Grosvenor, Tommy Hicks, Trula Hoosier, Kaycee Moore, Eartha D. Robinson. USA: BFI/American Playhouse/WMG/Geechee Girls, 1991.

Davidson, John. *Deterritorializing the New German Cinema*. Minneapolis: University of Minnesota Press, 1999.

Deleuze, Gilles and Félix Guattari. "Savages, Barbarians, Civilized Men." Section 1: "The Inscribing Socius." *Anti-Oedipus: Capitalism and Schizophrenia*. Trans. Robert Hurley, Mark Seem and Helen R. Lane. Minneapolis: Minnesota University Press, 1983.

Derrida, Jacques. *Given Time: I. Counterfeit Money*. Tr. Peggy Kamuf. Chicago: University of Chicago Press, 1992.

Detassis, Piera. ed. *Gianni Amelio: Lamerica: Film e storia del film*. Turin: Einaudi, 1994.

Double Happiness. Dir. Mina Shum. First Generation/New Views Films, released by Fine Line Features, 1995.

DuBois, Ellen Carol, and Vicky L. Ruiz, eds. *Unequal Sisters: A Multi-Cultural Reader in U.S. Women's History*. New York: Routledge, 1990.

Durham, Carolyn. "Euzhan Palcy's Feminist Filmmaking: From Romance to Realism, From Gender to Race." *Women in French Studies* VII (1999): 155–65.

Easthope, Antony. *Englishness and National Culture*. London and New York: Routledge, 1999.

Ebert, Roger. "*Lone Star* Holds a Mirror to America." *Chicago Sun-Times*. 3 July 1996: 37.

Ecker, Gisela. "'Heimat': Das Elend der unterschlagenen Differenz." *Kein Land in Sicht: Heimat—weiblich?* Munich: Fink (1997): 7–31.

Edge, Sarah. "'Women are trouble, did you know that Fergus?': Neil Jordan's *The Crying Game*." *Feminist Review* 50 (Summer 1995): 173–86.

Elia, Nada. "In the Making: Beur Fiction and Identity Construction." *World Literature Today* (Winter 1997): 47–54.

Elsaesser, Thomas. "Ethnicity, Authenticity, and Exile: A Counterfeit Trade? German Filmmakers and Hollywood." *Home, Exile, Homeland: Film, Media and the Politics of Place*. Ed. Hamid Naficy. New York and London: Routledge, 1995: 97–124.

———. *New German Cinema*. New Brunswick, NJ: Rutgers University Press, 1989.

Fanon, Frantz. *The Wretched of the Earth*. Pref. Jean-Paul Sartre. Trans. Constance Farrington, 1961. London: MacGibbon & Kee, 1965.

Feng, Peter. "In Search of Asian American Cinema (Race in Contemporary American Cinema, part 3)." *Cineaste* 21.1–2 (Winter/Spring 1995): 32–35.

Fiske, John. *Understanding Popular Culture*. Boston: Unwin Hyman, 1989.

Foucault, Michel. *Aesthetics, Method, and Epistemology*. Ed. James D. Faubion. Trans. Robert Hurely et al. Vol. II. NY: New Press, 1998.

———. *The Archaeology of Knowledge*. Trans. Alan M. Sheridan Smith. New York: Pantheon, 1972.

———. *Discipline and Punish: The Birth of the Prison*. Trans. Alan Sheridan. New York: Vintage, 1979.

———. *The History of Sexuality: An Introduction*. Trans. Robert Hurley. Vol. 1. New York: Vintage, 1978.

———. "What is an Author?" *Screen* 20.1 (Spring 1979).

Freud, Sigmund. *The Complete Psychological Works of Sigmund Freud, Vol. XIV*. Trans. James Strachey. London: Hogarth, 1969.

Friedberg, Anne. *Window Shopping: Cinema and the Postmodern*. Berkeley: University of California Press, 1993.

Friedman, Susan Stanford. "Women's Autobiographical Selves: Theory and Practice." *The Private Self: Theory and Practice of Women's Autobiographical Writings*. Ed. Shari Benstock. Chapel Hill & London: University of North Carolina Press, 1988: 34–62.

Friedrichsmeyer, Sara, Lennox, Sara and Zantop, Susanne, eds. *The Imperialist Imagination: German Colonialism and Its Legacy*. Ann Arbor: University of Michigan Press, 1998.

Gabriel, Teshome. *Third Cinema in the Third World: The Aesthetics of Liberation*. Ann Arbor: UMI Research Press, 1982.

Gegen Rassismus, Apartheid und Kolonialismus. Dokumente der DDR 1977–1982. Berlin: Staatsverlag der Deutschen Demokratischen Republik, 1983.

Gegen Rassismus, Apartheid und Kolonialismus. Dokumente der DDR 1949–1977. Berlin: Staatsverlag der Deutschen Demokratischen Republik, 1978.

Geisler, Michael. "'Heimat' and the German Left: The Anamnesis of a Trauma." *New German Critique* 36 (1985): 25–66.

Genette, Gérard. *Narrative Discourse: An Essay in Method*. Trans. Jane E. Lewin. Ithaca: Cornell University Press, 1980.

Ghosh, Bishnupriya, and Bhaskar Sarkar. "The Cinema of Displacement: Towards a Politically Motivated Poetics." *Film Criticism* 20.1–2 (Fall/Winter 1995–96): 102–13.

Gili, Jean A. "Entretien avec Gianni Amelio: un film non sur l'Albanie d'aujourdhui, mais sur l'Italie d'après-guerre." *Positif* 406 (1994): 25–31.

Gilroy, Paul. *The Black Atlantic: Modernity and Double Consciousness*. Cambridge, MA: Harvard University Press, 1993.

Ginsberg, Terri, and Kirsten Moana Thompson. *Perspectives on German Film*. New York: G. K. Hall, 1996.

Glancy, Diane. "Introductory Note." *Two Worlds Walking: Short Stories, Essays, and Poetry by Writers with Mixed Heritages*. Ed. Glancy and C. W. Truesdale. Minneapolis: New Rivers, 1994: xi–xii.

Gökberk, Ülker. "Understanding Alterity: 'Ausländerliteratur' between Relativism and Universalism." *Theoretical Issues in Literary History*. Ed. David Perkins. Cambridge: Harvard University Press, 1991: 143–72.

Göktürk, Deniz. "Turkish delight—German fright: Migrant identities in transnational cinema." *Transitional Communities*. Working Paper Series. WPTC-99–01. Oxford: University of Oxford Press, 1999.

———. "Turkish Women on German Streets: Closure and Exposure in Transnational Cinema." *Spaces in European Cinema*. Ed. Myro Konstantarakos. Exeter, England; Portland, OR: Intellect, 2000: 64–76.

Gordon, Robert. *Pasolini: Forms of Subjectivity*. Oxford: Clarendon, 1996.

Grass, Günter. "Im Hinterhof. Bericht über eine Reise nach Nicaragua (1982)." In: *Widerstand lernen. Politische Gegenreden 1980–1983*. Darmstadt/Neuwied: Luchterhand, 1984: 37–51.

Greene, Naomi. *Pier Paolo Pasolini: Cinema as Heresy*. Princeton: Princeton University Press 1990.

Greverus, Ina-Marie. *Auf der Suche nach Heimat*. Munich: Beck, 1979.

Guthmann, Edward. "*Lone Star*—Summer's Smart Sleeper Hit: Sayles Film Quietly Builds an Audience." *San Francisco Chronicle* 1 August 1996: D1.

Habermas, Jurgen. *The Structural Transformation of the Public Sphere: An Inquiry into the Category of Bourgeois Society*. Tr. Thomas Burger. Cambridge, Mass.: MIT, 1989.

Halbreich, Kathy, and Bruce Jenkins, eds. *Bordering on Fiction: Chantal Ackerman's D'est*. Minneapolis: Walker Art Center, 1995.

Hall, Stuart. "Cultural Identity and Diaspora." *Identity: Community, Culture, Difference*. Ed. Jonathan Rutherford. London: Lawrence & Wishart, 1990: 222–37.

———. "European Cinema on the Verge of a Nervous Breakdown." *Screening Europe: Image and Identity in Contemporary European Cinema*. Ed. Duncan Petrie. London: BFI, 1992: 45–53.

Halving the Bones. Dir. Ruth Ozeki Lounsbury. Ad Limina Productions, 1995. Distributed by Women Make Movies.

Hamill, Heather. "Hoods and Provos: Crime and Punishment in West Belfast." Diss. Oxford U, 2001.

Harcourt, Peter. "Imaginary Images: An Examination of Atom Egoyan's Films." *Film Quarterly* 48.3 (1995): 2–14.

Heilbut, Anthony. *Exiled in Paradise: German Refugee Artists and Intellectuals in America, from the 1930s to the Present*. New York: Viking, 1983.

Herring, Hubert. *A History of Latin America*. New York: Knopf, 1968.

Hill, John. "Crossing the Water; Hybridity and Ethics in *The Crying Game*." *Textual Practice* 12.1 (1998): 89–100.

Hinson, Hal. "'Chocolat': Landscape of Seduction." *The Washington Post* (14 April 1989): C1, C9.

hooks, bell. "*Exotica*: Breaking Down to Break Through." *Reel to Real: Race, Sex, and Class at the Movies*. New York: Routledge, 1996: 27–33.

———. "Postmodern Blackness." *Yearning: Race, Gender, and Cultural Politics*. Boston: South End Press, 1990.

Howe, Desson. "The Enticing Flavors of 'Chocolat.'" *The Washington Post, Friday Magazine* (14 April 1989): 33.

Hune, Shirley, Hyung-chan Kim, Stephen S. Fugita, and Amy Ling, eds. *Asian Americans: Comparative and Global Perspectives*. Pullman, WA: Washington State University Press, 1991.

Hutchinson, John. *The Dynamics of Cultural Nationalism: The Gaelic Revival and the Creation of the Nation State*. London: Allen & Unwin, 1987.

Iordanova, Dina. "Conceptualizing the Balkans." *Slavic Review* 55.4 (1996): 883–90.

Irigaray, Luce. "Women in the Market." *This Sex Which Is Not One*. Tr. Catherine Porter and Carolyn Burke. Ithaca: Cornell University Press, 1985: 170–91.

Jameson, Fredric and Miyoshi, Masao, eds. *The Cultures of Globalization*. Durham: Duke University Press, 1998.

Jameson, Fredric. *The Geopolitical Aesthetics: Cinema and Space in the World System*. Bloomington: Indiana University Press, 1992.

———. "Notes on Globalization as a Philosophical Issue." *The Cultures of Globalization*. Eds. Frederic Jameson and Masao Miyoshi. Durham and London: Duke University Press, 1998: 54–77.

———. *Postmodernism, or, the Cultural Logic of Late Capitalism*. Durham: Duke University Press, 1991. Reprint 1997.

Johnston, Claire. "Dorothy Arzner: Critical Strategies." *Feminism and Film Theory*. Ed. Constance Penley. New York: Routledge, 1988: 36–45.

Johnston, Sheila. "The Incredible Journey: Sheila Johnston talks to Xavier Koller." *The Independent* 28 June 1991: 19.

———. "The Long and Winding Road." *The Independent* 26 July 1991: 16.

Jordan, Neil. *The Crying Game*. London: Vintage, 1993.

Journey of Hope (1990). Dir. Xavier Koller, perf. Necmettin Cobanoglu, Nur Srer, Emin Sivas, Erdinc Akbas, Yaman Okay, Yasar Güner, Hüseyin Mete, and Yaman Tarcan. Switzerland: Mainline/Catpics/Condor/SRG/RTSI/Film Four, 1990.

Jousse, Thierry. "Jeux africains." *Cahiers du cinéma* 407–08 (May 1988): 132–33.

The Joy Luck Club. Dir. Wayne Wang, perf. Kieu Chinh, Tsai Chin, France Nuyen, Lisa Lu, Ming-Na Wen, Tamlyn Tomita, Lauren Tom, Victor Wong. USA: Buena Vista/Hollywood Pictures, 1993.

Kaes, Anton. *From Hitler to Heimat*. Cambridge, MA: Harvard University Press 1992.

———. "Leaving Home: Film, Migration, and the Urban Experience." *New German Critique* 74 (1998): 79–192.

Kain, Geoffrey, ed. *Ideas of Home: Literature of Asian Migration*. East Lansing: Michigan State University Press, 1997.

Kaleta, Kenneth. *Hanif Kureishi: Postcolonial Storyteller*. Austin: University of Texas Press, 1998.

Kaplan, Caren. *Questions of Travel: Postmodern Discourses of Displacement*. Durham and London: Duke University Press, 1996.

Kaplan, E. Ann. *Looking for the Other: Feminism, Film, and the Imperial Gaze*. New York: Routledge, 1997.

Karpf, Ernst, Doron Kiesel, and Karsten Visarius, eds. *Getürkte Bilder: Zur Inszenierung von Fremden im Film*. Marburg: Schüren, 1995.

Kauffman, Stanley. "Stanley Kauffmann on Films: Changes." *The New Republic* (17 April 1989): 28–29.

Kearney, Richard. *Postnationalist Ireland: Politics, Culture, Philosophy*. London and New York: Routledge, 1997.

———. *Transitions: Narratives in Irish Popular Culture*. Manchester: Manchester University Press, 1988.

Kenny, Kevin. *Making Sense of the Molly Maguires*. Oxford and New York: Oxford University Press, 1998.

Kermode, Mark. "Moving Stories." *Sight and Sound* 1.4 (August 1991): 21.

Kersten, Heinz. "*Blonder Tango.*" *So viele Träume. DEFA-Filmkritiken aus drei Jahrzehnten.* Berlin: VISTAS, 1996: 272–74.

Klawans, Stuart. Rev. of *Exotica*, dir. Atom Egoyan. *The Nation*, 20 March 1995: 397.

Kosta, Barbara. *Recasting Autobiography: Women's Counterfictions in Contemporary German Literature and Film*. Ithaca: Cornell University Press, 1994.

———. "Representing Female Sexuality: On Jutta Brückner's Film *Years of Hunger*." *Gender and German Cinema: Feminist Interventions*. Ed. Sandra Frieden [et al.]. Vol. 2. Oxford: Berg, 1993: 241–52.

Kristeva, Julia. *About Chinese Women*. New York and London: M. Boyars, 1986.

———. *Powers of Horror: An Essay on Abjection*. Trans. Leon Roudiez. New York: Columbia University Press, 1982.

Kuhn, Anna. "Bourgeois Ideology and the Mis(Reading) of *Ganz Unten*." *New German Critique* 46 (Winter 1989): 191–202.

Kuhn, Annette. *Cinema, Censorship and Sexuality 1909–1925*. New York: Routledge, 1988.

Kulaoglu, Tuncay. "Kebab and Curry: Von *40 qm Deutschland* zu *Lola* and *Bilidikid*—Ein Überblick über das türkisch-deutsche Kino. *Jungle World.* 10 March 1999. <http.//www.nadir.org/nadir/periodika/jungle_world/_99/11/26a.htm>

Kureishi, Hanif. "Bradford." *My Beautiful Laundrette and Other Writings*. London: Faber and Faber, 1996: 121–44.

Lamm, Hans Siegfried and Kupper, Siegfried. *DDR und Dritte Welt. Schriften des Forschungsinstituts der Deutschen Gesellschaft fur Auswärtige Politik e.V. Bonn*. Vienna: R. Oldenbourg Verlag, 1976: 54–55.

LaSalle, Mick. "Sayles Connects in *Lone Star*: An Old Murder Looms over Border Town." *San Francisco Chronicle* 21 June 1996: D3.

Levin, David J. "Community and Its Contents: Race and Film History in Percy Adlon's *Bagdad Café*." *Triangulated Visions: Women in Recent German Cinema*. Ed. Ingeborg Majer O'Sickey and Ingeborg von Zadow. Albany: SUNY, 1998: 117–28.

Ling, Amy. *Between Worlds: Women Writers of Chinese Ancestry*. New York: Pergamon, 1990.

Lipper, Hal. "A Director Full of 'Hope,'" *St. Petersburg Times* 5 July 1991: 10.

Lloyd, David. *Ireland After History*. Notre Dame: University of Notre Dame P in association with Field Day, 1999.

López, Ana. M. "Are All Latins from Manhattan? Hollywood, Ethnography and Cultural Colonialism." *Unspeakable Images: Ethnicity and the American Cinema*. Ed. Lester D. Friedman. Urbana: University of Illinois Press, 1991: 404–24.

Lowe, Lisa. *Immigrant Acts: On Asian American Cultural Politics*. Durham: Duke University Press, 1996.

Löwisch, Henriette. "Interview with Seyhan Derin: *ben annemin kiziyim* (*I Am My Mother's Daughter*)." *Triangulated Visions: Women in Recent German Cinema*. Ed. Ingeborg Majer O'Sickey and Ingeborg von Zadow. Albany: University of New York Press, 1998: 129–35.

Lugones, Maria. "Wicked Caló: a Matter of the Authority of Improper Words." Unpublished manuscript. 1998.

MacCabe, Colin. *The Eloquence of the Vulgar: Language, Cinema and the Politics of Culture.* London: BFI, 1997.

MacDougall, David. *Transcultural Cinema.* Princeton, NJ: Princeton University Press, 1998.

Marcus, Millicent. *Italian Cinema in the Light of Neorealism.* Princeton: Princeton University Press, 1986.

Marks, Laura. *The Skin of the Film: Intercultural Cinema, Embodiment and the Senses.* Durham and London: Duke University Press, 2000.

Martin, Helen, and Sam Edwards. *New Zealand Film, 1912–1996.* Auckland: Oxford University Press, 1997.

Martone, Mario. Interview in *La Repubblica.* July 16, 1998.

———. *Teatro di guerra: un diario.* Milan: Bompiani, 1998.

McClintock, Anne. *Imperial Leather: Race, Gender, and Sexuality in the Colonial Context.* London: Routledge, 1995.

McDonald, Lawrence. "A Road to Erewhon: A Consideration of *Cinema of Unease.*" *Illusions* 25, 1996: 20–25.

McHale, Brian. *Postmodernist Fiction.* New York and London: Methuen, 1987.

Mercer, Kobena. "Diaspora Culture and the Dialogic Imagination." *Blackframes: Celebration of Black Cinema.* Ed. Mbye Cham and Claire Andrade–Watkins. Cambridge, MA: MIT Press, 1988: 50–61.

Miller, Laura. "Virtue's Hack: John Sayles Makes Movies with All the Right Messages— and No Surprises, Madness, or Life." *Salon Magazine* 29 July–2 August 1996. <http://www.salonmagazine.com/weekly/movies960729.html>.

Mingalon, Jean-Louis. "Yamina Benguigui, la grande soeur cinéaste." *Le Monde,* February 2, 1998.

Minh-ha, Trinh T. *Woman, Native, Other.* Bloomington: Indiana University Press, 1989.

Mirzoeff Nicholas, ed. *Diaspora and Visual Culture: Representing Africans and Jews.* London and New York: Routledge, 2000.

Mitchell, Katharyne. "In Whose Interest? Transnational Capital and the Production of Multiculturalism in Canada." *Global/Local: Cultural Production and the Transnational Imaginary.* Ed. Rob Wilson and Wimal Dissanayake. Durham: Duke University Press, 1996: 219–51.

Mizejewski, Linda. *Ziegfeld Girl: Image and Icon in Culture and Cinema.* Durham: Duke University Press, 1999.

Mohanty, Chandra Talpade. "Under Western Eyes: Feminist Scholarship and Colonial Discourses." *Boundary: A Journal of Postmodern Literature and Culture* 12:3/13:1 (Spring/Fall 1984): 333–58.

———, et al. *Third World Women and the Politics of Feminism.* Bloomington: Indiana University Press, 1991.

Morley, David, and Kevin Robins. *Spaces of Identity: Global Media, Electronic Landscapes and Cultural Boundaries.* New York: Routledge, 1995.

Mudimbe, V. Y. *The Invention of Africa: Gnosis, Philosophy, and the Order of Knowledge.* Bloomington: Indiana University Press, 1988.

Mulvey, Laura. "Visual Pleasure and Narrative Cinema." *Visual and Other Pleasures.* Bloomington: Indiana University Press, 1989: 14–26.

My Father Is Coming, dir. Monika Treut. Filmwelt, 1991.

Naficy, Hamid. *An Accented Cinema: Exilic and Diasporic Filmmaking.* Oxford and Princeton: Princeton University Press, 2001.

————. "The Accented Style of the Independent Transnational Cinema: A Conversation with Atom Egoyan." *Cultural Producers in Perilous States: Editing Events, Documenting Change.* Ed. George E. Marcus. Chicago: University of Chicago Press, 1997: 179–231.

————. "Between Rocks and Hard Places: The Interstitial Mode of Production in Exilic Cinema." *Home, Exile, Homeland: Film, Media, and the Politics of Place.* Ed. Hamid Naficy. New York: Routledge, 1999: 125–47.

————, ed. *Home, Exile, Homeland: Film, Media and the Politics of Place.* New York: Routledge, 1999.

————. *The Making of Exile Cultures: Iranian Television in Los Angeles.* Minneapolis: University of Minnesota Press, 1993.

————. "Phobic Spaces and Liminal Panics: Independent Transnational Film Genre." *East-West Film Journal* 8.2 (1994): 1–30.

————. "Phobic Spaces and Liminal Panics: Independent Transnational Film Genre." *Global/Local: Cultural Production and the Transnational Imaginary.* Eds. Rob Wilson and Wimal Dissanayake. Durham and London: Duke University Press, 1996: 119–44.

————. "Theorizing 'Third-World' Film Spectatorship." *Wide Angle,* 18:4 (1996): 3–26.

Nakano, Mei T. *Japanese American Women: Three Generations 1890–1990.* Berkeley and Sebastopol: Mina Press, 1990.

Narayan, Uma. "The Project of Feminist Epistemology: Perspectives from a Nonwestern Feminist." *Gender/Body/Knowledge: Feminist Reconstructions of Being and Knowing.* Ed. Alison Jaggar and Susan Bordo. New York: Routledge, 1989.

Ney-Nowotny, Gertrud and Karl. *Joseph Schmidt. Das Leben und Sterben eines Unvergesslichen.* Vienna: Verlag Gerlach und Wiedling, 1967.

Noiriel, Gérard. "French and Foreigners." *Realms of Memory. Rethinking the French Past, vol. I. Conflicts and Divisions.* Ed. Pierre Nora. New York: Columbia University Press, 1996: 145–78.

Nussbaum, Martha C. *Love's Knowledge: Essays on Philosophy and Literature.* New York: Oxford University Press, 1990.

O'Sickey, Ingeborg Majer. "Staging Fables of Identity: Ethnicity, Gender, and Sexuality in Percy Adlon's *Salmonberries.*" *Seminar* 33.4 (1997): 407–18.

Ofodile, Gilbert. *I Shall Never Return: Eight Months in Communist Germany, A Nigerian Student of Journalism Reports.* Munich/Esslingen: Bechtle Verlag, 1967.

Ortner, Sherry. "Generation X: Anthropology in a Media-Saturated World." *Cultural Anthropology* 13.3 (1998): 414–40.

Oyono, Ferdinand. *Une Vie de boy.* Paris: Editions Juilliard, 1956.

Park, Mungo. *Travels in the Interior Districts of Africa: Performed in the Years 1795, 1796, and 1797, With an Account of a Subsequent Mission to that Country in 1805.* New York: Scribner's, 1816.

Parker, Saliha. "Unmuffled Voices in the Shade and Beyond: Women's Writing in Turkish." *Textual Liberation: European Feminist Writing in the Twentieth Century.* London: Routledge, 1991.

Pasolini, Pier Paolo. *Appunti per un'Orestiade africana. Trascrizione del commento e dei dialoghi a cura di Antonio Costa.* [Script of *Notes for an African Orestes.* Courtesy of the Fondo Pier Paolo Pasolini, Rome.]

————. *Scritti corsari.* Milan: Garzanti, 1975.

————. "Travestiti da poveri." *Accattone Mamma Roma Ostia.* Milan: Garzanti, 1993.

————. "Una visione del mondo epico-religiosa." *Bianco e Nero,* XXV: 6 (1964): 13–36.

Peters, John Durham. "Exile, Nomadism and Diaspora: The Stakes of Mobility in the Western Canon." *Home, Exile, Homeland.* Ed. Hamid Naficy. New York: Routledge, 1999: 17–41.

Petrie, Duncan, ed. *Screening Europe: Image and Identity in Contemporary European Cinema.* London: BFI, 1992.

Petty, Sheila. *The Archaelogy of Origin: Transnational Visions of Africa in a Borderless Cinema.* Halifax: MSVU Art Gallery & Dunlop Art Gallery, 1999.

Pevere, Geoff. "No Place Like Home: The Films of Atom Egoyan." Introduction. *Exotica.* By Atom Egoyan. Toronto: Coach House Press, 1995: 9–41.

Pflaum, Hans Günther, and Hans Helmut Prinzler. *Cinema in the Federal Republic of Germany.* Bonn: Inter Nationes, 1993.

Picture Bride. Dir. Kayo Hatta. Thousand Cranes Filmworks, released by Miramax, 1995.

Pratt, Mary Louise. *Imperial Eyes: Travel Writing and Transculturation.* London: Routledge, 1992.

Praunheim, Rosa von. *50 Jahre Pervers: Die sentimentalen Memoiren des Rosa von Praunheim.* Köln: Kiepenheuer & Witsch, 1993.

Ray, Robert B. *A Certain Tendency of the Hollywood Cinema, 1930–1980.* New Jersey: Princeton University Press, 1985.

Raymond, Janice. "The Politics of Transgenderism." *Blending Genders: Social Aspects of Cross-Dressing and Sex-Changing.* Eds. Richard Ekins and Dave King. London and New York: Routledge, 1996: 215–33.

Reid, Mark A. "Colonial Observations: Interview with Claire Denis." *Jump Cut* 40 (March 1996): 67–73.

Rimmon-Kenan, Shlomith. *Narrative Fiction: Contemporary Poetics.* London: Routledge, 1989.

Roberts, Paul E. "Caravats and Shanavests: Whiteboyism and Faction Fighting in East Munster, 1802–1811." *Irish Peasants: Violence & Political Unrest 1780–1914.* Eds. Samuel Clark and James S. Donnelly, Jr. Dublin: Gill and Macmillan, 1983: 64–101.

Rock, David. "War and Postwar Intersections: Latin America and the United States." *Latin America in the 1940s: War and Postwar Transitions.* Ed. David Rock. Berkeley: University of California Press, 1994: 15–40.

Romney, Jonathan. "Exploitations." *Sight and Sound* (May 1995): 6–8.

Rosello, Mireille. "Women Negotiating Cross-Cultural Experiences: Yamina Benguigui, Katherine Dunham and Zora Neale Hurston." Women's Studies Graduate/Faculty Colloquium, University of Illinois, 1998, unpublished paper.

Rosenbaum, Jonathan. "Godard in the Nineties: an Interview, Argument, and Scrapbook." *Film Comment,* 34:5 (1998), 52–60.

Rueschmann, Eva. *Sisters on Screen: Siblings in Contemporary Cinema.* Philadelphia: Temple University Press, 2000.

Rushdie, Salman. *Imaginary Homelands: Essays and Criticism 1981–1991.* New York and London: Penguin/Granta, 1992.

Said, Edward. *After the Last Sky: Palestinian Lives.* London and Boston: Faber and Faber, 1986.

———. *Culture and Imperialism.* New York: Vintage, 1993.

Sante, Luc. "French Colonial." *New York* 19: 5 (May 1989): 114.

Sayles, John. Dir. *Lone Star.* With Chris Cooper, Elizabeth Peña, Kris Kristofferson, and Matthew McConaughey. Castle Rock, 1996.

———. *Lone Star.* Unpublished screenplay. 2 January 1995.

Scarry, Elaine. *The Body in Pain: The Making and the Unmaking of the World.* Oxford: Oxford University Press, 1985.

Schatz, Thomas. *Hollywood Genres.* New York: McGraw-Hill, 1981.

Schickel, Richard. "Look, Ma, No Space Invaders!: John Sayles Makes the Summer Safe for Grownups." *Time* 22 July 1996: 95.

Schiller, Herbert I. *Mass Communications and American Empire.* 2nd ed. Boulder, San Fransisco, Oxford: Westview, 1992.

Schmidt, Joseph. *Deutsche und Englishe Soundtracks/Soundtracks from German and English Films*. Compact disk. Koch Schwann, 1996.

Sedgwick, Eve K. *Between Men: English Literature and Male Homosocial Desire*. New York: Columbia University Press, 1985.

Sesti, Mario, and Stefanella Ughi, eds. *Gianni Amelio*. Rome: Dino Audino Editore, 1995.

Seyhan, Azade. "Geographies of Memory: Protocols of Writing in the Borderlands." *German Cultures, Foreign Cultures: The Politics of Belonging*. Ed. Jeffrey Peck. Humanities Program. Vol. 3. American Institute for Contemporary German Studies, 1998: 73–88.

Shapiro, Michael. *Cinematic Political Thought: Narrating Race, Nation and Gender*. New York: New York University Press, 1999.

Sherzer, Dina, ed. *Cinema, Colonialism, Postcolonialism: Perspectives from the French and Francophone Worlds*. Austin: University of Texas Press, 1996.

Shohat, Ella, and Robert Stam. *Unthinking Eurocentrism: Multiculturalism and the Media*. London, New York: Routledge, 1994.

Shulgasser, Barbara. "*Lone Star* Is Classic Sayles: Full of Commitment, Ethics." *San Francisco Examiner* 21 June 1996: D3.

Sinka, Margit. "Tom Tykwer's *Lola rennt*: A Blueprint of Millenial Berlin." Glossen 11. 25 Dec. 2000. <http://www.dickenson.edu/departments/germn/glossen/heft11/lola.html>

Skármeta, Antonio. *Ardiente paciencia*. Santiago, Chile: Pehuén, 1986. Trans. Katherine Silver: *Burning Patience*. New York: Pantheon, 1987.

Sklar, Robert. *Movie-Made America: A Cultural History of American Movies*. Rev. New York: Vintage, 1994.

Smith, Sidonie. *De/Colonizing the Subject: The Politics of Gender in Women's Autobiography*. Minneapolis: University of Minnesota Press, 1992.

Soldini, Silvio. *Un'anima divisa in due: Sceneggiatura di Silvio Soldini e Roberto Tiraboschi. Con un'intervista di Gofredo Fofi all'autore*. Rome: Edizioni e/o, 1993.

Sontag, Susan. "Godot comes to Sarajevo." *The New York Times Review of Books*, vol. 40:17, 21 Oct. 1993.

Spickard, Paul R. *Japanese Americans: The Formation and Transformations of an Ethnic Group*. New York: Twayne, 1996.

Spivak, Gayatri Chakravorty. "Can the subaltern speak?" *Marxist Interpretations of Cultural Politics*. Eds. Cary Nelson & Lawrence Grossberg. Urbana: University of Illinois Press, 1988: 271–313.

———. "Subaltern Studies: Deconstructing Historiography." *Selected Subaltern Studies*. Ed. Ranajit Guha and Gayatri C. Spivak. Ed. Oxford University Press, 1988.

Stack, Oswald. *Pasolini su Pasolini. Conversazioni con Jon Halliday*. Parma: Ugo Guanda Editore, 1992.

Stack, Peter. "Something Else." *The San Fransisco Chronicle* 2 May 1991: E2.

Stam, Robert. *Subversive Pleasures: Bakhtin, Cultural Criticism and Film*. Baltimore and London: John Hopkins University Press, 1989.

Stone, Judy. "Odyssey of Turkish Kurds in Oscar Winner." 1 May 1991: E3.

Strauss, Frédéric. "Féminin colonial." *Cahiers du cinéma* 434 (juillet 1990): 29–33.

Taylor, Charles. *The Ethics of Authenticity*. Cambridge, Mass.: Harvard Press, 1992. 43–53.

Tekeli, Sirin. "The Meaning and Limits of Feminist Ideology in Turkey." *Women, Family, and Social Change in Turkey*. Bankok: Unesco, 1990: 139–59.

Teraoke, Arlene. *East, West, and Others: The Third World in Postwar German Literature*. Lincoln: University of Nebraska Press, 1996.

Thomas, Kevin. *Los Angeles Times* 26 April 1991: F17.

Tinazzi, Noël. "La parole a une valeur thérapeutique." *La Tribune*. February 4, 1998.

Tomlinson, John. "Cultural Globalization and Cultural Imperialism." *International Communication and Globalization*. Ed. Ali Mohammadi. London: Sage, 1997: 170–90.

Torgovnick, Marianna. *Gone Primitive: Savage Intellects, Modern Lives*. Chicago: Chicago University Press, 1990.

Trumpener, Katie. "On the Road: Labor, Ethnicity, and the New German Cinema in the Age of the Multinational." *Perspectives on German Cinema*. Ed. Terri Ginsberg and Kirsten Moane Thompson. New York: G. K. Hall, 1996: 733–43.

Veloso, Caetano. "Caricature and Conqueror, Pride and Shame." Tr. Robert Myers. *The New York Times*. 20 October 1991, Arts and Leisure Guide: 34 and 41.

Viano, Maurizio. *A Certain Realism: Making Use of Pasolini's Film Theory and Practice*. Berkeley: California University Press 1993.

Virilio, Paul. *War and Cinema: The Logistics of Perception*. Trans. Patrick Camille. London: Verso, 1989.

Vitti, Antonio. "Albanitaliamerica: viaggio come sordo sogno in *Lamerica* di Gianni Amelio." *Italica* 73:2 (1996): 248–61.

Volpi, Gianni, ed. *Gianni Amelio*. Turin: Edizioni Scriptorium, 1995.

Voss, Margit. "Von der Kraft zum Überleben." *Film und Fernsehen* 5/86: 2–3.

Wajcman, Gérard. "San Paolo Godard contro Lanzmann Mosé." *Carte di cinema*. New Series, 1 (Spring 1998): 65–67.

Walker, Alice, and Parmar, Pratibha. *Warrior Marks: Female Genital Mutilation and the Sexual Blinding of Women*. San Diego: Harcourt, 1996.

Walker, John, ed. *Halliwell's Film Guide*. New York: Harper Perennial, 1995.

Wheeler, Elizabeth A. "Bulldozing the Subject." *Postmodern Culture* 1:3 (1991). <http://muse.jhu.edu/journals/ postmodern_culture/ v001/1.3wheeler.html.> 25 February 1999.

White, Hayden. *Tropics of Discourse*. Baltimore: Johns Hopkins University Press, 1978.

Williams, T. Desmond, ed. *Secret Societies in Ireland*. Dublin: Gill and Macmillan, 1973.

Wolf, Markus. *Man without a Face: The Autobiography of Communism's Greatest Spymaster*. With Anne McElvoy. New York: Times/Random House, 1997.

Wood, Robin. "Ideology, Genre, Auteur." *Film Comment* 13.1 (January–February 1977): 46–51.

Xing, Jun, *Asian America Through the Lens: History, Representations and Identity*. Walnut Creek, CA: AltaMira, 1998.

Zizek, Slavoj. *Metastases of Enjoyment: Six Essays on Woman and Causality*. London: Verso, 1994.

Contributors

Barton Byg teaches German and film studies at the University of Massachusetts-Amherst where he is co-founding member of the faculty steering committee for the interdepartmental program in film studies and founder/director of the DEFA Film Library. His publications include the book, *Landscapes of Resistance: The German Films of Danièle Huillet and Jean-Marie Straub*.

David N. Coury is an associate professor of German and chair of Modern Languages at the University of Wisconsin–Green Bay. His primary fields of research are German cinema and the contemporary German novel. He has published articles on the New German comedy, Wim Wenders, Günter Grass, Heinrich Böll, and Paul Celan. Currently he is working on a book dealing with the role of the writer-intellectual in the public sphere.

Todd F. Davis is associate professor and chair of the Department of English at Goshen College. In addition to publishing numerous articles and reviews in such journals as *Critique*, *College Literature*, *Studies in Short Fiction*, *Mississippi Quarterly*, and *Yeats/Eliot Review*, Davis is the author of *Ripe*, a collection of poetry, and the co-editor of *Mapping the Ethical Turn: A Reader in Ethics, Culture, and Literary Theory*.

Rodica Diaconescu-Blumenfeld is associate professor of Italian and women's studies at Vassar College. She is author of *Born Illiterate: Gender and Representation in C. E. Gadda's Pasticciaccio* and the co-editor of *The Pleasure of Writing: Critical Essays on Dacia Maraini*. Her recent research has been in the area of Italian cinema, and she has published articles on Lina Wertmuller and Marco Risi. She is currently co-editing a collection of essays on the representation of the Balkans in European cinemas and is also working on a manuscript on the politics of cultural repression in classic and contemporary Italian cinema.

Carolyn A. Durham is Inez K. Gaylord Professor of French at the College of Wooster, where she also teaches extensively in the comparative literature and the women's studies programs. Her publications include *L'Art Romanesque de Raymond Roussel*; *The Contexture of Feminism: Marie Cardinal and Multicultural Legacy*; *Double Takes: Culture and Gender in French Films and Their American Remakes*; and numerous articles predominantly on French and American fiction and film, including essays on William Styron, Marianne Moore, Euzhan Palcy, Cyril Collard, Perez-Reverte, and others.

Mine Eren is assistant professor of German studies at Randolph Macon College. She specializes in twentieth-century German literature and culture, especially on minority literature and film. Her recently completed dissertation concentrates on the literary and cinematic output of Turkish women in the 1990s. Educated in Germany and the United States, she received her Ph.D. from Brown University in 1999 and a Masters degree from Ludwigs-Maximilians University in Munich in 1992.

Angelica Fenner received her Ph.D. in German and comparative literature from the University of Minnesota–Minneapolis. She currently teaches film studies in the Department of French and Italian at the University of Minnesota. Earlier essays on the Turkish-German cultural exchange and on East German cinema have appeared in various anthologies and in the journal *Camera Obscura*. She is completing a monograph on Afro-Germans in early West German films.

Norman S. Holland is associate professor in the School of Humanities, Arts, and Cultural Studies at Hampshire College, where he is also the associate dean of faculty for multicultural education. He has published widely on Latin American and Latino/a literature. He is a member of the *Confluencia* editorial board.

Mark Ingram teaches at Goucher College where he is primarily responsible for the French culture and civilization curriculum, but also teaches courses on contemporary Europe in the anthropology and history departments. He is the author of articles on French cultural policy in the *French Review* and *Quaderni*, and has contributed book reviews to *Anthropological Quarterly*. He is currently working on an ethnography of a touring French theater troupe during the Mitterand era.

Adam Knee is assistant professor in the English Department at Bucknell University. He holds a doctorate in cinema studies from NewYork University and has previously lectured at universities in Australia, Taiwan, and Thailand. His work has appeared in a number of anthologies, including *The Dread of Difference: Gender and the Horror Film*, *Cinemas of the Black Diaspora*, and *Representing Jazz*.

Florence Martin teaches literature and cinema of French expression and world literature at Goucher College. She has published *Bessie Smith* and is co-editor and co-author of *Resonances: Lectures Guyanaises*. Her articles on African diasporic culture and literature of French and English expression have been published in France (*Atlantiques, Europe, Les Cahiers de Corhum, Le Monde, Les Cahiers du Jazz*) and in the United States (*Études Francophones*, and forthcoming articles in *French Review* and *Studies in Twentieth-Century Literature*). She has contributed chapters to various volumes (*La Comédie Sociale* and *Feminist Companion to French Literature*) and is currently working on a book on French Guiana's literature in French.

Allen Meek studied and taught in the United States before returning to New Zealand to join the media studies program at Massey University. He is currently preparing his first book on media, place and identity. His publications include articles in the journals *Postmodern Culture*, *Screening the Past*, and *New Media and Society*.

Eva Rueschmann is assistant professor of cultural studies at Hampshire College, where she teaches courses on world literature and cinema, modernism, and cultural theory and criticism. Her book, *Sisters on Screen: Siblings in Contemporary Cinema*, was published by Temple University Press. Her other published work has appeared in anthologies such as *International Women's Writing: New Landscapes of Identity*, *The Significance of Sibling Relationships in Literature*, and in the journal *Literature/Film Quarterly*.

Kenneth Womack is associate professor of English and coordinator of the honors program at Penn State University's Altoona College. Womack has published numerous articles in such journals as *Mosaic*, *College Literature*, *Biography*, *Studies in the Humanities*, *Literature/Film Quarterly*, *TEXT*, and the *Yearbook of Comparative and General Literature*. He serves as editor of *Interdisciplinary Literary Studies: A Journal of Criticism and Theory* and as co-editor of Oxford University Press's celebrated *Year's Work in English Studies*. He is the co-editor of *Mapping the Ethical Turn: A Reader in Ethics, Culture, and Literary Theory* and the author of *Postwar Academic Fiction: Satire, Ethics, Community*.

Catherine Wynne is lecturer in English at the University of Hull, Scarborough campus. She has published articles on late nineteenth- and early twentieth-century British and Irish writing and on Arthur Conan Doyle and photography. She recently completed a book, *The Colonial Conan Doyle: British Imperialism, Irish Nationalism, and the Gothic*. She is currently working on cultural interactions with mesmerism in the nineteenth century.

Index